D0436619

UNIVERSITY OF WINNIPEG
515 PORTAGE & BALMORAL
WINNIPEG, MAN.   R3B 2E9
CANADA

To the Webster-Ashburton Treaty

A Study in Anglo-American Relations, 1783–1843

E
398
.J66

To The Webster-Ashburton Treaty

A Study in Anglo-American Relations, 1783–1843

by Howard Jones

The University of North Carolina Press
Chapel Hill

Cartography on pages x, 99, 135, and 155
by Marcy Johnston and Dariel Mayer

Copyright © 1977 by
The University of North Carolina Press
All rights reserved
Manufactured in the United States of America
ISBN 0–8078–1306–0
Library of Congress Catalog Card Number 76–58341

Library of Congress Cataloging in Publication Data

Jones, Howard, 1940–
    To the Webster-Ashburton treaty.

    "The Webster-Ashburton treaty": p.
    Bibliography: p.
    Includes index.
    1. Washington, Treaty of, 1842. 2. Northeast
boundary of the United States. 3. United States—
Foreign relations—Great Britain. 4. Great Britain
—Foreign relations—United States. I. United
States. Treaties, etc., 1841–1845. (Tyler). Bound-
ary, slave trade, and extradition. 1977. II. Title.
E398.J66   327.73'041   76–58341
ISBN 0–8078–1306–0

For Mary Ann, Debbie, Howie, and Shari

Contents

Illustrations

The peace of the Country when I reached Washington, on the 6th day of April 1841, was suspended by a thread, but we converted that thread into a chain cable of sufficient strength to render that peace secure, and so enable the Country to weather the storms of faction by which it was in every direction assailed.

————JOHN TYLER *to* DANIEL WEBSTER, 12 *Mar.* 1846
(WP [F20/26772].)

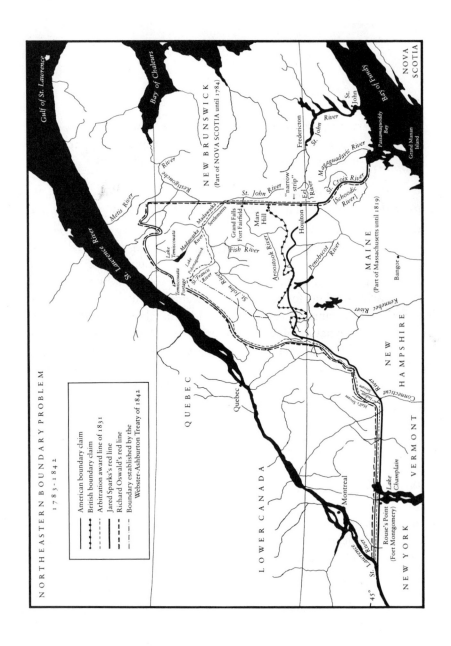

Preface

The primary purpose of this study is to show how the United States and Great Britain used the tactics of compromise to negotiate the Webster-Ashburton Treaty of 1842 and thereby reduce the threat of a ✓ third Anglo-American war. The theme of peace has enduring appeal. For almost a century after the Congress of Vienna there was no major war in Europe. An indirect result of this uniquely calm period on the Continent was the development of one of the most unusual and important international relationships ever recorded—that between the United States and Britain. Torn between mutual interests and burning animosities, this shaky Anglo-American understanding almost collapsed by 1842 when the elements working for good relations seemed about to give way again to war. But this time the diplomats would win, taking advantage of the complementary nature of the two nations' relationship, as well as their domestic and foreign troubles, to push them closer together after their last war in 1812–14.

Though the Webster-Ashburton Treaty was instrumental in maintaining peace between the Atlantic nations, there has been no full-scale, scholarly analysis of the settlement, and existing assessments are either incomplete or superficial. No historians have adequately placed the pact within the perspective of nineteenth-century Anglo-American relations, nor have they noted its effects on the international history of North America. Indeed, many have assigned the treaty to the background because of other important events during the 1840s, both domestic and foreign—in the United States, internal politics, Texas, Pacific coastal matters, the Mexican War; in Britain, internal political and economic problems, demands for social reform, Afghanistan, China, Egypt, France, Russia. Many writers seem to have overlooked the consequences of the treaty in their haste to move on to Oregon, Mexico, and the Civil War.

Close examination of the agreement shows that the crucial element lacking in Anglo-American relations after the War of 1812 was mutual trust, a deficiency that by the 1840s had increased the danger of war. If hindsight suggests no real threat of conflict in 1842, contemporary Anglo-American observers would not have shared this confidence. British and American documents reveal that each nation feared the other's motives and made contingency preparations for a war neither side wanted. Anti-British and anti-American feelings still ran deep. Though forces were operating for pacific relations, many veteran political, diplomatic, and military figures regretfully believed there was no way short of war to uphold both nations' prestige. The major personalities who virtually had at their command the decision for peace included Daniel Webster, John Tyler, Edward Everett, Lord Ashburton, Sir Robert Peel, and Lord Aberdeen. They confronted serious questions involving national honor and for that reason the pact they helped to secure deserves more attention.

Several factors justify a careful study of the Webster-Ashburton Treaty. In addition to the lack of a monograph on the subject, there is need to revise the harsh conclusions some historians have drawn about the treaty and the roles played in its negotiation by Secretary of State Webster and British Special Minister Ashburton.[1] This book attempts to show the importance of the settlement to Anglo-American relations, to establish the respectability of the two men's performances during their talks in Washington, and to place the treaty within the context of North American developments. New evidence uncovered in American, British, and Canadian archives necessitates revisions in the traditional story of the Webster-Ashburton Treaty. To cite examples, there was nothing discreditable about the "red-line map" controversy; the documents do not substantiate the charge that there was a private exchange of money between Webster and Ashburton; Webster did not sacrifice American interests for personal motives; his use of New England newspapers in arousing support for the northeastern boundary settlement was not a simple matter of "propaganda"; the agreement did not result entirely from open diplomacy. Webster and Ashburton signed the treaty because they considered it the wisest alternative to war—not because of the oft-claimed strategic distribution of money. In view of the adversity that confronted both men during the 1840s, an investigation into how they managed to resolve so many Anglo-American difficulties should tell us something about the peaceful settlement of international disputes.

There are other reasons for this study. An analysis of the treaty's formation alters the usual characterization of early nineteenth-century American foreign policy as "shirtsleeve diplomacy." The conduct of the negotiations and the reaction in the United States to the settlement show that some Americans had learned the value of compromise in diplomatic affairs. This study upholds the traditional view of isolationism during the nineteenth century—that the United States exploited Britain's domestic and foreign problems in negotiating a treaty that protected America's interests on this continent. It also illustrates that a major grievance by Americans throughout the period under consideration was their belief, however mistaken, that Britain refused to recognize the United States as a nation as worthy of respect as a European state. The Webster-Ashburton Treaty helped convince Americans that they had won British approval, and because of this it temporarily brought better relations.

If Britain and the United States after 1815 moved toward rapprochement, as several historians have argued, many issues still remained by the 1840s—some relatively minor in importance—that continued to provoke widespread anger on both sides of the Atlantic. Trust between nations should overcome differences by making negotiation the most feasible path to follow. But this was not always the case from 1815 to 1842. Some Britons, for example, countered Americans' complaints about British arrogance with insults. A London journal acidly remarked that before America "can deserve the name of a wise nation" it must rid itself of its republicanism, its nationalistic " 'fourth of July harangues,' [and its] nonsense about 'flying eagles and never-setting stars,' . . . and the infinite superiority of the Yankee over all mankind, past, present, and to come."[2] Each side was ready—almost anxious—to criticize and to believe the worst of the other, so that the slightest disagreement caused wrathful outbursts among both English-speaking peoples. This lack of trust forced the British to resort to a special mission.

In searching for forces pulling peoples and nations together, it is easy to ignore or to underestimate the power of issues driving them apart. No one can deny that by the middle of the nineteenth century social, political, and economic factors encouraged better Anglo-American relations; but too much emphasis on these elements obscures the fact that the growing connection was confined primarily to the Northern states and Britain. The South's contacts were with the Tories, an English party in decline.

Such a narrow approach also hides the important point that not all Atlantic spokesmen sought closer ties. One can argue that humanitarian reformers, for example, were sincere in their professed concerns, but he also can ask whether they were open to cooperation only insofar as this move aided their cause at home. The most significant reservation to the theory is that the complementary nature of the Atlantic relationship began to fade by the time of the American Civil War. During the 1840s the balance of trade shifted in favor of the United States; after the Civil War the Republic turned inward to reconstruct the nation and to experience its industrial revolution. In the meantime British skeptics sighed with relief that their reformers no longer could envy the United States, for it was becoming predominantly materialistic, and they declared with satisfaction that the United Kingdom had achieved what they considered to be the optimum social, political, and economic changes.[3] These observations raise serious questions about whether this alleged movement toward each other was a genuine manifestation of Anglo-American friendship.

Part of the explanation for Britain's watchful attitude toward the United States lay in its apprehension about the aggressiveness of America's form of government. Many Englishmen by the 1840s demanded reform at home, and it is no surprise that conservative spokesmen frequently denounced America. The democratic example across the Atlantic was no comfort to a country threatened with violence at home. *Blackwood's Edinburgh Magazine* of London attributed America's assumed inability to conciliate differences to its republicanism. According to the writer, the restlessness of that government placed the highest interests of the United States "at the mercy of the multitude" and generated an infantile approach to international affairs. John Croker, respected naval and political figure, warned of what happened to France when its so-called democratic revolutions rocked the country's foundations. Reformers in Britain, he said, were wrong when they claimed that America had undergone successful democratic upheaval. No undermining of property rights and no major societal changes had occurred. In addition, Croker pointed out, Britain did not have the physical capacity to absorb dissidents. A democracy must have room for the discontented; otherwise it will fall victim to its factions. He concluded, as did many others of the Napoleonic generation, that it was not healthy to follow the democratic standard of the United States.[4]

Some political leaders in both countries, surveying the domestic and foreign dangers, saw the great risks involved in another Anglo-American war and resolved to work toward cordial relations. They faced serious obstacles—including America's insistence upon states' rights. Though the new, conciliatory atmosphere in London and Washington was conducive to compromise, a formal settlement of the northeast boundary and other issues depended almost as much on maintaining harmony between America's state and federal governments. Negotiated agreements, the diplomats came to realize, were subject to approval of the American states directly involved in the particular question. At a time when few Americans considered the federal government the final arbiter of domestic disputes, presidential administrations often had to make policy according to wishes of states' rightists. This situation should not surprise students of slavery, tariffs, land questions, the national bank, and internal improvement programs—but historians sometimes forget that the doctrine of states' rights also affected America's foreign policy.

Most Anglo-American issues by the 1840s involved policy disagreements between local and national levels of government in the United States. The northeastern boundary, the *Caroline* affair, the Aroostook War, the African slave trade and the attendant questions of impressment and the right of search, the *Creole* incident and extradition, the growing dispute over Oregon—all showed the danger in allowing local events to determine national policy. The people of New Brunswick and Maine risked forcing two nations into war because of a long-standing boundary dispute. The *Caroline* crisis, which caused some to speak of possible conflict between Britain and the United States, resulted from aid New Yorkers illegally gave to Canadians rebelling against crown rule and from a deep-rooted American desire for continental union. Three years later the Atlantic nations resumed their threats of war when Alexander McLeod, a British citizen arrested for suspicion of murder and arson during the *Caroline* attack, went to trial in New York because the federal government lacked authority to prevent a state from trying a case affecting international relations. The Aroostook War, an outgrowth of the northeastern boundary dispute, started as a lumberjacks' brawl, but local events soon threatened to get out of hand. Slavery itself became entangled in foreign affairs. Southerners, already angry with Britain for claiming a right of search in suppressing the African slave trade, demanded a promise of noninterference with American shipping after Nassau authorities freed mutinous slaves of the *Creole*. And, though Oregon was not a serious issue in 1842, it had the potential to become one, if western migration continued. Handled one by one, these matters might not have become difficult. But they reached crisis stage in quick succession, so that, between 1837 and 1842, leaders of the two countries were almost never without problems.

In sum, Anglo-American relations were in deep trouble again by the 1840s. Mutual suspicions, America's states' rights doctrine, the uneasy political situation in the United States—all threatened to override the social, political, economic, and demographic forces encouraging conciliation.[5] Evidence indicates that the Tyler administration wanted to act decisively toward Britain. But the peculiar position of Maine in the boundary controversy and the fight within the Whig party between the nationalistic forces of Henry Clay and the few states' rightists following Tyler made it difficult to formulate policy. In a painstaking, almost desperate manner, the president sought to resolve his dilemma of having to please the states involved in the controversies, while acting resolutely toward the British government. When he threatened to revert to the "shirtsleeve" tactics of Andrew Jackson, Britishers saw consistency in America's approach to foreign policy.

A study of Anglo-American affairs during the 1840s strongly suggests that the Tyler administration based much of its British policy upon power politics. Though the president and his secretary of state, Daniel Webster, might have wanted to adhere to party doctrine or to ideological persuasions, they were realists who knew that meaningful diplomacy derives from carefully balancing the nation's priorities with its means of enforcement. It was doubtful that the United States could create an effective military barrier against British moves in North America; but it might secure a settlement favorable to American interests by taking advantage of the island kingdom's domestic and foreign difficulties, as well as the recently developed connections between the Atlantic nations.[6] Tyler and Webster at times only stumbled in this direction, but the outcome made it appear that they had carefully measured each step.

One cannot understand America's foreign policy during the 1840s without considering its domestic context. The State Department could not count on effective support from a national government too weak to control domestic concerns. Washington's diplomats had to resort to secret means. Another factor was the differing political ideologies of America's policy makers. Tyler's states' rights beliefs often ran counter to his secretary of state's adherence to nationalism.[7] Webster consistently disagreed with states' righters in Maine and New York, a stance that must have been difficult for the president to accept. Yet Tyler agreed with his secretary that national concerns took priority over private or state considerations. The administration's foreign policy was well conceived, but ineptly executed. As has been the case throughout America's history, rational approaches to diplomatic problems often got entangled in domestic politics and emerged in different form. Tyler's foreign policy was in large part the product of internal political factors that complicated and sometimes obstructed the decision-making and implementation processes.

In assessing America's relations with Britain during the 1840s, it is important to note Webster's influence on Tyler. If the secretary was not an avowed expansionist, he recognized the danger of having a potential enemy firmly established along America's borders. If he was an Anglophile, he still was cautious about British aims in North America.[8] Webster realized that the United States could not force Britain from the continent. Yet he understood that a military road in the north was important to London and exerted pressure at strategic points in securing a favorable settlement. Webster's background as a lawyer convinced him that the United States had to base its foreign policy on sound, legally defensible grounds. Throughout the controversies with Britain, he stressed the importance of adhering to international law—admittedly because it sometimes was to America's advantage. But Webster—and Tyler—knew that in dealing with Britain, a nation with a long legal tradition, their most effective weapon was a foreign policy guided by the national interest and supported by the laws among nations.

Thus this study offers a different perspective of nineteenth-century diplomacy between the United States and Britain. It is impossible to ignore the elements that led to division and ultimately could have caused war. Only by identifying the components of the derision that characterized much of Anglo-American history after 1815 can one determine the strength of the ameliorative factors. The hostility that can arise when two peoples know each other so well and associate so closely becomes plain from a study of the Atlantic nations' common history. An abiding lack of faith in each other's motives created a highly sensitive atmosphere that lasted throughout much of the early nineteenth century. At first glance the diplomats apparently achieved the Webster-Ashburton Treaty with little trouble—the natural culmination of a series of low-key talks that placed the stamp of placidity on the early 1840s. This assessment is inaccurate. The surface calm and apparent openness of their talks concealed shrewd maneuvering by both negotiators. Webster and Ashburton recognized the necessity of resorting to the ancient art of personal diplomacy in establishing mutual trust and bringing about more than the mere rhetoric of peace. More important than the public issues, they dealt with questions involving national honor and control of North America—vital interests that raised the specter of power politics. Recent events had reaffirmed the realization in British minds that in the future the United States intended to influence expansionist activities in North America. A major test of their rivalry over the continent was the northeastern boundary dispute.

Acknowledgments

I have incurred numerous debts in writing this book. Special appreciation goes to Maurice G. Baxter, Robert H. Ferrell, Irene D. Neu, and David M. Pletcher, who offered continuous advice and encouragement. Also important were the reassurances of Forrest McDonald and Grady McWhiney. The general tone of Anglo-American relations during the nineteenth century outlined here resulted in part from Frank Merli's persuasive arguments; he also helped immensely with style and content. A steady inspiration during the early stages of this study was Thomas D. Clark. Others who read all or portions of the manuscript and made useful recommendations were Lloyd Ambrosius, John Braeman, Thomas H. Etzold, Robert Gunderson, William Harris, Duncan Jamieson, Robert Johnson, James Jones, James H. Madison, James Rawley, John Schneider, Jack Sosin, Tom Thompson, and Eileen Walters. In addition, I want to thank the editors of The University of North Carolina Press, Matthew Hodgson, Malcolm MacDonald (now with The University of Georgia Press), Trudie Calvert, and Gwen Duffey, as well as the unidentified readers of the manuscript, all of whom offered excellent suggestions on improving my work. I alone, of course, am responsible for errors in fact or judgment.

Little progress would have been possible without the aid of the following archivists. Those in Britain who performed several tedious tasks included Tom L. Ingram of Baring Brothers in London, who read sections of the manuscript, and who also assured me there were no items relating to the treaty in the Baring family archives; R. A. H. Smith of the British Museum; Margaret Cash of the Hampshire Record Office; John L. Walford of the Public Record Office; Carole Rawcliffe of the Royal Commission on Historical Manuscripts, who confirmed my suspicions that there were no records of any collections of Lord Ashburton's papers in the United Kingdom except those in the Public Record Office. Patricia Kennedy and C. MacKinnon in Ottawa gave valuable help on the holdings in the Public Archives of Canada. In the United States I received assistance from John J. McDonough of the Library of Congress; Albert H. Leisinger, Ralph E. Ehrenberg, and Bob Richardson of the National Archives; William R. Erwin, Jr., of the William R. Perkins Library, Duke University; John D. Cushing of the Massachusetts Historical Society; John C. Dann of the William L. Clements Library, the University of Michigan. Also of great assistance were the library staffs of Indiana University and the Eli Lilly Library, both in Bloomington, the University of Nebraska, and the University of Alabama. Thanks go to the custodians of the Lord Palmerston papers and to the holders of the Edward Everett manuscripts in the Massachusetts Historical Society for allowing me to quote from their collections.

Others made vital contributions. Especially significant was the typing of Ruth Kibbey, Ellie Love, and Kitty Sassaman. Boyd Childress helped locate the illustrations, while my wife Mary Ann, daughter Debbie, and mother assisted me in reading proof. I also am indebted to Charles M. Wiltse, editor of the Papers of Daniel Webster, who allowed me to read a paper in manuscript on Webster which later appeared in the *Proceedings of the Massachusetts Historical Society*. In addition, his superb microfilm edition of the rich collection of Webster papers provided the primary source of American material comprising this work. I am grateful to the editors of the following journals for permission to use materials previously published as articles: *Capitol Studies*, *Civil War History*, *The Historian*, and *The New England Quarterly*. Financial assistance from the National Endowment for the Humanities, the Andrew W. Mellon Foundation, Indiana University, and the University of Alabama allowed completion of this study.

Finally, and most important, sincere gratitude goes to my parents, my wife Mary Ann, and my children, for they alone understand what went into this project.

UNIVERSITY   *Howard Jones*
Spring 1977   THE UNIVERSITY OF ALABAMA

To the Webster-Ashburton Treaty

A *Study in Anglo-American Relations, 1783–1843*

1. *The Great Northeastern Boundary Gap*

Americans saw the dispute over the northeastern boundary of the United States as a major British challenge to their sovereignty because it ✓ foreshadowed certain Anglo-American rivalry over North America. Though most observers in the 1790s did not consider the boundary an important issue, the ensuing debate over its location highlights the fragility of the republic's first decades. Despite the brave words of the Declaration of Independence and the Constitution, the grand philosophies of the first officers of the government, and the optimism among Americans in general, the experiment in New World republicanism might not have succeeded. Domestic opposition to the new national government is familiar to any student of American history. The opposition of foreign governments, especially that of Britain, has had less attention, perhaps because Americans have regarded their experiment in liberty as an internal proposition, unaffected by foreign nations. For years few European regimes looked upon the American government with respect, but the open disdain of the British was especially irritating. Americans believed, with little evidence, that London officials refused to consider either the Treaty of Paris of 1783 or the Treaty of Ghent of 1814 as a ✓ basis for good relations, and as a result did not move decisively to resolve the boundary.

Contentions between Americans and Britishers over the international boundary went on for more than a half century, and it is revealing to trace the course of the dispute as a case study of Anglo-American difficulties. From the end of the Revolution until the 1840s, the British ✓ seemed purposely to avoid a large view of the subject. The wording in the northeast boundary article of the Treaty of Paris was specific: "From the North West Angle of Nova Scotia, viz. That Angle which is formed by a Line drawn due North from the Source of Saint Croix River to the Highlands along the said Highlands which divide those Rivers that empty themselves into the River St. Lawrence, from those which fall into

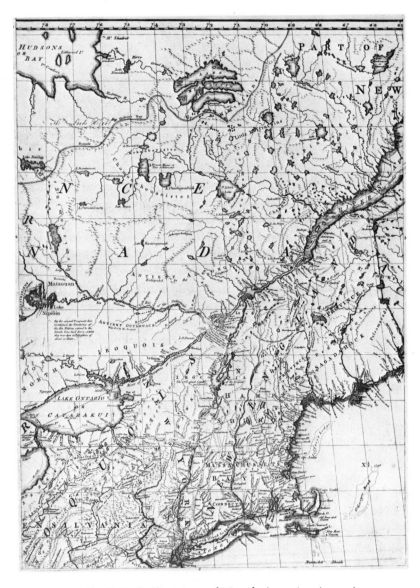

John Mitchell's Map of North America (1775)

the Atlantic Ocean, to the northwestern-most Head of the Connecticut River." But instead of resolving the question, the certainties of treaty language masked the uncertainties of North American topography, with long-lasting results. Indeed, these differences between Britain and the United States were not to be resolved until the Webster-Ashburton Treaty in 1842 finally ended the boundary dispute unwittingly created in the peace treaty of 1783.[1]

The many technicalities in plotting the northeast boundary generated the most serious Anglo-American arguments. The negotiators at Paris had used a 1775 impression of John Mitchell's famous *Map of the British and French Dominions in North America* (1755), the best map of its time, but the lack of surveys had forced the cartographer to guess at the location of many rivers and to omit important mountains and other land features. The Paris delegates had started their boundary at the St. Croix River—but no waterway of that name existed on the east coast of North America. A dispute developed over which of the region's rivers fitted the description of the St. Croix outlined in the treaty: the Schoodic in the west (the British claim), or the Magaguadavic in the east (the American). Title to some seven to eight thousand square miles of territory stocked with valuable timber and rimmed by a coastline allowing access to rich fisheries and vital waterways depended upon resolution of that problem.[2]

The Treaty of Paris created other cartographical problems as well. One concerned the northeast boundary's "highlands." Twenty years earlier the British government had used these slightly known ridges to divide the province of Quebec from Nova Scotia and New England, but they never had been surveyed. The treaty of 1783 specified a boundary that followed the highlands separating the flow of the waters of the St. Lawrence from those of the Atlantic. Did highlands mean mountains or only a watershed? This uncertainty caused another. The highlands formed the boundary to the northwesternmost head of the Connecticut River. No one afterward could determine which source of that river the negotiators meant. When Britishers contended for Indian Stream and Americans for Hall's Stream, the disputation added 150 square miles to the boundary argument.

There were still other difficulties. One arose from an erroneous survey of the forty-fifth parallel, the boundary along the top of Vermont and New York westward to Lake Erie; during the War of 1812 the United States unknowingly constructed a fort at Rouse's Point in British territory. Another question developed from the uncertainty of the international border running through the Great Lakes and to the Lake of the Woods.

Taken by themselves, these problems might have been susceptible to rapid solution; but they became intertwined with other matters to pose major obstacles to the establishment of harmonious Anglo-American relations.

In the period after 1783, Loyalists from Nova Scotia settled in the area between the Schoodic and the Magaguadavic and set off a dispute over the St. Croix that took a dozen years to resolve. The secretary for foreign affairs under the Confederation, John Jay, proposed a joint commission to settle the matter. Yet the British government rejected his overture—probably because it considered the entire subject relatively unimportant. Jay believed the situation was growing increasingly precarious and recommended that Massachusetts fortify key areas under "select and discreet officers" until Continental soldiers could take their place. Then, after adoption of the Constitution, the Massachusetts General Court in 1790 informed President George Washington that the British were encouraging settlers to occupy American territory. The president referred the question to the Senate, which soon repeated Jay's earlier proposal of a mixed commission.[3]

But European affairs intervened. When the British and French governments went to war in 1793, new, more pressing problems arose. John Jay, by this time chief justice of the Supreme Court, sailed for London the following year to defuse an explosive quarrel that had arisen from British interference with American commerce. The northeastern boundary question remained at best a secondary concern of both governments, but the European situation pressured William Pitt to settle some of his problems with the United States. Jay, however, failed to exploit his momentary advantage. He was surprised to receive a warm welcome from the king and queen, who were so cordial that the envoy decided not to mention his reception to the administration in Philadelphia for fear that Anglophobes might think the British government sought only to deceive him.[4] Southerners and Westerners remembered how willing he had been to forego navigation of the Mississippi River during the abortive negotiations with Spain in 1785–86. What could prevent him from giving up even more to win the favor of Britain, a country everyone knew Jay admired?

A small consequence of this British interest in rapprochement with the United States was a plan for settling the boundary, but even the business of resolving only a section from the Atlantic inland proved difficult. Jay's Treaty of 1794 marked the beginning of the modern history of arbitration when it provided that a three-member joint commission determine which river flowing into Passamaquoddy Bay was the St. Croix. Each government would name a commissioner, and these two men would choose a third. Two Americans and a Loyalist residing in Nova Scotia began work in the autumn of 1796.[5] Then the complications arose.

Almost immediately the Americans found themselves embarrassed, for they learned that the negotiators of 1782–83 had used a Mitchell map brought to Paris by the British representatives, a fact the American commissioner himself now uncovered by referring to letters written from Paris by Benjamin Franklin and John Adams. When the commission met in August 1797 at Adams's house in Quincy, the former diplomat, now president of the United States, stated that the Americans had consulted other maps in their quarters, even though he admitted that in drafting Article 2 he recalled using only a Mitchell. When the commissioners asked Jay (who also had been in Paris) about the matter, he agreed. The American side made another damaging admission. Adams and Jay confessed that in placing the boundary the delegates at Paris, both British and American, had not considered Mitchell's map conclusive.[6]

After considerable hassling, the commissioners succeeded in establishing only part of the northeastern boundary. The Schoodic, they announced, was the St. Croix intended by the treaty makers in 1783. The rest of the boundary, however, remained uncertain because there was no way to draw a line between the source of the St. Croix and the "highlands" mentioned in the treaty. No place in this northern area corresponded to the description in the treaty of 1783. A wide, irregular, elevated strip of land sprawled above the St. Croix, but there were no mountains. The British now claimed the St. John area, while the Americans argued that their country's territory stretched north of the Restigouche River (143 miles north of the British claim), along a line twenty miles inland from the lower St. Lawrence. Including the area around the Connecticut River's headwaters, the territory still in dispute after the commission filed its report in 1798 comprised a triangle of 12,027 square miles.[7]

The brief truce in the European war brought by the peace of Amiens in 1802 afforded a second opportunity to arrange the northeastern border. After the Americans informed British Foreign Secretary Lord Hawkesbury that they desired a settlement, their minister in London, Rufus King, a dignified, serious Federalist gentleman who expected immediate results in all affairs, received instructions to negotiate on the areas north of the St. Croix and through the Bay of Fundy. The United States appeared to have a good argument for several of the islands at the rim of Passamaquoddy Bay, but Secretary of State James Madison unfortunately made a tactical error in his directives that jeopardized his country's position. After defining the highlands above the St. Croix as "elevated ground dividing the rivers falling into the Atlantic," he wrote that the highlands of the treaty of 1783 were "now found to have no definite existence."[8]

Out of this confusion came the King-Hawkesbury Convention of 1803. Madison's instructions arrived in London in June 1802, a few days after King had departed on a three-month holiday in Europe. When the minister returned, he found difficulty in persuading Hawkesbury to devote time to the matter. At last came an understanding. There would be no problem in extending the line to the highlands, King wrote Madison with relief, as he and Hawkesbury had signed a convention for this purpose.[9]

The proposed agreement went to the Senate in October 1803, but with a message from President Thomas Jefferson that the northeastern boundary of 1783 was "too imperfectly described to be susceptible of execution." Although Secretary of the Treasury Albert Gallatin had urged approval, the president did not agree with Gallatin's reasoning. Oddly, Jefferson had submitted the treaty but recommended its defeat.[10]

The convention already had little chance for passage, but its downfall came primarily because the negotiators also had tried to patch a sector of the Canadian-American boundary on the other side of the Great Lakes, between Lake Superior and the Lake of the Woods, and the resultant proposal got entangled in the Senate's discussion of the Louisiana

Purchase. The British agreement had arrived in the autumn of 1803, not long after Jefferson's envoys had concluded the purchase treaty with Napoleon Bonaparte, and confusion quickly became apparent between the terms of the convention with Britain and the treaty with France. To deal with the matter, the Senate appointed a committee, chaired by the Anglophobic John Quincy Adams, and discussion soon focused on whether King and Hawkesbury had known of the purchase before signing the convention. Although King declared they had signed without knowledge, the committee decided that since no one understood the northern extremities of Louisiana it could not say whether there was conflict between the French and British agreements. Perhaps to salvage land claims farther north, the Senate in early February 1804 unanimously voted to accept all of the British convention except the portion concerning the Lake of the Woods boundary gap. The Pitt ministry, no doubt irritated with suspected American designs on Canada, refused this arrangement.

Other factors, such as resumption of the Franco-British conflict in May 1803, doubtless had an effect. There also may have been a mixture of American domestic politics. Jeffersonians, already suspicious of the British, perhaps had found their decision to vote against the convention easier because King was a potential presidential candidate on the Federalist ticket in 1804.[11] The King-Hawkesbury Convention thus expired, buried in the Louisiana Purchase and other seemingly unrelated matters.

The Americans and British made one more attempt to settle the northeastern boundary before going to war in 1812. James Monroe, minister in London, and William Pinkney, special envoy, signed a treaty with the British government in 1806 that involved commercial matters. Evidence indicates that both men considered America's commerce more important than any other subject. As a protégé of President Jefferson, Monroe cherished distinction in public service and might have signed almost any treaty with the British for the sake of accomplishment. Pinkney, a capable but stiff-mannered, cocksure lawyer, had been part of the Anglo-American commission established under Jay's Treaty to settle cases involving British seizures of American ships. This combination of talents augured ill for American interests. In addition to the commercial treaty, the envoys in 1806 hoped to reach a separate agreement dividing the islands in Passamaquoddy Bay. Monroe and Pinkney believed they had arranged the second convention, but when they sent back the first treaty on trade, Jefferson would not submit it to the Senate because the British government had not renounced impressment. By this time desertions had made the British navy so hard put to find seamen that it had begun to take suspect sailors found aboard privately owned ships of the United States. An unrelated issue—impressment—thus destroyed not only the commercial treaty of 1806, but also the possibility of a second convention on the boundary. A change in the British ministry further complicated matters. The Tories came back into power in March 1807 and opposed any agreements with the United States.[12]

The foregoing discussion shows that the major obstacle to an early boundary settlement was the United States—not Britain, as Americans unjustly claimed. The St. Croix commission decided in favor of the British, and when a war-conscious ministry in London found time to work for an agreement on the relatively unimportant northeast boundary, the government in Washington stalled and eventually rejected the pact. Though the Louisiana treaty, domestic politics, and the emotionally charged issue of impressment clouded responsible assessments of the boundary, the Americans themselves confused the question and must bear primary blame for obstructing its resolution.

The War of 1812 was integral to the northeastern boundary question because it convinced the British that they needed a military road between the Maritime Provinces and Lower Canada. The provinces—Nova Scotia and New Brunswick—long had been a source of naval supplies, seamen, and ships, while Lower Canada had become increasingly valuable to the crown because of its farmland and fisheries. The problem was how to defend such territories, especially Lower Canada. London's leaders could not rely on getting ships up the ice-choked St. Lawrence River in winter. During cold seasons British soldiers had marched on snowshoes through New Brunswick. Once they had maintained communication between Halifax and Quebec only by using a long overland route to the far north. In case of another war, British North America would be much more vulnerable to attack because of the expansion of roads and canals in the United States. During the winter the British might safeguard Lower Canada by maintaining troops at Kingston, Montreal, and Quebec, but without a fairly short overland route between the Maritime Provinces and Lower Canada, they could not reinforce the posts until spring weather opened the great river.[13]

The British effort to arrange better communication between the Atlantic Ocean and the Canadian interior began during the peace negotiations at Ghent in 1814. In the treaty of Christmas Eve, among other agreements, the two nations set up mixed commissions to deal with the boundary above the St. Croix, as well as with the undetermined sector between the Great Lakes and the Lake of the Woods. The American delegation—which included John Quincy Adams and Albert Gallatin—preferred to follow the precedent of Jay's Treaty by having three-member groups—one from each country, and the two choosing a third. There was no provision for arbitration, however. The British delegates accepted the first part of the proposal but rejected the second. They insisted that on each of the commissions there should be an American, a Briton, and a representative from a "friendly sovereign state," who in case of disagreement would hand down a binding decision. Adams, always suspicious of the British, immediately became defensive. Gallatin, more diplomatic in manner, enjoyed an extraordinary mixture of patience, wit, and generally agreeable disposition. He pushed hard to keep Adams at the peace table—especially when the British won on the issue of the boundary. British troops controlled many of the border areas, the Americans at Ghent were in no position to make demands, and so they compromised. The treaty provided for three commissions to settle the disputed portions of the North American boundary. The men could turn to arbitration if both governments agreed to do so.[14]

The Ghent boundary commissions were divided in results. Two were fairly successful. The first group gathered in 1816 and compromised a little more than a year later on ownership of the islands in Passamaquoddy Bay and the Bay of Fundy. The third, unable to fix the boundary from Lake Superior to the Lake of the Woods, nonetheless reached agreement in June 1822 on the line running through the Great Lakes. But the second commission, set up to determine the border between the source of the St. Croix and the intersection of the forty-fifth parallel with the St. Lawrence, failed miserably—primarily because its task was more difficult. At stake was Britain's overland communication. Three years of surveys led to a deadlock. Another delay followed, caused by American preoccupation with a boundary argument with Spain concerning Florida and by the series of events that led to the Monroe Doctrine. In the meantime other developments confounded the issue. Friendly relations among the commissioners all but disappeared. Someone stole the papers and equipment of a survey team. American citizens moved into the disputed region of Madawaska (claimed by the British) and declared loyalty to the United States. Maine became a state in 1820, and its officials refused to compromise on the area in question. The British commissioner, by now exasperated, believed that his American opposite was stalling. Finally, in 1822, the men filed their divergent reports. The bulk of the boundary around the hump of present-day Maine remained in dispute.[15]

The work of the second Ghent commission drew attention to several obstacles confronting a boundary settlement. The British needed a military road. The Americans wanted the hundred thousand acres of rich timberland at the head of the Connecticut River. And the two sides, as mentioned, had discovered the erroneous survey of the forty-fifth parallel. Fort Montgomery at Rouse's Point, an expensive project constructed during the War of 1812 and now called "Fort Blunder," stood awkwardly in British territory. It loomed as an important issue, and not merely because of embarrassment or cost. If the United States secured Rouse's Point, it would gain an important strategic advantage.[16]

The boundary question moved on, almost aimlessly. John Quincy Adams became secretary of state in the Monroe administration in 1817 and in two years had finished his settlement of border controversies with Spain by acquiring Florida from that country and securing a definite line between the United States and the viceroyalty of New Spain. By 1823, after Adams had halted Russian expansion south of Alaska, he perhaps felt that the time had come to complete the circle of his border calculations. In late July he directed the American minister in London, Richard Rush, to begin negotiation of several topics, including the northeast frontier. Adams wanted retention of Rouse's Point and Britain's recognition of America's right to navigate the St. Lawrence River. His instructions, however, were so ungenerous that they hindered a serious negotiation. In fact, his refusal to agree to any exchange of territory ensured failure. Adams's motives might have been partly political, since a candidate for the presidency in 1824—as he was—could not afford the opposition of Maine and Massachusetts. But Adams never had trusted the British, and for that reason alone may have taken his hard stand. The situation was not helped by Minister Rush, who shared Adams's intransigent attitude about Englishmen. When his British opposite in the Foreign Office proposed granting American navigation of the St. Lawrence in return for territory in northern Maine, Rush, in a remark worthy of his chief in Washington, crisply replied that the United States already had a right to the river.[17]

Two years later Adams, now president, tried again by instructing the minister in London, Gallatin, to reopen negotiations. Gallatin was to adopt any line acceptable to the Senate and the American people, but not to cede any part of Maine's territory or to renounce navigation claims to the St. Lawrence. The London talks began in the Foreign Office in November 1826 with the veteran of Ghent looking across the table at William Huskisson, also present at Ghent, and at Henry Unwin Addington, British chargé in Washington from 1824–25 and nephew of the former prime minister of the same name. After eighteen sessions Gallatin, tired of the difficult task, agreed in September 1827 to submit the boundary matter to arbitration by "some friendly sovereign or State," a contingency provided by the Treaty of Ghent.[18]

To pass the problem to an arbiter seemed sensible, but even this approach contained the potential of its own destruction. The first snag came in choosing an arbiter. When Adams had been secretary of state he had suggested the czar of Russia. In the autumn of 1826, Gallatin learned that the czar did not want to arbitrate the dispute. Having tangled with Secretary Adams in the summer of 1823, he had had enough experience with America's border problems. The contentious Americans had accepted the czar's offer of mediation during the War of 1812, hoping he would assist the United States in getting out of the war with Britain, but thereafter the thanks of the American republicans must have seemed hollow. Adams had warned the Russian government in 1823 to stay out of territory south of Alaska; and now the Americans were asking for the czar's help with another border dispute. London in 1827 tactfully proposed the king of the Netherlands. President Adams at first objected. William I, he said, was cousin of the king of England and had been an honorary general in the British army. But in June 1828 the president, himself tiring of the border issue and facing another election campaign, agreed to the appointment of William I.[19]

The border problem seemed unduly technical to a European

monarch accustomed to dealing with inhabited territory containing towns or cities—or at least some items of immediately ascertainable value. The sole duty of the king of the Netherlands or his representatives, presumably the latter, was to make a decision between the opposing American and British claims. William soon found that the solution to the controversy lay in the interpretation of maps. British and American negotiators at Paris in 1783 had used Mitchell's map, Gallatin admitted; however, that map, he added in a strange mixture of metaphors, was "only a skeleton, connecting the watercourses." He and Addington recommended that each side give the arbiter a Mitchell and any other supportive maps, along with a detailed defense of its claim. The British statement, duly prepared, reiterated the old demands by calling for a line extending north from the St. Croix to Mars Hill. Though that spot lay a hundred miles from streams emptying into the St. Lawrence, the British commissioner drew his line west from the hill so as to include the St. John River basin within British territory, a proposal that would permit a road joining the Maritime Provinces with Lower Canada and would give Britain the American-populated Aroostook Valley. The commissioner insisted that Britain indeed had rights to all western branches of the upper Connecticut.[20]

President Adams asked Gallatin to prepare the American case, and the minister willingly consented. To help in the project the president selected a judge on the supreme court of Maine, William Pitt Preble. Gallatin could not have known that his work with Preble marked the beginning of a long controversy over the boundary among Americans themselves and that as late as the 1840s both men still would be involved in the boundary problem. The two men gathered information during the next few months. Gallatin, since his return to America, had worked in Boston, Albany, and Washington, while Preble researched in New Brunswick. Near the end of 1828 they began collating their materials in a Washington hotel with the aid of fifteen assistants. The result was an eighty-seven-page booklet that was long enough for a novel, Gallatin told his wife, which King William did not receive until late December 1829. In support of the American claim Gallatin enclosed nineteen maps published between 1763 and 1781.[21]

Historians have debated whether Gallatin adequately prepared the American case. Samuel F. Bemis has asserted that if Gallatin had examined the map holdings of the British Museum he probably would have discovered a 1775 edition of Mitchell's map in the papers of King George III, which the British negotiators had used in the peace talks of 1782–83. Its red-line boundary, Bemis declares, substantiated the American claim to all of the disputed territory. According to this argument, Gallatin should not have relied on the Mitchell map because it did not show any highlands above the St. Croix. He even failed to tell the arbiter that the commissioners in 1782–83 had used a 1775 edition that, if inaccurate, constituted an improvement over the original published twenty years earlier. Frederick Merk, however, believes Bemis's criticism unfair. He has written that it is doubtful whether Gallatin could have turned up the King George map in the British Museum. Gallatin in 1827 had returned to the United States; possibly he could have gotten the map, had he stayed. But time would have run out on him, for in 1828 the museum's trustees resolved that no one could see materials pertaining to the treaty of 1783 unless in company of a trustee.[22]

Gallatin deserves criticism. After hearing arguments on the boundary he should not have depended upon the 1775 edition of Mitchell's map. In addition, the papers of John Jay contained a red-line map supporting American claim to the disputed territory. Though it did not become public until 1843, Gallatin might have discovered it earlier—had he researched Jay's papers. And one wonders why he was not curious about the King George III collection in the British Museum. Surely Gallatin's boundary discussions in 1814 and 1826–27 had suggested that a British map might have existed. If it was too late for him to dredge out the maps after 1828, there was no reason why he could not have acted earlier. Bemis's judgment is severe, but Gallatin's biographer, Raymond Walters, agrees with it. Some years later, in 1839, a discussion in Parliament led to the discovery that the King George map supported America's claim to the northeastern territory. Foreign Secretary Lord Palmerston immediately had the map interred in the Foreign Office, safe from American scrutiny.[23]

The king of the Netherlands meanwhile had made an award, in January 1831, and communicated his decision to Britain and the United States through their ministers at The Hague. Neither line claimed by the commissioners, William judiciously said, fitted the treaty of 1783, for it was impossible to locate the highlands described by the Paris negotiators.

After contending that neither the Restigouche nor the St. John emptied into the Atlantic but into the Bay of Fundy, William rejected both the American and the British cases and announced that the only solution was a compromise. His proposal awarded the United States 7,908 square miles of the 12,027 in dispute, but gave Britain the land necessary for the military road.[24]

The first reaction to the award came from the two Americans who had prepared their country's case. Preble, recently appointed minister to The Hague, argued in a note to King William's minister for foreign affairs that the arbiter had exceeded the powers granted him. The king's only responsibility was to choose between the competing claims. Preble repeated his charge to the British representatives at The Hague and forwarded his commentaries to the American secretary of state. After returning to Maine he published an anonymous pamphlet entitled *The Decision of the King of the Netherlands* in which he declared that Maine should reject William's compromise. The national government, he said, had no constitutional right to cede a state's territory without that state's consent. Before the award Gallatin warned that an arbiter might not make a decision on the basis of material presented; "an umpire, whether he be a King or a farmer," he said, might try to "split the difference." He now called the decision unfair and said the United States should not abide by it.[25]

For the government in Washington the king's decision presented problems. Though the British government agreed that William had violated his instructions, it was willing to accept the award. The problem was that Maine protested the compromise settlement as an infringement of its rights. A legislative committee reported that the arbitral agreement had not authorized the arbiter to substitute a new line and that the king should have made a choice between the American and British proposals. President Andrew Jackson privately favored the award, but politics prevented him from supporting it publicly. His political friends in Maine and Massachusetts warned that such action would drive Maine out of the Democratic party at a time when he sought to build a machine in the East to complement those in the South and West. The president believed the treaty line of 1783 unworkable and wanted immediate acceptance of the Netherlands award. Cabinet members, however, urged him to avoid responsibility for a decision by refusing to submit the award to the Senate for consideration. Ask that body only for advice, they said, and let it take ✓ blame for the outcome. Jackson let the matter lie for several months, but then gave in to states' righters from the Northeast. In his annual message of 1831 he announced he would send documents to the Senate and expressed hope that it would manage a settlement without violating the rights of Maine. Ten years later he privately admitted regret about having accepted his cabinet's advice and wished he had actively supported the ✓ award. An acquaintance reported that he said this was the only time in his life when he had let subordinates overrule his judgment.[26]

In the meantime, Jackson quietly did his best to get the border line established. He proposed that Maine receive a million acres of public land in exchange for giving up claim to territory north of the St. John and east of the St. Francis rivers. The offer was so attractive that even Preble considered it, and in February 1832 he met in Washington with the congressional delegation from Maine. Next morning he wrote Governor Samuel Smith that all of the state's representatives in Congress recommended accepting the award in return for the land indemnity. ✓ Secretary of State Edward Livingston agreed with Preble that before any arrangement became final it would have to meet Maine's approval.[27] About a week later Governor Smith confidentially gave his correspondence with Preble to the legislators in Augusta. The legislature went into secret session.

The result, nonetheless, was contrary to the president's wishes. When people in Maine learned that the legislature was meeting in Augusta with leaders of the Jacksonian party, suspicion spread that the Democrats, accused of being Anglophiles, might sell American territory to the British. Newspaper headlines appealed to national and party prejudice: "MAINE IN THE MARKET!" and "OUR FELLOW CITIZENS TRANSFERRED TO A FOREIGN POWER FOR CASH OR LAND!"—while Maine's legislature alternately blew hot and cold over Jackson's proposal, which did have attractive qualities. For giving up land north and east of the arbitration line the state would receive a million acres in Michigan ✓ territory worth about $1,250,000. Governor Smith appointed Preble and two others as commissioners to deal with the national government. Preble then had a change of heart. In Washington, much to the disappointment of the Jackson administration, he and his colleagues told their state's senators that it was "exceedingly desirable, if not indispensable" that the Senate refuse the line proposed by the king of the Netherlands. Public pressure from Maine had prevailed.[28]

The Senate in Washington now entered the dispute. The Foreign Relations Committee recommended acceptance of the arbitral decision, but in June 1832 the Senate rejected it by vote of 21 to 20. It then resolved, 23 to 22, that the president reopen negotiations to determine the line established in 1783. Secretary of State Livingston suggested to the British minister, Charles Bankhead, that Washington host the meetings. He hinted that if the two countries could not locate the boundary the United States might be able to set up a compromise line because of a recent understanding with Maine. But when he proposed that Britain grant navigation rights on the lower St. John, Foreign Secretary Palmerston declared that he could not combine the navigation and boundary issues. Then Maine's legislature killed all hopes of compromise by announcing that no agreement between the federal government and Britain could be binding unless approved by a majority of the state's people assembled in town meetings.[29]

In the spring of 1833, Secretary Livingston again tried to arrange joint commissions with an arbiter to resolve disagreements. Realizing he could hope only for the line of 1783, or more properly, for Maine's interpretation of it, he tried to persuade the new British minister, Sir Charles Vaughan, to accept a boundary extending northeast or northwest from the source of the St. Croix to the highlands. The secretary admitted that the line would not run due north in accord with the precise treaty stipulation ("due North from the Source of Saint Croix River to the Highlands"). But Vaughan feared that any modification of the line might take territory from New Brunswick. He eventually informed the government in Washington that if Britain submitted to "the pretensions of the State of Maine," the United States would benefit from every defect in the Treaty of Paris.[30] The British government thus could accept neither the American version of the treaty line of 1783 nor an American alteration. And even if by chance the two countries reached agreement, it would be subject to approval by town meetings in Maine.

In the years after 1783, Americans unfairly complained that the essential reason for failure to settle the northeastern boundary was British refusal to treat them as a nation worthy of respect. The truth was that London's leaders faced one problem after another that unavoidably forestalled a major boundary settlement. Though the St. Croix commission of the 1790s had determined the boundary line for a short distance, events in Europe dominated diplomacy until 1815. Thereafter, diplomatic discussion, including arbitration, had not worked. But this was not Britain's fault, as Americans charged. Several important works show that the British sought accommodation with the United States throughout this period.[31]

The primary obstruction to a border settlement was the United States. Time and again boundary commissions, some dominated by Americans, decided in Britain's favor. More than once Washington's leaders rejected agreements Americans themselves had negotiated. Indeed, one wonders if they hoped that delay might lead to a more favorable de facto line brought about by Americans settling in the disputed area. Yet there were other factors. By the early 1830s Maine had entered the controversy and had begun to force the issue. Politics persuaded Jacksonians to be cautious about alienating that state's voters. When the president offered land in Michigan to Maine, he encouraged state officials to hold out for more. It was ironic that Jackson tried to placate states' righters in Maine at the same time he threatened to use the Force Bill against South Carolina nullifiers.[32] The issues, of course, were different: Maine posed no threat to the Union, only an annoyance to the Democratic party. Yet the affair revealed Jackson's willingness to yield to political danger. If he had declared himself in favor of the arbitral award, it might have met Senate approval. The Democratic party might have suffered a minor setback, but would not have lost the election of 1832. A border settlement at this early time would have reduced the danger of an Anglo-American confrontation in the 1840s, but despite assertions by Americans, Britain was not the source of the trouble. In any event, resolution of the boundary had to await a crisis along the Canadian border in 1837–38.

2. *The* Caroline *Affair*

Late in 1837, during the Canadian rebellion against Britain, one of the most potentially explosive events in Anglo-American relations since the War of 1812 occurred. The *Caroline*, a privately owned American steamboat whose owner was accused of giving illicit aid to the insurgents, was captured, burned, and sunk near Niagara Falls by Canadian volunteers under command of two British officers at nearby Chippewa, Colonel Allan MacNab of the militia and Captain Andrew Drew of the Royal Navy. Because the vessel had been destroyed on their side of the Niagara River and an American had been killed, Americans along the New York-Canada border immediately demanded war with England. The event, they declared, had violated national honor. Government leaders in London and Washington faced the task of preventing this inflammatory incident from developing into a third Anglo-American war.

The rebellion in Canada encouraged America's border residents to think again of ending British rule in North America. Hurt by the growing depression, wanting to carry the democratic banner into Canada, or simply coveting land there, they assisted insurgents seemingly affected by the "spirit of '76." Interest in Canada was not new. A considerable number of Americans deeply regretted that British dominion in North America had not been removed in 1783, and they always had seemed committed to an early form of manifest destiny—continental union. Though expansionist aims in the United States eventually turned to the Gulf and Pacific shores, Americans along the Canadian border wanted the northern areas as well. Self-government in Canada would lead to separation, they hoped; meanwhile, infiltration would prepare its inhabitants for union with the United States. Anti-Jackson newspapers during the late 1820s urged the United States government to buy Canadian lands to offset the contemplated purchase of Texas, and there was talk that the nation should exchange Oregon territory for Upper Canada and the area around Montreal. The *North American Review* declared that union of Canada and the United States would lessen the chance of hostilities. Admitting that such a bond should result only from Canada's request, it nonetheless urged private citizens to encourage the move.[1]

When the Canadian rebellion broke out, many Americans openly sympathized with the insurgents' objectives. Among the complex issues were demands for election of all officials, more popular participation in government, and a new banking system.[2] Drawing on examples from the American Revolution, the rebels established vigilance committees, committees of public safety, committees of correspondence, and Sons of Liberty. The British Constitutional Act of 1791 had not granted popular government, and by dividing the colony into Upper and Lower Canada it did nothing to encourage the British in the western province to mix with the French in the east. Though the government of Upper Canada had conceded a partly democratic franchise, the legislative council and executive (neither chosen by the people) could defeat any measure proposed by the elected assembly.

Plans to eliminate British influence in North America were developed in meetings along both sides of the border from Lake Champlain to Lake Michigan. Attracted by the promise of money and land, the first "Patriot" army in the United States was organized in Buffalo, New York, in mid-December 1837. Open recruiting followed, and in about a month the number of enlistments had reached nearly a thousand. Supporting organizations appeared, some of which, such as the Canadian Refugee Relief Association and the Sons of Liberty, disappeared after the first unsuccessful attempts to invade Canada. But secret societies like the Hunters' Lodges and Chasers, similar to the Masons, dedicated themselves to the elimination of British influence in North America and eventually spread between Vermont and Michigan and into Canada and the southern states.[3]

Newspaper opinion leaves the impression that most Americans opposed active government interference with the rebellion, but that they did not mind a neutrality favoring the rebels. The Albany *Argus* did not discourage individual participation and hoped that Canadian independence would allow the United States to settle the northeastern boundary and secure navigation of the St. Lawrence River. When Lord John Russell's parliamentary resolutions of March 1837 rejected Lower Canada's demands for self-government and precipitated the rebellion, the *National Intelligencer* declared that the British government deserved to lose Canada. Yet like the *Argus* it advocated neutrality. The *Intelligencer* went a step farther, however, and questioned the moral right to intervene.[4] Freedom would result without aid from the United States, it predicted; and political similarities might incline the province to gravitate to the United States.

President Martin Van Buren faced numerous obstacles in attempting to restrain Americans from interfering with Canadian affairs. He dutifully warned that anyone aiding the rebels would receive no assistance if captured. But the Neutrality Act of 1818 only provided punitive measures after the fact; it did not establish steps by which the president could *prevent* filibustering. If Americans were arrested for helping the rebels, there was no guarantee of punishment; juries were reluctant to convict alleged offenders. Nor could Van Buren rely on military force, for the army numbered only 7,130 men in December 1837, 4,000 of whom were fighting Seminoles in Florida. He could not count on civil officials; they either were inefficient or sympathized with the rebel cause and refused to enforce the laws. The situation was dangerous politically as well, for although Van Buren's Democratic party was actively expansionist, it desired no war with the British. His long association with the aggressive Andrew Jackson, normally an asset, now made Democrats wonder if Van Buren's peaceful measures were temporary.[5] Thus the president was in an unenviable position. If he adopted repressive measures his party could suffer politically—especially in his own New York; if he did not, the Whigs could charge him with wanting war with England. Confronted by Whigs and dissatisfied Democrats, by an economic depression, and by the weakness of neutrality legislation, Van Buren tried to keep peace.

After the insurgents failed to take Toronto in early December, their chieftain, William Mackenzie, and about twenty-five others established a provisional government on Navy Island on the Canadian side of the Niagara River and prepared to invade the mainland. The island, seemingly formidable because its banks were from ten to twenty feet high and almost everywhere perpendicular to the surrounding waters, was about a mile above the falls and directly across from Schlosser on the American side. Its sole occupants, a widow and her son, had converted its only building into a tavern that had become a rendezvous for outlaws. The rebels, by now attracting more supporters, received artillery and other weapons from New York arsenals, while rumor spread along the border of an impending attack on Chippewa. Some observers estimated the number of men on Navy Island at five thousand, including several Americans, but there were actually about a tenth that many. Mackenzie issued a proclamation calling for democratic reforms, and his men raised a flag of twin stars and a new moon peering through the clouds. Colonel Rensselaer Van Rensselaer of Albany, an American chosen by Mackenzie to lead the rebel army, readied his little force for battle. At this point the lieutenant governor of Upper Canada, Sir Francis Bond Head, warned Van Buren of the imminence of war.[6]

Before the government could decide what to do about the crisis developing on Navy Island (soon called the "Island of Liberty"), the *Caroline* arrived in the Niagara area. The forty-five-ton American steamer, owned by William Wells of Buffalo, left that city's harbor early on 28 December with a license to carry passengers and cargo between Buffalo and Schlosser. Though Head concurred with the British militia commander at Chippewa, Colonel Allan MacNab, who said he had information that someone on Navy Island had hired the *Caroline* to transport men and war materials, Wells later argued that he had not made a contract but had made his boat available, admittedly at exorbitant rates, to anyone wanting to cross the river. During the twenty-mile trip from Buffalo to the Niagara region, the *Caroline*'s crew raised the American ensign. Someone on the Canadian shore near Black Rock Dam opened fire on the boat, but no injuries resulted. When it arrived the next day at Navy Island several passengers disembarked and the crew unloaded cargo. The *Caroline* then left for Schlosser on the American side of the river and arrived around three o'clock in the afternoon. It made two more trips to Navy Island that day, bringing men each time. Though Wells claimed that his boat had transported no war materials to the island, he admitted that on one passage it carried a six-pound cannon. Curiously, he dismissed this as unimportant because the gun belonged to a passenger.[7] Early in the evening mechanical difficulties caused the crew to chain the *Caroline* to the dock at Schlosser.

Several other incidents made MacNab determine to destroy the steamer. An officer of the British navy had set out to round Navy Island in a small boat to investigate the strength of the fortifications, but as he gazed through his spyglass, a cannon opened fire on him. That same day muskets were fired from Grand Island (American soil) at Chippewa. Perhaps not knowing that the *Caroline* was moored in American waters at Schlosser, MacNab assured a New York attorney that he had no intentions of invading American territory and ordered Captain Andrew Drew of the navy to destroy the boat.[8]

According to Drew's later report to MacNab, five boats carrying forty-five volunteers left at eleven o'clock that night, expecting to find the *Caroline* at Navy Island. Pushing across the Niagara with the falls thundering to their left, the men rowed into the breakwater of the island. Not finding the *Caroline* at the wharf, they moved on, locating the steamboat about midnight—within American waters. Drew nevertheless ordered his men to move their boats slowly toward the vessel. Within a hundred yards the *Caroline*'s sentry spotted them in the moonlight and called, "Who comes there?"—once, twice, three times—and demanded the countersign. "Friend," finally answered Drew, now less than twenty yards away. "I'll give the countersign when I get on board!" The sentinel opened fire, but the men already were boarding, armed with cutlasses, pikes, and pistols. The British party drove the thirty-three sleepy passengers and crew to the shore and had control in less than ten minutes.[9]

While British and American witnesses testified that no one on board the *Caroline* was armed and that Drew's men took the boat quietly, their story is unlikely. For one reason, New Yorkers had expected a British attack on Navy Island earlier that day—29 December—and had gathered at Schlosser to watch. These circumstances suggest that at least the *Caroline*'s crew would have been armed. Since the boat had been *chained* to the dock, not moored by rope in the usual manner, the officers on board must have expected trouble. In addition, three men in the boarding party, two of them officers, received gunshot and knife wounds during the attack, and a stage driver from Buffalo, Amos Durfee, died from a shot through the forehead while standing on the dock nearby. Though the question of whether anyone on the *Caroline* was armed may not seem worth argument, it *was* important to the British participants who later sought to defend their actions against the charge of massacre leveled by American newspapers and other sympathizers with the rebellion. In the excitement of the attack the British volunteer force perhaps mistook its men for the enemy, although some witnesses said that the moonlight must have illuminated the red arm patches worn by Drew's men. Shepard McCormack of the British navy, a member of the boarding party who was wounded severely during the melee, said almost a year after the event that he had met resistance from three men on the *Caroline* and had seen many others carrying swords and pistols.[10]

Because of the swift current of the Niagara and the proximity of the falls, Drew decided not to tow the *Caroline* to the British side. Making sure no one, dead or alive, remained on board, he ordered it set afire. Considerable time elapsed before the crew managed to break the chain holding the *Caroline* to the dock, pull the boat to the middle of the river, and start the fire. Flames quickly enveloped the wooden hull, and the three-foot-long flag fell from the stern. Wells's risky investment had cost him $4,600.[11]

Eyewitness accounts mistakenly claimed many victims in the struggle over the *Caroline*. Misinformed, Drew told MacNab that his men had killed five or six, while a witness swore that a black man lay dead on the wharf. A Canadian testified that in a Queenstown bar he overheard two British participants boast that they had slaughtered everyone aboard. In a more plausible story the commander of the boat, Gilman Appleby, told the New York grand jury that he had encountered a British soldier named Angus McLeod on the deck who screamed, "Down, you damned Yankee!" and momentarily held his sword against Appleby's chest. Several others on the *Caroline* testified that the boarding party cried out, "G——d damn them! Give them no quarter! Kill every man! Fire, fire!"[12]

It was indeed an awful massacre—according to the newspapers. Dubbing MacNab the "Robespierre of the age," the Livingston *Register* of Geneseo, New York, urged the "Eagle of the North" to avenge national honor on the principle of "Blood for Blood." *Niles' Register* reported that British soldiers had killed all but two or three of the thirty persons aboard and sent the boat over the falls. The *National Intelligencer* warned that destruction of the *Caroline* had seriously endangered peace. Nearly 150 men had boarded the boat, it said, and after giving three cheers for Queen Victoria they killed twenty-two. Several New York newspapers claimed that British soldiers had butchered everyone on board the *Caroline*. Weeks after the event, Mackenzie tried to rekindle American hatred by publishing a paper called *The Caroline Almanac*, which showed the boat in flames, its terror-stricken passengers on the rail, as it drifted over the falls. The New York *Herald*'s correspondent in Buffalo declared: "Surely war with England was unavoidable."[13]

Settlers in western New York began arming, their newspapers carried military orders, the frontier was inflamed. By early February 1838, the Niagara County court had issued a murder indictment against MacNab, Angus McLeod, and others. According to a poem published at the time,

> As over the shelving rocks she broke,
> And plunged in her turbulent grave,
> The slumbering genius of freedom woke,
> Baptized in Niagara's wave,
> And sounded her warning Tocsin far,
> From Atlantic's shore to the polar star.

In a brief article entitled "Quick on the Trigger," the *Herald* announced that New York theaters were preparing a patriotic play based upon destruction of the *Caroline*. Government actions in Canada further incensed Americans. The legislature of Upper Canada celebrated the *Caroline* victory by presenting swords to MacNab and Drew, and Lieutenant Governor Head and the Canadian press publicly approved the attack.[14]

Many in New York demanded war with Britain. Rochester politicians delivered inflammatory speeches to huge crowds of irate citizens, while in Albany, according to the New York *Herald*, there was a "silent, sullen, settled determination of vengeance" among "young, active, hardy, and daring men," who bragged in the streets that they would dine in Toronto in a couple of weeks. At a public meeting chaired by the mayor and attended by fifteen hundred people in the city's park, great disorder followed cheers of "Hurrah for the patriots!"; "Three groans for Mac-Nab!"; and "Down with Sir Francis Head! Off wid his head!"[15]

The situation in Buffalo was more disturbing. The New York *Herald* recorded that men beat drums while soldiers marched, "convulsively" grasping their muskets. Citizens readied cannon to defend the city, while a West Point cadet, "a splendid fellow," led a company of volunteers down to Grand Island, planted the flag, and swore to protect the United States. Highlighting events was the public funeral of Amos Durfee. In the evening of 30 December, the *Herald* reported, the rebels exhibited his draped body in front of the Eagle Hotel, its "pale forehead, mangled by the pistol ball, and his locks matted with his blood!" After placing his remains on the veranda of city hall they advertised the funeral by coffin-shaped posters. Nearly three thousand persons attended the obsequies the following day. With the coffin resting on the steps of the courthouse before the jammed public square, an Episcopal clergyman offered a prayer for Durfee, and the *Herald* reported that a young attorney gave a "speech more exciting, thrilling, and much more indignant than Mark Antony's."[16]

President Van Buren learned of the *Caroline* affair just before an Executive Mansion dinner on 4 January. General Winfield Scott, Henry Clay, nineteen Whig friends, and three or four Democrats had arrived; but long after time for dinner, the president had not appeared. After a while the guests learned he was in a cabinet meeting, and the Whigs jokingly asked the Democrats if Van Buren planned to resign. Eventually the chubby little president, drawn and pale, entered the room and went directly to Clay and Scott. Informing them blood had been shed, he ordered Scott to the Niagara border. The secretary of war was writing instructions that moment.[17]

Van Buren then invoked the neutrality proclamation, ordered out the militia, and warned that anyone interfering was subject to arrest and punishment. Turning to Congress, the president asked for military appropriations and announced that he would seek reparation for the *Caroline*. Congress immediately set aside such important matters as the subtreasury issue, John C. Calhoun's proslavery resolutions, and the Mexican claims dispute and began an extensive, bitter debate on the new crisis.

Most congressmen did not want war with Britain, but many from all sections of the country feared its imminence unless the Van Buren administration secured reparation for the *Caroline*. The indignant Representative Millard Fillmore of New York told the House that MacNab's orders to destroy the *Caroline* had been especially infuriating because the colonel had offered assurances just before the attack that the United States need not fear invasion. Fillmore disgustedly pointed out that Drew disobeyed orders, yet MacNab had praised him. Representative John Quincy Adams of Massachusetts expressed fear that the United States was in danger of war. Several congressmen railed in anger at the alleged massacre, a "foul, wilful, deliberate, unmitigated murder," exclaimed Waddy Thompson of South Carolina. Richard Menefee of Kentucky drew criticism from all sides when he declared that he could not favor war because there was no great principle involved in the *Caroline* incident, such as the right of search and impressment of American seamen. "No principle involved! Great God!" exclaimed Thompson. "No principle involved in the invasion of our territory by a hostile band of another nation, and the murder, with fiendish atrocity, of our sleeping and unoffending citizens?" In the Senate, John C. Calhoun of South Carolina urged calm, while Henry Clay of Kentucky considered the event atrocious and wholly unjustifiable, but wanted peace and called on the British to make reparation. Thomas Hart Benton of Missouri seemed to express the sentiment of both houses when he angrily concluded that full redress was imperative.[18] Congress appropriated $625,000 for defense of the northern frontier.

The diplomats finally took over. The Department of State and the Foreign Office exchanged many notes through March and helped to alleviate the crisis by moving the focus of attention to the moderates who favored peace. Secretary of State John Forsyth, influential Jacksonian Democrat and former senator from Georgia, urged reparation for the destruction of American property and murder of American citizens.[19] Lord Melbourne's government, however, delayed reply. Assumption of responsibility for the act clearly would have made Britain the aggressor, disputing reports that there had been no intention to invade American territory. No one seemed to realize that until British officials called the attack a "public act" (committed under government orders), participants were subject to prosecution by New York courts.

Over a month after the incident the British minister in Washington, Henry Fox, explained to Forsyth that the "piratical character" of the *Caroline* and the inability of New York to enforce American neutrality laws had justified destruction of the boat wherever it was found. Labeling the *Caroline* a "pirate," Fox knew, authorized all states concerned to destroy it. He might have added that the United States' declaration of neutrality, though not formal recognition of the Canadian insurgents, was akin to regarding Navy Island as a state at war—hence liable for breaches of law. Although piracy usually is associated with offenses on the high seas, the crown's law officers in late February 1838 supported Fox's reasoning by saying that under the dire circumstances destruction was justifiable by the law of nations and that the place of the boat's mooring could not be construed as neutral territory. Forsyth countered that the *Caroline* had not been engaged in piracy, for the owner had registered it in Buffalo as a freight and passenger boat and it had been flying the American flag. A resident of Canada, however, later claimed convincingly that Wells had chartered the *Caroline* to the Patriots in Buffalo for $6,000 a month.[20]

Back and forth went the diplomatic argument. The American minister to Britain, Andrew Stevenson of Virginia, declared to British Foreign Secretary Lord Palmerston that one of the most sacred principles in public law was immunity of neutral territory during war. Since there was no imminent danger to British forces in December 1837, he argued, London could not justify the invasion. Settlement of the matter, Stevenson concluded, belonged to the national governments, not to subordinate officers.[21]

Though Palmerston promised only to consider the minister's note, informal discussion with the foreign secretary convinced Stevenson that the British government would acknowledge the attack as a public act, justified by the law of nations. Canadian officials admitted that Drew had dealt with the *Caroline* according to the "Usages of War." It was an act of "necessity," Palmerston declared, caused by the "impending destruction" of British control over the situation. The truth was that there was no way Britain could evade responsibility: Canadian volunteers had destroyed the boat in an effort to suppress the rebellion against the crown; the lieutenant governor of Upper Canada had approved the act publicly; the provincial assembly had awarded swords to MacNab and Drew. Palmerston's silence could be interpreted as approval of the act. He may have hoped to gain from delay; after all, the *Caroline* had been destroyed without the London government's permission or foreknowledge. Whatever his strategy, it was not until nearly six months after Stevenson's request for reparation that the foreign secretary instructed Fox, on 6 November 1838, to admit that destruction of the *Caroline* was a public act. For some unexplained reason—Fox later said it was because there was never a question that the *Caroline*'s destruction was a public act—the British minister did not inform the United States of his government's decision for two years. He perhaps assumed that his labeling the steamboat's activities as piracy implied that its destruction was justified by self-defense and that such act was "public"; but his failure to make this point clear allowed a bad situation to become worse.[22]

General Scott meanwhile had proceeded to the frontier. Secretary of War Joel Poinsett had instructed the fifty-two-year-old soldier to assume command of American forces along the Canadian border and to request militia from the governors of New York and Vermont. Poinsett did not authorize the use of army regulars, and the New York *Herald* wryly commented that the government had sent him on a "fool's errand." Scott surely had enough to do. According to his own perhaps exaggerated account, he was to restore order along a frontier eight hundred miles long, enforce weak neutrality laws, and protect the United States from British attacks—all through "rhetoric and diplomacy."[23]

Scott encountered many problems. Moving through territory untouched by railroads, he, his aide, and a black servant traveled mostly at night in a huge sleigh pulled by four horses, each man taking turns warming himself under a stack of fur robes. At one point exhaustion and a stomach ailment forced the general to bed, but during his healthy days he marched before American troops at every chance, a stately military hero, over six feet tall and dressed immaculately in blue and gold uniform. Perhaps these exhibitions were ostentatious, but they assured some observers that he intended to keep order. A resident of Buffalo noted the secure feeling "this yellow-plumed, gold-laced hero" gave to everyone. Crowds, often hostile at first, gathered to hear Scott denounce American interference with British affairs. In most cases his calling the *Caroline* incident a national outrage received applause. Britain owed the United States reparation and an apology, he said, but only the president and Congress should deal with the matter. Unarmed, except for his sword, he thanked God for America and challenged his listeners: "I tell you, then, except it be over my body, you shall not pass this line—you shall *not* embark."[24]

Scott apparently convinced Colonel Van Rensselaer to abandon the war effort. At a meeting with the rebel leader near Niagara Falls on the night of 13 January 1838, he told the young man that the rebels' cause was hopeless. Though there are no records of the conversation, Scott's lecture might have brought Van Rensselaer to a decision—or bolstered one already made. In any case, the insurgents left Navy Island the following day and retreated to Fort Malden near Buffalo. Governor William Marcy of New York had Van Rensselaer arrested on 15 January, but he soon was free on bail and planning another invasion. Shortly thereafter he jumped bail and fled to Canada where the authorities promptly arrested him; this time he stayed in jail.

Other border incidents taxed Scott's patience, but fortunately his moderating influence prevailed. Perhaps because of Scott, but certainly because of the lack of strong insurgent leadership, the rebellion proceeded disastrously, and by late 1838 it was over. During the first week in November rebels in Lower Canada rose in revolt; apparently the Hunters planned to invade the upper province. But the rebel attack was poorly organized and was led by a general who marched behind his men. Van Buren issued another neutrality proclamation that same month, and in early 1839 he again resorted to Scott. Canadian officials soon spoke of the improved feeling along the border, and interest in secret societies quickly waned. By the end of the year most Americans had reservations about intervening in British affairs.[25]

The British government in the meantime had sent a special mission to Canada led by Lord Durham to resolve the insurgents' problems peacefully. After arriving in Quebec in early 1838, he dispatched his wife's brother, Colonel Charles Grey, to Washington to settle some of the touchy border issues. Both countries increased patrols along neighboring waters. They even circumvented the Rush-Bagot agreement of 1817 by instituting, for the first time, joint patrol of the Great Lakes. When Durham produced his report in February 1839, reformers welcomed his recommendations for union of the two Canadas and establishment of popular government. But the ensuing Canada Union Act of 1840 only unified the Canadas; not until 1848 did Lord Elgin's ministry recognize the principle of responsible government. Most important to Anglo-American relations, the ideas contained in the Durham Report helped to eliminate the causes of the rebellion and lessened the possibility of collision between Britain and the United States.[26]

If the governments in London and Washington had not insisted on peace in early 1838, the *Caroline* affair might have combined with the northeastern boundary and other Anglo-American differences to embroil the two countries in war. The basic issues over national honor were present, as they had been prior to the War of 1812. What more explosive events could have happened than for British soldiers to have invaded American territory, destroyed American property, and killed an American citizen? When one considers that these acts were committed by Britain, a country many Americans believed would do anything to win control of North America, it was no small accomplishment that British and American diplomats preserved the peace.

Though Britain and the United States seemed dangerously close to conflict in early 1838, close analysis reveals that war fever noticeably declined except along the Canadian frontier, and that many congressional members from all sections of the country were satisfied only to criticize the Van Buren government for not acting immediately and forcefully to secure redress. Few wanted war. Even British Minister Fox, no admirer of the United States, discerned that it was primarily irresponsible members of the press, political opportunists from New York, and small numbers of unthinking private citizens who demanded war. The Richmond *Enquirer* happily remarked in mid-January that excitement had diminished. While the Washington *Globe* urged peace throughout the crisis, the *National Intelligencer* gratefully announced that the "tragico-comico Navy Island affair" was about to end. General Scott's energetic course was a factor. Several British leaders expressed faith in his "high character" and "known discretion." A steadying influence surely was Van Buren's belief that Palmerston truly sought conciliation. The foreign secretary's confidence in the president's "Friendly Spirit" and "perfect good faith" also was important, as was the preoccupation of both nations in other matters. In addition to domestic issues, Britain had problems in Afghanistan, Egypt, and China. Even the emerging Texas question made British leaders hesitant about protesting Canadian affairs.[27] The United States also had problems. Besides the depression, it had to deal with Mexico and with the slavery question. Most important, diplomats and government leaders from both countries realized that neither side could afford a war.

3. The Aroostook War

The Canadian rebellion hardly had ended when a second border crisis developed—this one between New Brunswick and Maine. Though the ensuing incidents were bloodless, the so-called "Aroostook War" sharpened concern over the unsettled northeastern boundary by raising the issue of national honor and threatening the balance of power in that section of North America. Uncertainty over the line's location had encouraged intrusions by both Canadians and Americans. Though contemporaries believed that much of the area was virtually worthless, it contained good farmlands and rich pockets of timber. In addition, the British had learned during the War of 1812 that they needed land for a military road between Halifax and Montreal. This need aroused suspicions of Americans who were already anti-British and again increased the danger of war.

By the 1830s both Canadians and Americans called the richly forested strip of land lying between them the "disputed territory." British desire for a military road, perhaps a railroad, between their Maritime Provinces and the Canadian interior; their rivalries with the United States over the timber and rich soil of the Aroostook and Madawaska valleys; competing local patriotisms that often got entangled with questions of honor; mutual hatreds stemming from many recent events—all these underlined the fact that by the close of the decade it had become of vital concern that the British claim in the area did not coincide with the American claim. The Aroostook War, then, was the outgrowth of the long-standing northeastern boundary dispute, the expanding Anglo-American interest in North America, and the deep-seated Anglophobia in Maine that had become increasingly dependent upon the doctrine of states' rights.

When Maine entered the Union in 1820 as part of the Missouri Compromise, its northern boundary was surely the least of Congress's worries. Even in the latter part of the decade, the state was not important politically to the Democratic administration in power, for the Jacksonians won office again and again, despite their failure in the early 1830s to build a strong machine in the Northeast. Maine's internal policies, however, led to problems along the border. Its leaders had issued liberal land grants to farmers along the western frontier, but the new landowners found it more profitable to rent their animal teams to lumbermen than to work what they thought was untillable land. As timber camps moved farther into the forests, settlers from New Brunswick who also had received land titles, along with many who had not, moved into the disputed territory as well. Trouble was predictable.

If border incidents were not vitally important to the governments in London and Washington, they became so to those in New Brunswick and Maine. To prevail over the northern areas, Maine had to establish a line of communication other than the St. John River, which the British controlled, since that waterway flowed into the Atlantic by way of New Brunswick. The state ordered a path cut through the woods by 1833, and by the time the Aroostook War began, a road was open to the upper Aroostook River, a southern branch of the St. John. In 1837 geological reports from both Maine and Massachusetts asserted the richness of the region's soil. When Britain tried to negotiate for land suitable for a military road, Maine refused. But because the Aroostook's economy depended upon navigation of the St. John, the British possessed a strong bargaining position.[1]

The Melbourne ministry in London thought that, pending final settlement of the boundary, it had a legitimate claim to the disputed territory. It was impossible to carry out the terms of the Treaty of Paris of 1783, British leaders claimed, and until the two nations arranged a compromise the country first exercising jurisdiction in the territory should continue to do so. Minister Fox later explained that this claim rested upon an Anglo-American understanding that had evolved over the years. Foreign Secretary Palmerston declared that his country's only motive was to maintain safe custody of the disputed territory by preventing lawless people from despoiling the land.[2] Given Britain's known interests in North America, Maine's citizens found little solace in this assurance.

The British theory of jurisdiction faced its first test in early 1837, when the Maine legislature ordered a census in the northern area. Henry Clay and eastern Democrats had sponsored a congressional bill that would distribute proceeds from public land sales to the states, and since the amount allotted would be in proportion to population, Maine understandably wanted to count inhabitants in the unsurveyed north as its own. New Brunswick officials arrested the state's land surveyor for trespassing. The Canadian province's "Warden of the Disputed Territory," James MacLauchlan, promised the man his release if he left the area, and the solicitor general carefully informed him he could fulfill his responsibility to Maine by presenting a note from British authorities confirming the threat of imprisonment. The surveyor refused the offers.[3]

Citizens of Maine found the arrest outrageous. The governor informed Washington that his state expected reparation from Britain, and Secretary of State Forsyth, without seeking an explanation from the British, instructed Minister Stevenson in London to make this demand. The Melbourne ministry simply replied that it would exercise jurisdiction in the disputed territory, as it had done since before 1783, until the two nations settled the northeastern boundary. In the meantime Canadian officials warned of rumors that Maine was sending militia to the frontier.[4]

Palmerston considered the border events merely a nuisance and seemed willing to accept almost any form of compromise. Yet he realized that Maine's position in the controversy presented great difficulties. The state staunchly opposed any alteration in the treaty provisions of 1783, and the United States Senate undoubtedly would not approve a treaty denounced by Maine. As a result the state had a virtual veto over any settlement that conflicted with its interpretation of the Paris treaty. To satisfy dissidents in Maine, Palmerston proposed that a new joint commission of survey attempt to locate the treaty line, adding that the state must be party to the agreement. The government in London had little confidence in the measure, but did not want to reject a possible means of resolving the issue. The joint commission would search for geographical features meeting the description in the treaty of 1783. If it failed, Palmerston indicated, compromise was the only alternative.[5]

The Van Buren administration in Washington, at the time more concerned about events along the New York border, did not wish to alienate Maine and immediately rejected Palmerston's call for a new survey because, Forsyth explained, the British conditions had converted a commission of survey to locate the treaty line into a search for a compromise line. Maine would not accept the proposal.[6]

Months of inaction by the national government encouraged Maine to set up its own boundary commission. The Democratic governor, Edward Kent, told the Augusta legislature in March that the state could not assent to compromise until the two national governments had demonstrated that the treaty line of 1783 was inoperable. About a week later the assembly resolved that if neither Britain nor the United States authorized a survey commission before 1 September the governor would designate his own team. When Kent warned the president of this development, the long-patient Van Buren testily replied that the national government would not ignore the state's interests. Senator Reuel Williams of Maine introduced a bill calling for a joint commission of exploration and survey, and Daniel Webster of Massachusetts and James Buchanan of Pennsylvania supported the motion. But during the summer, before Congress could act, Maine sent its surveyor general to the Aroostook Valley, and the governor appointed a commission. Its three members soon reported, to no one's surprise, that the line of 1783 was executable.[7]

By the beginning of 1839, after over a half century of surveys, countersurveys, head scratching, map comparing, cajoling, and arguing, the governments of Britain and the United States had achieved only mutual frustration. The frontier stood open to both New Brunswick and Maine. Canadian and American loggers exploited the rich timber. Settlers did not know whether they were British or American. An island once holding title to most of a continent now was expected to deal on equal terms with former colonies. A nation had not decided whether it would adopt the nationalist ideas of Alexander Hamilton or the states' rights principles of Thomas Jefferson. The governments in London and Washington should have negotiated a settlement, but the Van Buren administration was hamstrung by Maine, while Melbourne's government was not convinced the matter warranted an effort and might well have been bored over such a petty issue.

Yet something had to be done. Reliable sources estimated that several hundred thousand dollars worth of timber had been taken from the disputed area within the past fifteen years. Governor Kent's successor in early January 1839, John Fairfield (also a Democrat), warned the state legislature of the probable loss of $100,000 worth of timber that winter alone. As Kent had stressed that the border problem affected "only this frontier state," Fairfield agreed that it was not national in scope and repeated that Maine's character was at stake. The legislature immediately appropriated $10,000 for defense of the territory.[8]

The situation then became more ominous. The lieutenant governor of New Brunswick, Sir John Harvey, normally was slow to anger, but Maine's actions had pushed him beyond his limits of endurance. After learning that Maine's land agents were in the disputed territory, he issued a proclamation in February warning that he would use troops if American soldiers entered. His announcement came too late. Nearly two hundred volunteers from Maine already had started for the troubled region. Their leader was the state's land agent, Rufus McIntire, nearly seventy years old and spoiling for an encounter with the British. Searching the Aroostook Valley for intruders, his "posse," as it was called, arrested over a dozen "trespassers," including New Brunswick's warden of the disputed territory, James MacLauchlan himself. A short time later a band of fifty Canadians seized McIntire and two companions and jailed them at Fredericton. When a Maine militia officer protested, he was imprisoned with McIntire.[9]

The McIntire incident caused great excitement throughout Maine. Democratic newspapers called for immediate action, while the Whig press, normally conciliatory toward Britain, urged the state to avenge this territorial invasion. In answer to New Brunswick's indignation over MacLauchlan's arrest, McIntire's replacement as land agent, Charles Jarvis, bitterly warned that if the so-called warden tried to enforce any law against him, he would "consider the approach to my station, by an armed force, as an act of hostility, which will be met by me, to the best of my ability."[10]

The government in Augusta was equally active. In a message to the legislature, Governor Fairfield advised sending three hundred reinforcements to the Aroostook and asked for ten thousand militia in addition to the thousand already drafted. He asserted, probably correctly, that even though Harvey denied authorizing McIntire's arrest, Canadian officers had sanctioned it by a warrant issued under authority of the February proclamation. Fairfield concluded with an impassioned plea that the state defend its "spirit of independence and self-respect." The legislature unanimously appropriated $800,000, and within a week ten thousand militiamen were on their way to the Aroostook Valley. After calling for assistance from Governor Edward Everett of Massachusetts, Fairfield, at long last, appealed to President Van Buren for federal soldiers to "cooperate with the forces of this State in repelling an invasion of our territory." Finally, the governor warned Harvey that if Canadian troops tried to drive out Maine's forces, the state would retaliate.[11]

In the meantime the lieutenant governor gained support from residents of New Brunswick and England. The province's newspapers criticized Fairfield for interfering with a national problem and charged Maine with invading British territory. Surely, they added, the Van Buren administration could not countenance such blatant interference with international affairs. The St. John *Herald* feared invasion of the city, and the commander of New Brunswick's militia delivered a spirited address to his "gallant warriors" preparing to stop further "encroachment." In London there was opposition to war with the United States, but the press thought conflict almost inevitable because Americans seemed determined to bring about Canadian independence and end British influence in North America. According to a deposition received by Harvey, a resident of Maine originally from New Brunswick warned that if Americans met no resistance at the Aroostook, they soon would erect barracks and fortifications on the Madawaska and Fish rivers.[12]

Despite Harvey's efforts, there seemed no way to prevent bloodshed. Supported by promises of military aid from the lieutenant governors of Lower Canada and Nova Scotia, he ordered the seizure of illegally cut timber and placed proceeds from its sale in a "disputed territory fund," presumably to compensate landowners for timber removed. He then released McIntire on a "parole of honor," even though New Brunswick's attorney general argued that the man had acted under orders of a state, thus violating the law of nations, and that London should decide the case. Harvey said his aim was to force the matter before the governments of Britain and the United States by replacing civil officials with the military. But his note to Fairfield arrived too late. Wagons, arms, powder, and blankets were on the way to Maine's "soldiers" gathering in Bangor, and the lieutenant colonel in charge of New Brunswick's militia was convinced that the state would *go the whole hog*. Even though Fairfield directed the release of MacLauchlan on similar terms as those meted

THE
UNIVERSITY OF WINNIPEG
PORTAGE & BALMORAL
WINNIPEG, MAN.   R3B 2E9
CANADA

to McIntire, troops from Maine, chanting that they would whip the "warriors of Waterloo," were about to meet those of New Brunswick.[13]

The Aroostook War had begun, a glorious event for residents of Maine. The "Red Shirts" of the New England state, as they were christened, were off to fight the "Blue Noses" of New Brunswick. A letter to a state congressman reported that the threat of conflict had brought "pomp and circumstance" to almost every town in Maine. Legislators exhorted Americans to cast off the British yoke, and patriots responded by pulling out swords and muskets their grandfathers had used in the Revolution, donning new uniforms, and drilling every day before huge crowds. At Houlton, the last town before the Aroostook, observers noted that after the troops attended chapel they marched out to what they believed would be a righteous war. Protests from the Reverend Caleb Bradley had no effect. Referring in his diary to warmaking as madness, he declared that the "wicked ambition of unfeeling demagogues" had brought on this "contemptible, disgraceful, horrible, abominable" event.[14] His vehemence seemed justified, for Maine's politicians were stirring up Anglophobes, and sheer emotion was rushing the state into a skirmish with New Brunswick. While lumbermen and others from both sides shared blame, Maine's Democrats encouraged the controversy. Whigs were unable to retreat from a position they had advocated earlier; and newspapermen urged everyone to battle.

The war promised to be splendid. Editors and political spokesmen waved the flag, songwriters and poets laureate rapturously bolstered morale. Newspapers sent correspondents to Augusta, Bangor, and Houlton. The Bangor *Whig* printed a column or more for several weeks describing hardships endured by the men, while the Belfast *Republican* simply issued the challenge of "Maine and her soil, or BLOOD!" The Augusta *Journal* proclaimed, "*Let the sword be drawn and the scabbard be thrown away*" and called on the state to show "a little of the spirit of '76." The Augusta *Age* urged Maine to "fall back upon its original sovereignty," while the Massachusetts press blamed the almost certain war with Britain upon the Van Buren administration's failure to resolve the boundary problem and imaginatively declared that Governor Fairfield had opportunity "to become second only to Moses and Washington." In a rousing speech to Maine's troops departing from Augusta, Fairfield declared that the "spirit of patriotism which lighted up the fires of the revolution, glows in the bosoms of our citizens with undiminished force." Men in Boston curled their whiskers and sported mustaches, for without these decorations, they declared, they could not shout with honor, "WAR! WAR!" Newspapers printed the "Soldier's Song" denouncing the redcoats and the "Maine Battle Song" with these lines:

> Britannia shall not rule the Maine,
> Nor shall she rule the water;
> They've sung that song full long enough,
> Much longer than they oughter.

Massachusetts citizens became irate upon learning that an American sat in a Canadian jail for whistling "Yankee Doodle" and would not be released until he whistled "God Save the Queen." When Governor Everett urged caution, one opponent called him a traitor and another quipped:

> Ye Yankee of the Bay State,
>   With whom no dastards mix!
> Shall Everett dare to stifle
>   The fire of seventy-six?[15]

There can be no doubt that Americans everywhere, not merely in the Northeast, supported the doughty patriots of the Aroostook War. The legislatures of Alabama, Virginia, Maryland, Massachusetts, Pennsylvania, Ohio, Indiana, and Kentucky all promised aid. The brigadier general of the Illinois militia offered military assistance, and a resident of New York assured Fairfield of troops from every state in the Union.[16]

Though primarily sympathetic to Maine, newspaper editors around the country seemed cautious about continuing these steps toward war. The idea of conflict with Britain was not attractive to several Boston and New York newspapers. Though the Richmond *Enquirer* complimented Fairfield for upholding the honor of America and the interests of Maine, the Massachusetts press questioned the apparent capability of a state to push nations into war. The Boston *Patriot* simply labeled Maine's efforts "an experimental lesson in the science of nullification." After the *National Intelligencer* expressed relief that "great mental or physical power" did not unite often with "mischievous propensities," it sarcastically added that the boundary question was a game in Maine to be won by the political party that succeeded in "driving the ball furthest." Next day Reuel Williams angrily retorted in the Senate that his state had united to secure its *"whole territory"* and would shed blood before yielding to Britain. The normally Anglophobic New York *Herald* seemed divided in its stand. It denounced the lumberers and legislators who had caused the crisis, yet it could not resist the temptation to insult Canada. After declaring that the Montreal press contained much editorial bombast, the *Herald* wryly commented that if talking won a war the United States would not have a chance. Everyone knew what Canadian courage was; "as the little boy said to his school fellow—'You only wait till my big brother comes, and then see how I'll whip you.'"[17]

President Van Buren, ruminating in Washington about what the Panic of 1837 had done to the country, not to mention his own chance for a second term, perhaps wondered what his predecessor General Jackson might have done if the panic had occurred a year before. The new president looked upon the excitement along the Maine border (wherever that border lay) with indifference approaching boredom, and yet he could not sit and do nothing. The Democracy of Maine supported two senators, and that was important in itself. Moreover, there was the question of example, when so many anti-Jacksonians throughout the country might raise their ugly heads. Van Buren knew the value of letting sleeping dogs lie and would have liked to do nothing, but the moment was upon him and inaction was impossible.

The president faced his dilemma with indecision. This stance had worked well during the *Caroline* crisis, for it allowed the furor to pass without further incident. But domestic politics made circumstances more complex in New England. If he failed to defend Maine, then, as Governor Fairfield had remarked, "God only knows what the result would be politically." Van Buren did not want war with Britain, but he believed Maine's claims were just. At a cabinet meeting on 24 February, he denied New Brunswick's authority in the disputed area, but criticized Maine for not informing the provincial governor of the proposed military measures. He appealed to the British minister in Washington to recall all armed men from the Aroostook Valley. After assuring Fairfield of national support in case of hostilities he urged him to make haste slowly. In a message to Congress on 26 February, he nonetheless declared that there was no basis for the British claim and that Maine might disperse all trespassers. He succeeded in gaining the enmity of almost everyone.[18]

Members of Congress probably were delighted to see Van Buren shoved to the front of the Maine argument, for that gave them more leeway to develop their own subtleties. In the Senate, Buchanan quoted from two diplomatic conversations that he said disproved the British argument. In 1832 the American secretary of state had explained to the British minister in Washington that until the two nations settled the boundary question they should not exercise jurisdiction beyond the territory then occupied. In reply the next year, Buchanan showed, a newly appointed British minister had agreed with the American position. Webster in the meantime aroused the ire of the present British minister, Henry Fox. The Massachusetts senator drew his customary applause from the galleries when he declared that if the two nations did not settle the boundary issue by 4 July 1839, the United States should run the line of 1783 and occupy the territory in question. Benton told the Senate that his government must protect Maine from the British, while Clay and Calhoun also urged national intervention.[19]

Congress eventually emerged with a policy. The Senate Foreign Relations Committee unanimously declared that Britain did not have exclusive control over the disputed area and moved that the president repel the invasion. That same day, 28 February, the House Committee on Foreign Affairs resolved that Congress authorize the president to resist British aggression.[20]

The result of the congressional debates was a bill signed by Van Buren in early March empowering him to stop British encroachments in the disputed area and to appoint a special minister to London to settle the northeastern boundary question. In a nearly unanimous vote—all senators approved the bill, while the vote was 201 to 6 in the House—Congress appropriated $10 million for armaments and authorized the president to call out fifty thousand volunteers. The force of the bill stunned Fox. The United States could not have shown a "greater parade of preparation" if Britain had announced intentions to return America to colonial status. Palmerston feared that any border incident might cause war.[21]

In the course of trying to determine what to do, the Van Buren administration contemplated appointing a special minister to Britain, but contention in the Democratic party made Van Buren decide against such a move. Secretary of State Forsyth had suggested Webster for the position, and when Secretary of War Joel Poinsett disapproved because the senator's stand was "too much inclined to a *war* aspect," Webster showed a memorandum explaining his policy on the boundary. His suggestions were the same tried by earlier administrations, except he emphasized that the negotiations should be friendly and informal. The first step, he claimed, was to secure Maine's approval of a compromise line; arbitration was the alternative. Palmerston's skepticism about the success of a special mission surely made Van Buren's decision easier, but for political reasons the president eventually decided against the move.[22]

While Congress debated, Fox and Forsyth signed a memorandum on 27 February 1839 designed to prevent hostilities. They proposed that New Brunswick would agree not to force Maine's posse from the Aroostook area if the state would withdraw its men voluntarily. The two antagonists also were to release imprisoned civil officers. Thus both sides could retreat gracefully. In the future they would cooperate in stopping trespassing in the disputed territory. The proposal, temporary in nature, was not to affect the ultimate agreement on territorial possession. Fox knew he had made a concession by opening the question of jurisdiction, but believed it necessary to lessen the chance of war. Palmerston and Van Buren immediately approved the agreement. Senator Williams was hesitant, while only one of his state's newspapers, the Whig Portland *Courier*, argued that it was acceptable. The others urged Maine to continue preparations for war.[23]

Van Buren now turned again to his troubleshooter, General Winfield Scott. Secretary of War Poinsett instructed the soldier to leave immediately for the border and to use the Fox-Forsyth memorandum as a basis for maintaining peace. If Britishers refused to evacuate the disputed area the commanding general would order regulars to join Scott along the northeastern frontier; these, with the militias from Maine and Massachusetts, would provide enough men to "enforce the determination" of the national government. As Scott prepared his departure from Washington, he told Van Buren and Poinsett that if they wanted war, "I need only look on in silence"; if they wanted peace, he could assure them of nothing. Van Buren's reply was a call for peace with honor.[24]

Fortunate it was, of course, that no one had done any fighting while the general was on his way. In fact, the embarrassing truth was that New Brunswick's men were poorly provisioned and that Maine's troops, according to a competent observer, wanted only to go home. After the

Americans discovered that nearly all British subjects in the disputed territory were peacefully engaged in farming or lumbering, they constructed several blockhouses at what they proudly called Fort Fairfield and laid a huge boom across the Aroostook in a futile attempt to prevent passage of timber. In the meantime, the British troops, expecting an attack, had gathered in Madawaska, but there was no confrontation. The only serious incident was a barroom brawl in Houlton, Maine. British and American soldiers had been drinking together when some hotspur offered a toast of success to Maine, and the result was a few bloody noses, one broken arm, and the imprisonment of several participants in the fray. Maine's forces suffered other mishaps. One soldier died of measles, and a farmer at Fort Fairfield was killed by a bullet that ricocheted from a rock during a peace celebration. The war, it seemed, was ending largely on its own. Maine's militiamen were tired and cold after their six-week-long trek in the wilderness, but they marched home proudly, deriding the regulars stationed at Houlton.[25]

Scott meanwhile had to placate the political forces behind the crisis. Accompanied by Captain Robert Anderson, later the Union defender of Fort Sumter, and by Lieutenant E. D. Keyes, also to distinguish himself in the Civil War, the general established quarters at the governor's house in Augusta in early March. En route he had asked Governor Everett of Massachusetts to keep the militia ready and in Portland had heard a state senator declare that he would rather see Maine "deluged in blood, and every field bleached with the bones of our citizens" than concede anything to British arrogance! Scott recorded in his memoirs that almost everyone was dissatisfied with "diplomacy, parleys, and delays" and expected him to take the Aroostook Valley by force.[26]

Scott proved to be an adept diplomat. He conferred with Governor Fairfield and the council three times a day for about a week, until he had heard their arguments and won their trust. At the same time he privately communicated with Lieutenant Governor Harvey in Fredericton. Scott quickly realized that his problem was not New Brunswick but faction-ridden Maine. Fairfield noted the political ramifications involved and sent the legislature a message denouncing the Fox-Forsyth memorandum, but implying that peace was possible through Scott's almost identical compromise. Scott suggested that when New Brunswick renounced its claim to exclusive jurisdiction, the Maine legislature should empower the governor to withdraw the state's forces from the disputed territory. A posse would remain, armed or unarmed, depending upon the circumstances.[27]

Though the Whigs were a minority in the Maine legislature, Scott needed their support and moved carefully to get it. They had avoided the general (himself a Whig) because he seemed to have crossed party lines by working with Van Buren, and Scott had to be careful not to alienate the Democrats. His reception in the legislative hall in Augusta was encouraging. Soldiers and officers, comrades in arms during the War of 1812, were friendly. Scott assured them that if war came he would be glad to fight "shoulder to shoulder—breast to breast." According to his memoirs, he persuaded a Whig state representative, George Evans, to invite the governor and leaders from both parties to dinner. At one end of the table sat Scott with the Whigs, at the other end Fairfield and the Democrats. When Scott appeared to be making no progress with the Whigs, Evans whispered an assurance that the general "was as good a Whig as the best of them," and a cordial atmosphere immediately developed.[28] Scott's account sounds apocryphal. Probably both parties finally had understood where their policies had led the state and gladly took advantage of an opportunity to escape war.

Scott now had to win Harvey's support for the compromise. He encountered no difficulty in New Brunswick. Though enemies during the War of 1812, the two men had earned the respect of one another and had become friends in the period afterward. Scott assured him that Maine would withdraw from the disputed area if the provincial government publicly declared it did not intend to expel the state's troops. He explained that Fairfield wanted a posse in the territory to prevent further trespassing. Some men would stay near the boom across the Aroostook River, while the rest would work on a road from Bangor to the Fish River (in the disputed territory). Until settlement of the new boundary, New Brunswick would occupy the upper St. John Valley around the Madawaska River, and the Aroostook Valley would belong to Maine. In mid-March, Fairfield urged acceptance of Scott's compromise with a succinct explanation of the doctrine of states' rights:

The respective States of the Union are Sovereign and independent, except so far as that sovereignty has been restrained or modified by the Constitution of the United States. The General Government is one of limited and defined powers. The power to alienate the territory of a State, or to transfer a portion of it, or the jurisdiction and possession of it, to a foreign power, for an indefinite period or for one hour is no where, is no where granted. An assumption of such a power on the part of the General Government, it is believed, would always meet the Stern and uncompromising opposition of this State.

The Maine legislature unanimously approved Scott's compromise. New Brunswick agreed to the terms shortly thereafter.[29]

That long month in 1839 had passed without conflict. The Aroostook War did not develop into a physical encounter for several reasons, but perhaps the most important were that leaders in London and Washington worked against it and that both countries had other, more serious problems. The restraint of Van Buren, the Scott mission, the sudden realization on both sides of the border that war was a distinct possibility, the assurances of American goodwill through diplomatic exchanges—all helped to convince the Melbourne ministry that the Washington government wanted to prevent hostilities. Minister Fox mentioned Van Buren's friendly tone several times, and Lord Russell in Parliament expressed his government's confidence in the president. Palmerston himself, no admirer of America, believed the two nations had been able to avoid war because of commercial ties.[30]

Despite the relief among Americans and Britons, the two nations seemed to assume that because they had averted conflict in 1839, war would not occur in the future. As if nothing had happened, Maine's senate unanimously called on the United States government to establish a joint commission with Britain to mark the boundary line in accordance with the treaty provisions of 1783. In case of disagreement, Maine was to be "sole judge" of the outcome. If the British objected, the state would urge the American government to take all disputed land. The two nations again exchanged projects and counterprojects for commissions of survey and continued discussing rivers, lakes, and highlands. At one time a few citizens in Maine talked of cutting a canal through part of the disputed territory, and at another spokesmen in both nations considered inviting three scientists from other countries to arbitrate the matter. The first idea never received serious attention, while Fox dismissed the second with the wry comment that leaders of Britain and the United States, not "mere Professors," should deal with the question. Later, at Portland in June 1839, Secretary of State Forsyth unsuccessfully tried to raise support for a settlement. The following month Palmerston, hoping another survey would keep the border quiet, sent a commission into the disputed area. Predictably, its report affirmed Britain's title to all territory in question. By December, Governor Fairfield wrote President Van Buren that British forces already had violated the Scott compromise by moving into the disputed area near Temiscouata Lake. A familiar refrain was his call for the federal government to defend Maine.[31]

Britain and the United States should have taken advantage of the momentary lapse in controversy over the border to arrange a lasting settlement, but they turned instead to other matters and soon resumed their dialogue over location of the line. In Washington, some congressmen still spoke of war, but much of their discourse clearly was inspired by politics. The American public quickly turned to more pressing economic and political problems, while the British people showed little interest in the question. Members of Parliament made surprisingly few references to the northeastern frontier of the United States—probably because of the rise of greater issues elsewhere. Warden MacLauchlan in the meantime complained about the activities of Maine's posse in the disputed territory, and during the year following the Aroostook crisis, officials in both Canada and England expressed so much dissatisfaction with the weak leadership they believed Lieutenant Governor Harvey had shown that he soon was recalled to London.[32] The North American boundary remained a problem only to the few people directly involved—to those scattered Americans and Britons living along the still undefined border between New Brunswick and Maine.

4. The Case of Alexander McLeod

The case involving Alexander McLeod, a largely unknown Canadian sheriff accused of murder and arson during the *Caroline* affair, came closer to causing conflict between Britain and the United States than any other event in the years 1815 to 1841. To Americans, he symbolized British ruthlessness; to Britons, his arrest proved the republic's lack of respect for international law. The excitement caused Anglophobes along the New York-Canadian border to protest British violations of their sovereignty and to appeal to the rights guaranteed by the Revolutionary War. When the federal government seemed unaffected by their pleas to protect the national domain, these border patriots indignantly informed the administration in Washington that if it would not guard the country's northern limits, they would settle the matter and force McLeod to stand trial in New York as a warning to future British aggressors. As during the Maine border crisis in 1839, troops marched, diplomats maneuvered, and local politicians and newspaper editors sought to make national policy. New Yorkers raised questions of national honor and resurrected the bitter memory of the *Caroline*, causing many Americans and Britons to fear a third war between Britain and the United States.

The *Caroline* affair was no longer a major concern of Anglo-American diplomacy by the middle of 1838, but memories of the event irritated inhabitants of the Niagara frontier for the next few years. Incidents continued along the border as Americans persistently urged Canadian dissidents to break from British rule. Secret societies encouraged patriots and unemployed workers along the waterways from New York to Michigan to raid towns in Upper Canada. New Yorkers commemorated the *Caroline* with public meetings and memorials condemning Britain and elected officers of a "Republic of Canada," including the former commander of the *Caroline* as "Admiral of Lake Erie." Canadian and American officials suppressed the "republic," and the British government executed its leaders or sent them to Australia. Yet there remained on record in Niagara County an indictment for murder and arson against twelve alleged participants in the destruction of the steamboat. Between April 1838 and mid-1840, New York authorities arrested several Canadians under the indictment, but had to release them because of lack of evidence. Then, in late 1840, state officials arrested Alexander McLeod after he reportedly boasted in a tavern in Buffalo that he had killed an American during the *Caroline* attack.

Before 1840, McLeod's name would have raised few eyebrows on either side of the American-Canadian border. The immigrant Scot had become deputy sheriff in the Niagara district of Upper Canada, and when the insurrection broke out in the 1830s he worked as a secret agent for the crown. He soon became a soldier in the guards and rose to the rank of sergeant, later colonel, of the volunteers. Late in 1837 he fled from a mob in Buffalo after gathering information about the *Caroline*'s early activities.[1] A victim of personal hatreds and patriotic malice, McLeod quickly became a habitual target for New York state law.

His arrest was a complicated affair. In September 1840 he was taken into custody in Manchester, New York, for participating in the *Caroline* attack. He argued his innocence, even shouting to a large crowd outside the jail that had he been part of the expedition he surely would not deny it. Released for lack of evidence, he soon was rearrested and taken to Niagara. But his brother's name, Angus, was on the warrant by mistake, and McLeod was released again. In the meantime a New Yorker brought suit against him for embezzlement. To secure witnesses for his defense McLeod traveled to Buffalo. On his way home he was arrested in Lewiston, New York. McLeod won the civil case, but was unable to secure dismissal of the charges relating to the *Caroline* incident. After a long examination before a New York magistrate, he was confined to jail in the county seat at Lockport on suspicion of murder and arson.[2]

At this point British officials intervened. McLeod had appealed to the civil secretary of Upper Canada, who sent an investigatory agent to Lockport. In the meantime the province's attorney general decided to help McLeod line up witnesses and arrange bail. Minister Fox in Washington suggested that McLeod put up the money and escape into Canada. There was no official reaction to this idea. Two attorneys from Lockport agreed to defend McLeod and obtained bail of $5,000. Fox asked Secretary of State Forsyth to intervene and repeated what he called the "well-known" fact that destruction of the *Caroline* was a public act and thus the law of nations required London and Washington to deal with the matter.[3]

The situation quickly headed toward an inglorious muddle. With regret, President Van Buren explained that the federal government had no power to interfere with the state's proceedings. Having seen his Democratic party go down to defeat in November, and being from New York himself, the lame-duck president obviously would rather see his successor, the Whig William Henry Harrison, burdened with McLeod. The position of Van Buren's Democratic colleagues was more important. No friends of the British, they did not want to force New York to release McLeod, and Governor William Seward, a Whig who also was personally opposed to the president, denied that the federal government had authority to do so anyway. Stalling for time, Van Buren asked Forsyth to send him the State Department's transcripts of depositions relating to the *Caroline* incident.[4]

The administration's inaction encouraged Congress to enter the scene. Southerners in the House justifiably labeled Van Buren's reply to Fox a "good State Rights paper" and argued that the British had invaded American territory, while Millard Fillmore, a rising legal and political figure from New York, hoped the jury would acquit McLeod but warned that if it found him guilty the state would have to execute him. Francis Granger, also from New York, assured the House that McLeod would receive a fair trial; but, like Fillmore, he believed that if the jury returned a verdict of guilty the state would fulfill its duty. If Britain should begin hostilities—why, then, western New York would react as patriotically as it did in 1812.[5] Apparently his memory was short.

Some Americans believed it was time to go to war again with Britain to show the rulers of the old country that America had come of age. Newspapers sensed the opportunity. The Philadelphia *Public Ledger and Daily Transcript*, in an article entitled "THE CAROLINE MURDERS," argued that the British demand for McLeod's release was an insult. If the United States surrendered him, Britain should free the Americans captured during the Canadian rebellion and make reparation for those individuals it had executed. Insistence upon McLeod's release would meet "RESISTANCE TO THE LAST!"[6]

British subjects and their government were indignant about McLeod's imprisonment, and it is fair to say that if in the United States there was sentiment for a third war with the British, so in Britain there was feeling that Brother Jonathan, for a third time, needed his nose adjusted. In a note to Minister Stevenson in London, Lord John Russell, now colonial secretary, warned of the explosive effect McLeod's execution would have in the United Kingdom. In the meantime Fox demanded McLeod's release, members of the House of Lords complained that the American Congress had insulted Britain, and Palmerston privately warned Stevenson that the McLeod case could lead to collision. The American minister thereupon urged Van Buren to prevent an execution, for he was convinced that such an act would mean war. That same day, 9 February, Palmerston ordered Fox to leave the United States if New York executed McLeod, for war surely would follow.[7]

By early 1841, neither the safety of the Empire nor of the Republic seemed at stake in the affair, and emotions cooled. Englishmen professed to believe either that McLeod would be free on bail or that New York would discharge him after a mock show of force. Some felt confident either that the United States was afraid to fight the British again or that the South would refuse to go to war over peculiarly Northern affairs like the *Caroline* or McLeod. Others seemed sure that Governor Seward would avert an execution.[8] Van Buren's reluctance, or perhaps inability, to act forcefully had made his tactics appear to be a stroke of genius. Perhaps a more important factor was that the British and American publics were becoming accustomed to the disparaging remarks political leaders had cast at each other across the Atlantic over the past seventy-five years.

Tempers had calmed only temporarily, however, for McLeod's ordeal in New York had just begun. After defense counsel arranged bail, a county judge at Lockport ordered McLeod's release. In the meantime rumor spread that the prisoner intended to jump bail and escape into Canada. Since it was near dusk and an animated crowd of people had gathered, the town's law officials wisely decided to hold McLeod until morning. Two days later, however, another judge remanded him to custody and set new bail at $7,000. Also in the month of February, a Court of General Sessions of the Peace met in Lockport and charged McLeod on seventeen counts of murder and arson. Governor Seward requested a member of the New York Supreme Court to preside over the trial and directed the state's attorney general to head the prosecution.[9]

The threatened mob action, the indictment in New York, and the certain trial threw the governments in Washington and London into a quandary. Van Buren had hoped local authorities would settle the matter amicably, but his policy of drift had bankrupted. British officials also had groped for a solution. Fox had demanded McLeod's release on the grounds that no American court had the right to try an alien, and yet Upper Canadian officials had raised bail, an action implying that the state of New York had jurisdiction. The county judges had complicated matters when, without conferring with either national or state officials, they permitted bail in a capital case affecting Anglo-American relations.[10]

The House of Representatives in Washington now took the initiative. Almost two weeks after McLeod's indictment, its Committee on Foreign Affairs presented a report by Francis Pickens of South Carolina, which was in reality a manifesto for states' rights as well as an extended critique of the United Kingdom's policies toward the United States over the past few years. Predictably, it condemned the British for destroying the *Caroline* and for demanding McLeod's release, but it then insisted that the president's attempt to exercise authority over issues not stipulated in treaty or law was a violation of state powers. The governor general of Canada called the findings "ridiculous," and Minister Fox regarded them as "highly offensive." On the House floor there was surprising concurrence with the British reaction. Some members denounced the report as a virtual declaration of war, while others warned that it might interfere with negotiations over McLeod. After considerable debate the House voted to print the report anyway.[11]

At this point, in March 1841, the Whigs assumed power in Washington, and, considering how complicated the McLeod affair had become, they promised a welcome change from the uncertainties of President Van Buren. The new president, William Henry Harrison, was a novice in political and diplomatic affairs and yet this may have been fortunate, for he brought a novice's simple views to the case. On the *Caroline* and McLeod incidents he took the stand one might expect from a former general: the invasion of American territory had violated sovereign rights, but McLeod personally was not responsible. Though the *Caroline* had aided the rebellion against the crown, the British government owed the United

Daniel Webster

States an apology and reparation. The president, through his secretary of state, Daniel Webster, would attempt to move proceedings to the United States Supreme Court if the court in New York convicted McLeod. Once there, the administration hoped to enter a nolle prosequi. In the interest of peace, Harrison would send United States Attorney General John Crittenden to Albany to ask Governor Seward to intervene.[12]

Harrison's choice of Webster as secretary of state was a major asset in dealing with the McLeod case. The former senator from Massachusetts, fifty-nine years of age and in excellent health, was an impressive figure. Almost five feet ten inches tall, endowed with huge chest and shoulders, large head, big, dark eyes, and thick, black eyebrows and hair, his appearance suggested physical and intellectual strength as well as integrity. "Black Dan," friends had called him. He often wore a blue coat with brass buttons, a white shirt with ruffles, and a wide black cravat that enhanced the size of his neck. According to a British critic of the United States, Webster was a living lie "because no man on earth could be so great as he looked." He was a wise selection to head the Department of State. He had visited England in 1839 and had made many friends. He had served as legal adviser to the House of Baring. During Webster's stay in England, Palmerston had suggested to Queen Victoria that the British government relax protocol for him, "a person upon whom an act of civility would be usefully bestowed." Even Fox was confident of a peaceful settlement. Webster's approach to diplomatic relations with Britain was not novel, but he made a good impression during a precarious time.[13]

Despite these hopeful signs, America's relationship with Britain had become hazardous by the time Webster became secretary of state. The London press carried menacing headlines, while Sir Robert Peel, soon to be prime minister, told a cheering House of Commons that as much as he opposed war, Britain might have to defend honor. Lewis Cass, American minister in Paris, wrote Webster that "*one who knew*" informed him that if the Americans executed McLeod, Fox's certain departure from the United States would be the "*casus belli.*" Secretary of War John Bell prepared to defend the Atlantic coast, while Minister Stevenson in London, without consulting Washington, advised Commodore Isaac Hull at Marseilles to move the American naval squadron closer to home. After a friend warned Webster that war would follow McLeod's execution, Stevenson informed him of a notice at Lloyd's inviting bids for transporting soldiers to Canada.[14]

As a Whig, Webster was a strong nationalist, and therefore his public statements and actions relating to the McLeod case officially reversed the policy of the Van Buren administration. Whereas Forsyth had deferred to New York by maintaining that Britain could not avow the *Caroline*'s destruction as a public act, Webster rejected this narrow states' rights view and agreed with the British that international law could not justify ✓ punishing an individual for an act committed under military orders. Yet the secretary knew that America's legal system did not authorize him to intervene in New York. Consequently, he prepared to transfer the case to the United States Supreme Court on a writ of habeas corpus. Contrary to his statements before Congress in 1846, Webster then asked a friend and highly regarded politician and lawyer from Utica, Joshua Spencer, to be McLeod's counsel. Evidence indicates, however, that Spencer already had accepted a similar invitation from the British government.[15]

Seward's position in the affair now began to emerge. When the federal government moved to bring the case before the Supreme Court, he sent his own attorney general to Lockport to block the attempt. Despite calls of politics, the governor undoubtedly was sincere in wanting a fair trial. If at the same time his efforts could bring discomfort to the British, so much the better. In the spring of 1841 he apparently informed Attorney General Crittenden, Secretary of War John Spencer, and one other unidentified person in a private meeting that McLeod had an alibi and that the jury probably would acquit him. There is evidence that Seward confidentially assured the men that in case of conviction he would halt an execution. Five years after the McLeod case, Seward wrote a friend that in that same 1841 meeting he had asserted that if McLeod were convicted, he, as governor of New York, would "interpose [his] Constitutional power to prevent the sentence from being executed." After writing that he meant this letter of 1846 for Webster's viewing only, Seward noted that he eventually appealed to Crittenden to recall his "assurances" about McLeod's safety. There is no record of a reply.[16]

Seward's statements are difficult to reconcile with those of the secretary of state, for in 1846, as a senator, Webster told Congress that as for "the intimation of the Governor of New York" that he would use his pardoning power, the "entire detail is imaginary, and altogether destitute of foundation in fact."[17] Either there was a breakdown in communication, or someone did not tell the truth. Whatever the case, it is likely that Seward never promised anyone he would pardon McLeod if convicted, but *implied* it when he repeatedly said he could not do anything until after the trial. In this way he protected himself. By not opposing the trial he satisfied New Yorkers who insisted the state had jurisdiction; at the same time he could prevent an execution that the British had warned would lead to war.

Such was the condition of affairs when General Winfield Scott, a good soldier and not infrequently a good politician, appeared again to settle a series of border troubles. Ordered to Buffalo by the secretary of war in mid-March, he arrived late in the month and found the frontier fairly quiet. After authorizing a patrol of the Niagara River, he persuaded the owner of the *Caroline* to drop his damage charges against McLeod, an act the general believed would "disembarrass" the case. Fillmore warned him of the danger to McLeod's life, and Scott notified commanders from Detroit to Lake Champlain to be ready for trouble.[18] He then returned to Washington, stopping briefly in Rochester on 10 April to face the unpleasant task of acting as pallbearer in the funeral exercises held there for President Harrison, who had died of pneumonia after only a month in office.

The new president, John Tyler of Virginia, held a view of the McLeod case similar to that of Harrison, but whereas the general had enjoyed a wide following and might have persuaded acceptance of his course in the affair, Tyler soon found himself facing almost every obstacle imaginable. In his first message to Congress he promised to uphold American honor. Confident that negotiations with Britain would resolve the McLeod matter, he shared Webster's belief that since the British government had assumed responsibility for the *Caroline*, New York should release the defendant on a writ of habeas corpus.[19]

Tyler's new position was not enviable. A Jacksonian until the South Carolina nullification crisis of 1833, he had been part of the states' rights wing in Congress that helped to establish the Whig party. But the Whigs steadily moved toward nationalist principles. The sudden death of Harrison had catapulted Tyler into the presidency, the first time this had happened to a vice-president, and the Virginian soon discovered that his opposition to the nationalist ideas of Henry Clay and other Whigs put him at odds with almost everyone in the administration. When he vetoed Clay's national bank bill, everyone in the cabinet resigned except Webster, whose decision to stay was regarded by Fox as important to good Anglo-American relations. Affirming loyalty to the president, Webster explained that he wanted to complete the northeastern bound- ✓ ary negotiations.[20] The secretary probably was affected also by the fact that he had greater political power within the Tyler administration than outside it. In any case, the president was without a party; and Webster soon would be in nearly the same position. These political developments promised to have both domestic and foreign repercussions.

Unable to unify the country, and eventually accused of inconsistency in his states' rights views, Tyler quickly antagonized Seward by accepting Webster's poorly conceived advice to appoint McLeod's chief counsel, Joshua Spencer, as United States district attorney for the northern district of New York. No act could have confirmed more fully the state's fear of federal interference with the trial. Spencer's official position made him appear to be the spokesman for both McLeod and the national govern- ment. Questions even arose that the Tyler administration was in league with the London government when some people suspected, correctly, that the British had paid Spencer's retainer.[21]

At best, Tyler and Webster probably regarded Spencer's appoint- ment as a means of maintaining intimate communication with defense counsel, and perhaps with the client, during the trial. In a note marked official and confidential, Webster asked Spencer to notify Washington of developments in the case. Tyler may not purposely have linked Spencer's appointment with his position as defense attorney for McLeod. Indeed, Webster apparently had not immediately informed the president of Spencer's connection with the case. Tyler assured Seward that Spencer had received no orders from him to serve as McLeod's counsel and claimed he had not heard that Spencer had agreed to lead the defense until four days before the commission for federal district attorney left the State Department, yet he made no effort to hold the appointment. Becoming a bit disturbed with Seward's protests, Tyler briskly told him that the national government had duties to perform and that New York had licensed Spencer to practice in its courts. Surely the state's "great and magnanimous people," Tyler said sarcastically, would not deny the national government's power to guarantee counsel even to the lowest individual.[22]

Seward, already under pressure from his constituents, was justified in being upset over the president's handling of the McLeod case. The truth was that Tyler had made little effort to work with New York. Both he and Webster should have realized that the timing of Spencer's new appointment was ill-advised. Not only was the trial date approaching, but Seward was wrangling with the president's home state of Virginia over the slavery question. Tyler and Seward exchanged several indignant letters on the *Caroline* and McLeod affairs, but their correspondence on these matters virtually ceased by late May 1841. Webster maintained contact with the governor throughout the controversy, and this may have helped to smooth the dangerous situation. Tyler, however, could see no good in discussing the matter further with Seward.[23]

The Tyler administration was deep into the McLeod case, whether it admitted it or not, and the House of Representatives too worked its way into the affair. Some members sought to embarrass the Tyler administration, others to affirm the right of New York to defend the border. Many did not have their facts straight. John Floyd of New York offered a resolution, later tabled, that the president disclose whether he had ordered the attorney general to Albany and whether the national government had made secret arrangements to free McLeod. He also wanted to know why the president had directed General Scott to the area. Charles Ingersoll of Pennsylvania, longtime Democratic opponent of Webster, labeled the moves unconstitutional and added that it was surprising that the secretary had not tried to defend "this English pet" before the Supreme Court with the British legation in attendance to make sure justice prevailed. The United States, Ingersoll dramatically proclaimed, was at the brink of war because of Webster's cowardly surrender to the British.[24]

Perhaps it was because the secretary of state had remained loyal to Tyler, or perhaps it was in the nature of strong-willed men like Webster to gravitate to the center of political controversy, but antiadministration members of the Senate soon focused their criticisms on him. They rebuked Webster for attempting to release McLeod without first securing redress for the *Caroline* and declared that he had violated New York's rights by sending Crittenden to Albany. James Buchanan of Pennsylvania denounced the British and argued that McLeod was accountable only to New York because he had invaded that state's neutral territory. In answer to the defense of Webster offered by William Rives of Virginia, Buchanan sardonically referred to the poet who said, "Two bodies with one soul inspired." *Harrison*, he added, would not have submitted to British threats. John C. Calhoun of South Carolina declared that the British had to make reparation for the *Caroline* before the United States could release McLeod, while Missouri's Thomas Hart Benton, another stern critic of Webster, complained that the secretary of state had created a ridiculous situation: Seward's attorney general would prosecute McLeod, and Tyler's attorney general would assist the defense.[25]

About this time the federal government's attempt to free McLeod on a writ of habeas corpus failed in the New York Supreme Court. In delivering the opinion Judge Esek Cowen ruled that by the law of nations a public war—between nations—could not exist unless there was "actual concurrence of the warmaking power." Since neither queen nor Congress had declared war, peace had existed at the time of the *Caroline* attack. In answer to the British argument of self-defense, the judge pointed out that the steamer had not assaulted Canada. The decision to destroy the *Caroline*, he concluded, was a judgment of death, and the soldiers were the executioners. The court refused to grant a writ of habeas corpus but ordered a change in venue so the trial would take place in Utica, some distance from the troubled Niagara area.[26]

Cowen's decision received mixed reaction. Though several noted jurists in the United States were critical, the New York *Herald* expressed the views of many when it praised the ruling but warned that the British minister's certain demand for his passport would result in war. Despite spirited remarks by the British press, Minister Stevenson in London believed that the course followed by the Tyler administration satisfied the ministry of Lord Melbourne. Indeed, Fox was convinced of the federal government's good intentions, but shrewdly noted that it was "hopelessly embarrassed" by this dilemma.[27]

Webster was prepared for Cowen's decision. While the New York Supreme Court was in session, the secretary passed through Albany and advised McLeod's lawyers to prepare an appeal on a writ of error. As mentioned earlier, he believed that if he could get the case before the United States Supreme Court, the president could discharge the defendant on a nolle prosequi. Minister Fox was dubious about Webster's strategy, and a judge in Washington remarked that the president had no authority to order a nolle prosequi in criminal cases brought before a federal court. But Webster's plan was not tested, for McLeod preferred a prompt trial before a New York jury to an indefinite wait in prison while counsel worked the case through the state court of errors to the federal courts. He told Spencer that only a verdict of not guilty would satisfy people on both sides of the border.[28]

Across the Atlantic, official British reaction to events in New York had become surprisingly tame. Perhaps this was because London's spokesmen regarded the McLeod affair as another indication of the shortcomings in America's federal system of government; or it might have been because of the hesitation of Melbourne's faltering ministry to consider hostilities with the United States and add another problem to the long list it had accumulated already. Though the duke of Wellington thought war with the United States "probable," others in England professed to believe that America would not risk war and that commercial ties would hold the two nations together. Governor General Lord Sydenham in Canada assured Lord Russell in the Colonial Office that New York ultimately would release McLeod, but added that the prisoner had to stand trial to gratify the American "braggadocios" who would not be satisfied until they had "bullied" the British government.[29]

Palmerston's actions showed the circuitous nature of the ministry in London. He already had drawn a contingency war plan, yet he told Fox of his "entire confidence" in the "just intentions" of the American government and claimed to understand its "Embarrassing position." He even directed his consul in New York *not* to interfere with the state's judicial proceedings. At one time the foreign secretary privately concurred with Stevenson's explanation of the jurisdictional problems arising in a federal system of government, but later declared in the House of Commons that international law did not permit a country to refuse redress because of its domestic institutions. Since the United States demanded reparation for the *Caroline*, Palmerston concluded, Britain had a right to expect McLeod's release.[30]

Then came a much-needed change in the British government. In September 1841, Sir Robert Peel, leader of the Conservatives, succeeded Melbourne as head of the ministry; no less important was his choice of the conciliatory Lord Aberdeen as foreign secretary. The new prime minister was noted for his interest in expanding trade with the United States, while Aberdeen, scholarly and formal in demeanor and a studious believer in peaceful international relations, stood in stark contrast with the rambunctious, unpredictable nature of his predecessor, Lord Palmerston. More important, Peel and Aberdeen wanted to relieve the tension with France resulting from Palmerston's aggressive diplomacy and had decided that resolution of the "American problem," as one historian has called it, would pressure the government in Paris to seek better relations with the new London ministry. "Great times ahead!" proclaimed the normally anti-British New York *Herald*; "A new Cabinet in each country!" Tyler was relieved to see a softened tone in the new British ministry.[31]

Another factor conducive to settling Anglo-American difficulties was the appointment of a new American minister to England. By the time the short-tempered Andrew Stevenson left the Court of St. James's he had fallen into such disrepute in Britain that Aberdeen only reluctantly had allowed him final audience with the queen. Tyler sent as his replacement a professor of Greek at Harvard and editor of the *North American Review*, Webster's friend Edward Everett of Massachusetts. As Everett was similar to Aberdeen in courteous manner and easy temperament, his selection seemed likely to improve communications between the countries.[32]

Just when emotions seemed calmer, the British learned that in September, Canadian volunteers had entered Vermont and seized an American, James Grogan, who had been accused of arson in Canada. The press stirred excitement along both sides of the border, and some newspapers expressed the belief that the execution of McLeod might lead to retribution. The Peel ministry immediately launched an investigation to determine whether reparation was due to the United States. Grogan soon was released, with indemnification, but his arrest and probable guilt caused Britishers to speak of war with the United States, and the stock market plunged temporarily.[33] In this atmosphere, Americans and Britons awaited McLeod's trial.

While diplomats and government leaders argued principles, and newspapermen and politicians warned of war, McLeod sat in the Oneida County jail at Whitesboro awaiting his trial at Utica, four miles away.

Patriots along the border seemed determined to make trouble, and rumor circulated that the Hunters' Lodges intended to hang him. After someone stole cannons from state arsenals, Governor Seward stationed guards around the jail and readied the militia. Scott followed by confidentially ordering Brigadier General John Wool and fifty soldiers into the vicinity of Utica. Wool conferred with Spencer and various local officials and received approval from an Oneida County judge to dispatch soldiers to town during the trial. Although William Mackenzie and other Canadian rebels had arrived in Utica, Wool believed with Seward and Scott that there was little danger to McLeod.[34]

The London government, three thousand miles away and not immediately aware of these precautions, anxiously followed the proceedings in New York and finally resorted to contingency preparations for war. In a dramatic move Aberdeen repeated Palmerston's earlier action by ordering Fox to leave Washington if McLeod were executed. A series of resolutions by the Colonial Society calling for McLeod's release added to the pressure already on the Foreign Office. When a member of Parliament asked if the secretary of the admiralty had orders related to the McLeod case, Peel commented darkly that at the moment it would be unwise to reveal the government's plans. A few days later Peel sent Aberdeen and other officials a memorandum urging tighter defense measures. The following day, 18 October, the prime minister met with Aberdeen and other members of the ministry to prepare for what Peel called the "*possibility* of War" with the United States. He wrote Wellington that the admiral would send two more ships to Gibraltar, one to Halifax, another to Bermuda if needed, and several heavy frigates and steamers to the area of Plymouth. In a "Most Private" note, Peel warned his secretary of state for the colonies that the first area attacked by the United States would be Bermuda.[35]

President Tyler also adopted emergency measures. To avoid war, he would refuse Fox a passport and keep him in Washington until British leaders reflected on the matter. Tyler also promised constitutional amendments to prevent a recurrence of similar problems. Surely, he told Fox, Britain would not go to war over a defect in the American Constitution. Even though Aberdeen considered Tyler's plans "unusual and extraordinary," he believed they showed "unequivocal proof" of America's desire for peace. Peel, however, told the queen that the steps

Tyler contemplated were unjustifiable. The president should grant Fox's passport upon request and send a special minister to London to make reparation.[36]

While the tempo had increased on the international front, the initial flurry of excitement in Utica had disappeared. Sheer distance from the touchy Niagara area was a factor, while another was the outward show of military force by American authorities. Talk of war no doubt sobered some enthusiasts, and many probably felt they had achieved their goal: the trial would take place in New York. Whatever the reason, the sheriff had no trouble keeping order in the town. Spencer was sure he would prove his client's innocence, claiming as a major asset that the circuit judge had no feeling for the patriots. Judge Philo Gridley was to preside at the trial after Seward's original choice, Judge Samuel Nelson of the New York Supreme Court, had become ill. It became apparent that more and more people in Utica seemed satisfied that McLeod had nothing to do ✓ with the *Caroline* affair and should go free.[37]

At long last the trial began.[38] Spectators entered the courtroom on 4 October in an orderly manner, their behavior a contrast to what many had predicted; throughout the trial the courtroom was no more than one-third filled. Shortly after nine o'clock in the morning, Gridley entered, accompanied by four judges of the Oneida County court. Jury members, several of them Quakers and opposed to capital punishment, already were seated. The trial would last from ten to twelve hours a day for eight days. Each session's proceedings would fill thirty newspaper columns. During the reading of depositions the jurors would become so drowsy that the court stenographer compared them to twelve convicts sentenced to death, "broken down in mind and body."[39]

A little before ten o'clock in the morning of the first day of the trial, the guards conducted McLeod into the courtroom. The Utica *Observer*'s reporter described him as between forty and fifty years of age, above average height, physically strong, with red hair and whiskers. Dressed in a black suit and blue cloak, he seemed a gentleman at ease.[40] Despite the testimony against him he would show no emotion throughout the trial. One wonders if the government in London or the one in Canada—or even the one in Washington—had assured him of his safety.

Any weakness in the prosecution's case would have been plain only to the discerning listener. Its opening statements dramatically proclaimed that McLeod's offense was the blackest of all crimes. After reading Cowen's July decision in its entirety, the state's attorney general, Willis Hall, argued that the attack on the *Caroline* violated only New York law and that the federal government had no jurisdiction. McLeod had been one of the strongest supporters of the expedition; he had traveled to Buffalo to see if the *Caroline* were going to Schlosser and had persuaded others to join the attack. On several occasions, Hall declared, McLeod had brandished a pistol and a bloody sword, exclaiming that he had taken them from a damned Yankee.[41]

Several witnesses swore that McLeod had participated in the *Caroline* attack. The commander of the vessel assumed that McLeod had been the one who hit him with a sword, and a resident of Chippewa testified that while he stood on shore and watched the *Caroline* burn he heard McLeod say there still were people on board and only the sentry had been armed. Though McLeod had been more than ten feet away and facing the opposite direction, the witness amazingly identified him by voice and with the aid of a flickering light from a window. Another under oath said that on 29 December, the day of the *Caroline* attack, McLeod was with Captain Andrew Drew, leader of the boarding party, in the back room of a tavern in Chippewa. McLeod had asked the witness to leave because he had private business with Drew. The morning after the *Caroline*'s destruction, the witness continued, McLeod bragged to a crowd that he had killed a Yankee or two. A fourth witness thought he saw McLeod get into one of the boats that left for Schlosser, though the defendant was more than ten feet away and stood in the shadow of willow trees. Another person testified that a week after the *Caroline* affair McLeod boasted in a bar in Niagara, Canada, that he had killed Amos Durfee: "By God I'm the one," McLeod said, and waved his pistol as the weapon.

The prosecution's case lacked credibility for many reasons. Spencer pointed out that several of the witnesses had participated in the rebellion against Britain in the 1830s and now were in concert to convict McLeod. Some were Hunters, one had a record of testifying for money, another already had been charged with perjury by Judge Gridley. Others admitted hating the defendant, and no one could give the names of persons present when he allegedly boasted his part in the attack. Another point of confusion was that McLeod's brother Angus bore a remarkable resemblance to him and that it was probable that Angus *had* taken part in the *Caroline*'s destruction. It also seemed peculiar that witnesses remembered only one sentence of McLeod's statements and that the wording was similar though they heard him in different places. According to one account, ten days after destruction of the steamboat McLeod displayed a bloody pistol, and—*horribile dictu*—a sword with blood on six inches of the blade. "Human blood so carefully hoarded!" exclaimed defense counsel.[42]

The defense then presented its case. Depositions from Drew and Colonel Allan MacNab, commander of British militia forces at Chippewa in 1837, maintained that McLeod had not been one of the volunteers, while one from a British naval officer seriously wounded in the fray also asserted that the defendant was not there. Four witnesses personally attested to McLeod's innocence: a retired British officer, his wife, son, and daughter. All swore that McLeod spent the night of 29 December at their house nearly four miles from Chippewa. Hall warned against the man's testimony because of McLeod's "too successful influence" over the family—one of the officer's daughters lived with McLeod—but the defense urged the jury to consider that many participants in the act could not recall McLeod's presence, especially after the prosecution argued that he practically had engineered the attack.[43]

There could be little doubt of the outcome. On 12 October, Gridley charged the jury. Less than half an hour later it declared McLeod not guilty. The prisoner, silent throughout the trial, rolled his eyes, said nothing, and left the courtroom. Four days later, accompanied by the sheriff and a small detachment of American soldiers, McLeod was safely out of the United States, across the Niagara River. He later received a warm welcome in Montreal.[44]

As before the trial, stories circulated afterward that the federal and state governments had been in collusion to assure McLeod's acquittal. Minister Fox heard of what he called a "shameful and atrocious" arrangement—had the prisoner been convicted, he said, Governor Seward would have suspended execution until the federal government secured British reparation for the *Caroline*. He also reported that at least two persons had intended to testify to seeing McLeod shoot Durfee, but either they had taken fright or the state and federal governments finally had realized the gravity of the situation and kept them out of the way.

Rumors to this effect had become so widespread by May 1841 that Seward assured the New York assembly there had been no deal.[45]

It is unlikely that there was any explicit agreement between New York and Washington, but this conjecture does not imply that the Tyler government would have permitted McLeod's execution had the jury declared him guilty. The relationship between Webster and Seward never had been close, and the outspoken rivalry between Tyler and the governor raises doubt that they could have reached agreement.[46] The two executives' correspondence, as mentioned, became so bitter by the eve of McLeod's trial that Tyler refused to discuss the matter with Seward further. Had the court sentenced McLeod to death, however, the situation would have changed drastically. There can be little doubt that the Tyler administration would have intervened—forcefully if necessary—to prevent an execution that could have led to war.

One result of the McLeod imbroglio was that early in December 1841, Tyler urged Congress to pass a law allowing the federal government to remove from state courts cases that involved the country's international obligations. Aberdeen had recommended to Minister Everett in London a constitutional amendment, and Fox had urged Tyler to ask Congress for a law remedying the situation. Choosing the latter approach, Webster asked Senator John Berrien of Georgia to draft a bill; he received it in January 1842, and it became law on 29 August. "An Act to provide further remedial Justice in the Courts of the United States" authorized federal judges to issue writs of habeas corpus to remove cases having international ramifications from state to federal courts; it also sanctioned the release of aliens held for acts committed under order of a foreign government (i.e., "public acts").[47]

The matter still was not closed. Four years later, in 1846, Democrats in Congress accused Webster, then senator from Massachusetts, of federal interference with the McLeod trial. Leaders of the move, his old enemy, Charles Ingersoll, chairman of the House Committee on Foreign Affairs, and Daniel Dickinson, senator from New York, asserted that the Washington government had violated New York's jurisdiction by trying to prevent the trial, that Webster had warned Governor Seward recklessly and needlessly that unless McLeod was released New York City would be "laid in ashes" by the British, and that he had paid Spencer $5,000 from government funds to lead the defense. When challenged by Webster, they could produce no evidence for their claims. The former secretary was in a safe position. Ingersoll was unable to prove federal interference with the trial, nor could he uncover an alleged letter confirming the threat against Seward, and the evidence establishes that the British government paid Spencer's fee.[48]

The Peel ministry agreed with McLeod that the United States should make reparation for his eleven-month ordeal, but Aberdeen's public stand was only formalistic. He assumed that the government in Washington would make amends and asked Everett in London what redress would follow. The foreign secretary, however, instructed Fox not to embarrass the president by making a "premature demand." Nothing resulted, and the British government later was unsympathetic toward McLeod. He sued New York for eleven months of false imprisonment, but lost, and later petitioned the Canadian assembly for compensation. In 1845 a legislative committee in Ottawa recommended that the crown consider the request, and the government in London eventually awarded him an annual pension of £200. Still unhappy, McLeod in December 1854 brought his case before the claims commission established under the convention of 1853 between Britain and the United States. The commissioners deadlocked, and the umpire rejected the claim because "the entire matter had been ended as a subject of international discussion."[49]

Despite dissatisfaction on both sides of the Atlantic, the outcome of the McLeod case suggested that the tone of Anglo-American diplomacy had improved. Peel's resolution was a welcome change from the indecisiveness of Melbourne, for at least the Americans would know what direction the new ministry was taking. And even though Tyler and Webster had not always performed admirably, they had convinced the British government of their sincere desire for peace. Americans were encouraged by the realization that Palmerston's aloof attitude toward the United States had given way to the conciliatory nature of Aberdeen. To those who resented Palmerston's seemingly warlike behavior, this was a most needed change.

Beneath the Americans' furor over the *Caroline* and McLeod affairs had run deep indignation over apparent British reluctance to deal with the United States as an equal. The event of 1837 had insulted American honor, they argued, and Washington's attempt to stop McLeod's trial was a clear violation of New York's sovereignty by an administration that for some inexplicable reason had taken Britain's side in the controversy. If the United States government had been able to put up a bold front, the Melbourne ministry might have issued an apology and redress for the *Caroline* in early 1838, and there would have been no McLeod affair. To most everyone McLeod himself was not the issue. Once it was plain that he would stand trial, hardly anyone questioned his innocence. Anglophobia had reappeared because of the United Kingdom's apparent opposition to America's claims to sovereign rights. Another factor was that over the Washington government's objections, Palmerston and others unrealistically observed that local difficulties should have no bearing on national and international policy. Clearly, the longer the McLeod case dragged, the more elaborate and forceful the opposing arguments became, and the more serious would be the potential results.

Britain and the United States thus survived the most serious threat to their peace since 1815. Though one may dismiss Palmerston's threats as saber rattling—his well-known practice—it is not easy to do the same with the secret military preparations made by two recognized opponents of war—Peel and Aberdeen. Seward probably would have pardoned McLeod had he been convicted. If he had not, the Tyler administration would have had an unhappy choice: possibly to go to war with Britain— if the Peel ministry had upheld its official position—or openly to interfere with New York's jurisdiction and risk internal conflict. Weak as the Washington government was, neither alternative would have been attractive. A confrontation with New York—if indeed the state had refused to surrender McLeod—no doubt would have strengthened its spokesmen's resolve to defend what they perceived to be the national interest. Patriots along the American border, supported by anti-Britishers outside New York, were convinced that they alone were upholding the country's integrity and refused to compromise what they understood to be America's honor. Already disenchanted with both Van Buren and Tyler, New Yorkers by 1841 had found themselves in a strange paradox: Anglophobia was their bulwark of national honor and the doctrine of states' rights its guarantor. Opposing them was a president who shared their states' rights views, but who with Webster had a different interpretation of the national interest. McLeod's acquittal was fortunate for all.

5. *Slavery and National Honor*

Before 1841, American Southerners showed little interest in the problems hindering the establishment of good Anglo-American relations. Border incidents in the North were remote, peculiarly local, and seemingly capable of resolution with little difficulty by the two national governments. By the early 1840s economic ties fostered by the South's growing cotton trade with Britain appeared to have eliminated the possibility of serious disagreements. Yet Southerners who had lived through the War of 1812 remembered British violations of America's sovereignty by their practice of impressment. The issues that now developed over the African slave trade and America's interstate traffic in slaves revived this anti-British feeling. Not only did these matters involve questions of American honor—impressment, visit and search, freedom of the seas—but by the 1840s they had the potential of causing a major confrontation over slavery. Southerners protested British search tactics as an infringement of America's freedom of the seas—a reminder of impressment—and called on the Washington government to defend national honor. Their sincerity is impossible to determine, but some Southern papers argued for maritime rights and national integrity when their real concern was whether these British abuses would encourage more slave rebellions. By the end of the 1830s the South, just embarking on the politics of slavery, joined the expanding list of people and nations with grievances against the government in London.

The basis for these long, protracted disagreements lay in the efforts by both countries to suppress the African slave trade. Britain had abolished it in 1808, the same year the United States forbade further importation of slaves. In 1833 the British government prohibited slavery in the Empire and then refused to allow slaves in its territorial waters or on the high seas—even if they were on other nations' ships. The United States was lax in enforcing its laws against the traffic, and since its leaders opposed any search of their ships by British vessels seeking to suppress the practice, slave traders from other nations soon sought refuge under the American flag. The Republic thus found itself perpetuating the illegal business. A touchy affair occurred in November 1841: British authorities in Nassau liberated all slaves from an American brig, the *Creole*, forced into the Bahamas by its mutinous cargo of slaves.

The *Creole* incident resulted in a complex, heated dispute that brought together the scattered complaints about British attempts to end the African slave trade. Slavery undoubtedly lay at the root of it, but spokesmen for the American government did not make the peculiar institution the basis of their protests. They argued, instead, that interference with their ships violated freedom of the seas and therefore insulted America's integrity. In the African slave-trade controversy Americans declared that British search policies could lead to impressment—never recognized by the United States as permissible in international law—while the British countered by offering assurances against its use in peacetime. In the *Creole* affair the London ministry proclaimed that slaves entering British territory automatically became free because of municipal law—the Emancipation Act of 1833. But even the staunch abolitionist John Quincy Adams denied Britain the right to board American ships in peacetime. A right of search, he told the British minister in Washington, was worse than the slave trade because it "would be making slaves of ourselves."[1] Truly, patriotism made strange bedfellows.

The emotional foundation of the bout over the *Creole* was the fact that both the London and Washington governments had taken a stand against the African slave trade and, by chance, had done so in the same year. Article X of the Treaty of Ghent of 1814 expressed moral condemnation of the practice and implied that both nations would take strong action against it. Yet only the British navy possessed sufficient power to suppress the trade. Leaders in London urged the American government to allow their naval captains to search all ships flying the American flag, but Washington refused. Many agreed with John Quincy Adams that this was a poorly disguised attempt by the United Kingdom to secure the right of search in peacetime.[2]

After the War of 1812 the British took the initiative in trying to suppress the African slave trade. Their foreign secretary in 1818, Lord Castlereagh, persuaded the European monarchs at the Conference of

Aix-la-Chapelle to allow mutual search in peacetime. He and his successor, George Canning, urged the United States to join. Americans
declined. Yet a strong group in Congress opposed the slave trade, passed
strict laws against it in 1818 and 1819, and the following year labeled the
practice piracy, punishable by death. When House committees in 1821
and again in 1822 recommended establishing a mutual right-of-search
policy with the British, a pact seemed imminent.[3]

John Quincy Adams, now secretary of state, sought an alternative to
mutual search. Always suspicious of the British, he proposed a joint-
cruising plan that would emphasize cooperation. If the United Kingdom
also construed the slave trade as piracy by the law of nations, execution
of the provision in peacetime would be acceptable. He soon instructed
the American minister to London, Richard Rush, to sign a convention
whereby Britain would define the slave trade as piracy and work with the
United States for its suppression. Rush did so in 1824, but domestic politics intervened. The Senate amended the convention to exclude American
coastal waters from its jurisdiction and then refused to consent to it. The
effect of American reluctance to cooperate in suppressing the African
slave trade cannot be calculated, but British cruisers alone liberated
almost 149,800 slaves from 1810 to 1864.[4]

The United States refused the British call for mutual search primarily
because of fears for its national honor and its maritime principles and
because of the influence of proslavery advocates. It should have been
clear that impressment had become unnecessary after conditions in the
Royal Navy had been improved, that its exercise in peacetime was
purposeless, and that no law could stop the British from using it in war.
Admission of the right of visit and search might have raised questions
about America's freedom of the seas, but it could not have endangered
national independence. Certainly politics was a factor, as was American
fear that the agreement was a guise for British search. Adams, however, had his own explanation. The secretary of the treasury, William
Crawford of Georgia, was his rival candidate for the presidency in
1824 and was worried about his Southern constituents. "Crawfordism,"
Adams bitterly commented, "had taken the alarm lest this concert between the United States and Great Britain for suppressing the slave-trade
should turn to a concert for the abolition of slavery."[5] Though only five
Southern senators voted against the convention, there can be little doubt

that concern for slavery contributed to its failure. Many Southerners, highly influential in the government, either were sincere in their appeals to national honor or were afraid that destruction of the trade would encourage Northern abolitionists to legislate slavery from the United States. Perhaps their feelings were a mixture of both.

The British tried again in the 1830s. Only two months after John Forsyth, a slaveholder from Georgia, assumed the post of secretary of state in 1834, he received a note from the British minister in Washington inviting the United States to sign treaties with Britain and France to stop the slave trade. Forsyth refused. Participation, he said, would cause delayed voyages, for American ship captains accused of slaving would have to return home for trial. An agreement to suppress the traffic also would violate America's maritime rights. The United States would handle American slavers with its own patrols.[6]

Despite Washington's reluctance to cooperate, the London government worked closely with several European and South American nations to stop the slave trade. British leaders remembered that before they signed a convention with France, the French flag had protected slavers, as had those of Spain and Portugal. By a series of intricate agreements, British vessels by 1840 patrolled much of the western coast of Africa and maintained blockades at the mouths of major rivers, so only those slave ships flying the American flag were safe from British search.

Slave traders therefore abused the American stars and stripes, and British efforts to stop the trade seemed hopeless. A slave ship, whether Brazilian, Portuguese, or Spanish, could carry an American citizen who professed to be its captain. If a British cruiser stopped the vessel on its outward crossing to Africa, the "captain" showed alleged American papers and prevented a search. If an American cruiser halted a slave ship on its outward voyage it likewise would go free; there were no slaves on board, and despite the objections of the British foreign secretary, Lord Palmerston, the United States Congress would not enact a law against ships carrying slave-trade equipment.[7] Once a slaver reached the African coast and took on cargo, it lowered the American flag and raised its own. The reason was practical: if a British cruiser stopped the slaver, its courts merely would condemn the ship and sell it, but if an American patrol halted a slaver flying American colors, its jurists might prosecute the captain and crew as pirates under American law and sentence them to death.

Not all Americans opposed mutual search to halt the slave trade. Some believed that the British were not using the practice to gain commercial control or to insult America. The commander of the American schooner *Grampus*, Lieutenant John Paine, patrolled the African coast and on numerous occasions saw slave traders from other nations abuse his flag. Finally, without authorization from Washington, he signed an agreement at Sierra Leone in March 1840 with Commander William Tucker of the British *Wolverine* allowing mutual search to suppress the slave traffic if there were reasonable grounds for suspicion. If a detained ship proved to be American and was engaged in the trade, it would go to an American cruiser captain; if not American, the British would have jurisdiction. Before the United States government could disavow Paine's action, Palmerston used the agreement to defend British capture of America's *Iago* and *Douglas*. In a third seizure involving the *Tigris*, the Massachusetts circuit court held that there had been no grounds for the action, and the British commander admitted having had no orders to stop American vessels. Reparation eventually followed.[8]

The argument over the slave trade became intricate when British leaders tried to make a distinction between a "visit" and a "search." Palmerston maintained that British naval officers could not trust the American flag as proof of nationality; they had to examine the ship's papers. Yet such action, he insisted, constituted only a visit, for a search would include examination of cargo. The State Department was not convinced. Andrew Stevenson, American minister to London and a Virginia slaveholder, denied a difference between the terms and declared that under no conditions was the practice acceptable. When Lord Aberdeen became head of the Foreign Office in September 1841, Stevenson did not wait to see if British policy might change, but instead challenged the new foreign secretary with a veritable lawyer's brief. Since violations of municipal law were punishable only in the country that passed the law, he argued, Britain could not enforce treaties or domestic statutes against the United States by visitation, detention, or search. British inspection of American papers during time of peace constituted "national degradation."[9]

Aberdeen nonetheless tried to assure the United States of his good intentions. The British government, he repeated, could not renounce the right of visit and still hope to suppress the slave trade. The British public demanded enforcement of laws against the traffic, and because of this and his own feelings against slavery, he had to condone the boarding of American ships. Fraudulent use of the American flag necessitated examination of a ship's papers. But the new prime minister, Sir Robert Peel, was worried. War with the United States could occur, he warned, unless British actions were "clearly defensible" by international law. Aberdeen suggested that if the visit determined the ship was American, the British officer would leave immediately. In case of injury, he said, London would grant compensation.[10]

By this time other British leaders seemed to be moving toward Aberdeen's proposal. A former secretary of the admiralty, John Croker, assured Peel that the right of visit was justified, but added that the government should make reparation for injury or delay. Peel seemed to agree. The prime minister believed that if a naval officer could go no further in his investigation than to examine a ship's papers, the visitation was ineffective; and if he could, the visit became synonymous with search. Perhaps it would have been practical for a British officer dissatisfied with the papers to have sent the ship into port for a search, but the Peel ministry apparently dismissed this option—if it considered it at all. Both the delay and its appearance of direct interference with American shipping would have discouraged the idea. To prevent an incident with the United States, Peel recommended that commanders exercise extreme discretion, report every case by letter, and include a detailed account of the seizure. Such tedious measures, he hoped, would discourage abuse. Private letters among British leaders show that their essential concern was not to insult America or to gain commercial advantages but to halt the African slave trade.[11]

The British government then tried to set up an international organization to end the traffic—perhaps hoping to pressure the United States to join. In late 1841, Foreign Secretary Aberdeen sponsored a meeting in London to promote the mutual right of search for suppressing the trade. The Quintuple Treaty, negotiated in December by representatives of Austria, Britain, France, Prussia, and Russia, labeled the trade piracy and provided that captains and crews of slave ships stand trial in their countries' courts. It was a "Holy Alliance," Aberdeen proudly announced. The United States should join the great powers of Christendom in abolishing the trade. If it refused, he warned, the American flag would not prevent visitation by signatory nations. When Washington spokesmen argued that no government ever had claimed this privilege in peacetime, Aberdeen cited instances in the Gulf of Mexico where American commanders boarded ships, regardless of what flag was raised. Edward Everett, recent successor to Stevenson at the Court of St. James's and mildly opposed to slavery, took advantage of Aberdeen's moderate tone and urged redress for past seizures of American ships. Such action, Everett believed, would allay excitement in the United States, prove the sincerity of the foreign secretary's efforts at conciliation, and perhaps bring about America's signature on the treaty. Aberdeen was agreeable.[12]

At first Everett and Aberdeen's efforts seemed likely to persuade the government in Washington to cooperate with the British in stopping the trade. In light of Aberdeen's reasonable attitude, Everett asked Secretary of State Webster, whose views were cautiously antislavery, why the United States should not become party to the Quintuple Treaty. In exchange for America's signature, Britain could renounce impressment and agree to confine interference with American vessels to African waters. In this way, the minister continued, there could be no danger to national honor. But President Tyler, a Virginia slaveowner but opposed to the African slave trade, was wary of alienating isolationists, Anglophobes, and slaveholding interests, and he balked at the suggestion. Webster's feelings remained obscure. When France refused in February 1842 to ratify the London treaty, Everett again pushed for American participation. The United States should exploit Britain's problems with the French and secure guarantees against impressment, he declared to the secretary of state.[13] Yet, either because of traditional fears of involvement in European affairs or because of political conditions at home—or both—Everett's admonitions received no encouragement from Washington.

The controversy over search might have drifted longer had it not been for the interference at this point of Lewis Cass. As minister to Paris, the rotund, former senator from Michigan—the "Michigander," Senator Jefferson Davis of Mississippi suggestively called him—became a sort of uninvited overseer of Anglo-American relations. His motives were unclear. Without instructions from Washington, he involved himself in the search controversy with Britain—either because of his long-standing anti-British feeling or to use his post to support a cause that might prove politically beneficial. Perhaps both factors were important. He defended his actions by saying he had done nothing more than fulfill his responsibilities as diplomatic agent. When the London government urged France to ratify the Quintuple Treaty, the Northern Democrat seized upon the search issue to criticize the British again and perhaps to use it, according to a responsible British observer, as a "Stepping Stone to the Presidential Chair."[14] Cass's protests put Tyler into the awkward position of either having to approve the minister's unauthorized actions or appearing to oppose him for political reasons.

Cass's public stand on the African slave-trade issue embarrassed the administration in Washington; it also enhanced his political future by drawing support from Americans who disliked the British. In the confusion over the Quintuple Treaty, he anonymously published a pamphlet entitled *An Examination of the Question Now in Discussion Between the American & British Governments, Concerning the Right of Search. By an American*. His identity did not remain secret; when asked if he wrote it, he did not deny authorship. Though the essay first appeared in French, published in Paris in February 1842, it soon came out in English and German editions, and thereafter received wide circulation in Europe and the United States.[15] It encouraged a confrontation with the British over competing maritime policies and stirred Anglophobes in both the North and the South.

The pamphlet contained a curious logic. The minister warned that the Quintuple Treaty would help the British gain supremacy on the seas, for in almost every incident their cruisers would conduct the search. He indignantly asked who had given Britain the right to be the "great Prefect of police of the Ocean?" Cass conceded that if a British officer encountered a ship flying the American flag, he might board it if strongly suspicious of its nationality. Though this admission appeared to grant everything London's leaders had wanted, Cass declared that visit was a *privilege* allowed by the United States, not a *right* belonging to Britain. If the officer proved to be wrong but committed no injury, London still was to make reparation—thereby acknowledging trespass. In case of injury, of course, reparation had to follow. The point was that the United States could not grant the British a perpetual right to search American ships; this admission would violate America's maritime sovereignty and sustain the principle behind impressment. Cass agreed that a general search policy would aid suppression of the African slave trade, but he did not consider it indispensable to success. More helpful would be efforts by

Brazil, Portugal, and Spain—the destinations of slavers—to close their slave markets. He then reminded the French foreign minister, François P. G. Guizot, that France's signature on the treaty would incur an obligation to follow the search policy—even against the United States.[16]

The Tyler administration reacted to the pamphlet with uncertainty, largely because of the possible political ramifications. Cass in the meantime informed Secretary Webster that many distinguished men on the Continent approved it and that it had helped to shift opinion in France against the treaty. The president soon publicly approved Cass's conduct—probably because he hesitated to rebuke a leading candidate for the Democratic nomination for the presidency in 1844. Webster at first told Cass he was doing a "respectable" job in Paris, but eventually chastised him for interfering with America's relations with Britain. Correspondence between the men became so bitter that when the United States did not secure British renunciation of the right of search, Cass resigned his post in Paris and publicly blamed the Tyler administration for the failure. For the time being, however, the secretary of state tried to soothe Everett, who had become incensed over Cass's intervention in Anglo-American concerns. The administration, he implied to the minister in London, had been slow to criticize Cass's behavior because it had not had time to assess the situation.[17]

Everett bluntly expressed his opinion that the pamphlet interfered with negotiations between Britain and the United States. Because of Cass, the United States could receive blame if France refused to ratify the treaty; and if France signed over his protests, American prestige would suffer. Everett expressed surprise at the Paris minister's vehemence, for when Cass was a member of President Jackson's cabinet, he showed no dissatisfaction with the Anglo-French treaties of 1831 and 1833 that condoned the right of search. It was wrong, Everett declared, to "electioneer" upon the question of peace with Britain.[18]

Cass unjustifiably took credit for France's ultimate decision to reject the Quintuple Treaty. He claimed his intervention had convinced Guizot; and the French minister, always skeptical about British motives and therefore wanting to appear on friendly terms with the United States, apparently let him believe this. Actually, Cass's pamphlet did not appear until after both Guizot and the Chamber of Deputies had decided to oppose the treaty. Members of the Chamber long had been bitter because the Melbourne ministry in London originally drew the treaty without asking assistance from France. Aberdeen's efforts intensified these feelings. The French also resented Britain's attempt to monopolize suppression of the African slave trade—especially when Her Majesty's naval officers assumed the right to search French ships. More important, Britain's recent triumph over France in the Near East rekindled the long-standing hatred and caused Aberdeen to design his foreign policy toward building better relations with the French as well as with the Americans. In fact, part of the foreign secretary's reason for conciliating the United States was to weaken the Franco-American relationship and thereby to improve British relations with the government in Paris. Cass can claim little credit for the outcome. France's enmity for the British was stronger than its opposition to the slave trade.[19]

The slave-trade issue caused deep resentment against the British, yet for several reasons it never erupted into conflict. One reason was that many Americans had little interest in slavery—particularly in the African slave trade—and another was that British officers stopped few American ships. Even when they did, news of the seizures arrived weeks afterward. Nor could the few Americans engaged in the slave trade protest visitation, for slaving was piracy and punishable by death. Another consideration was that advocates of antislavery did not want to encourage the African slave trade by opposing British search tactics. Finally, abolitionists in both Britain and the United States had not yet won much support. Thus, a major controversy did not develop over the African slave trade, but it remained a constant irritant in Anglo-American relations.[20]

The argument over the African slave trade was low-key, but the slave mutiny on the American brig *Creole* became entangled with it, reviving many of the issues over slavery and national honor and threatening to inflame the South against Britain. Not only did the affair involve American domestic politics, but it intimately concerned relations between the governments of Britain and the United States. Disposition of the case raised arguments and counterarguments similar to those that were to echo through American politics for two decades and result in the Civil War; it also would affect future negotiations between the countries. Because the *Creole* revolt occurred in 1841, not 1861, it eventually took its place as a minor incident in antebellum history. Yet its potentially explosive nature justifies more attention than it has received. The *Creole* √ affair caused Southerners to consider having to fight the British again.

In its details—the event itself and its ramifications—the *Creole* case constituted a microcosm of the ideas and actions of later years. The vessel had sailed from Hampton Roads, Virginia, for New Orleans in October 1841 with a small crew, a cargo of tobacco, 135 slaves, and 6 white passengers. For nearly eleven days the brig made its way down the coast and during the evening of 7 November prepared to enter harbor at Abaco Island in the Bahamas the following morning. About 9:30 that night, nineteen slaves rose in mutiny. Casualties were light on both sides because there was little resistance to the revolt and because its leaders helped to restrain the others from killing the whites on board. Only one white man—owner of thirty-nine slaves on board—was killed in the scuffle, while two other whites, including the ship's captain, were hurt. Two blacks who took part in the revolt were wounded seriously, one of them later dying.[21]

After a brief discussion, the nineteen blacks ordered the crew to set sail for Nassau, New Providence, a British possession. There, a few days later, the British attorney general decided that the Emancipation Act of 1833 applied to any slaves entering the islands and freed those blacks not / involved in the insurrection, but held the nineteen accused of mutiny and murder until instructions came from the government in London. Despite strong protests by the American consul at Nassau, it is doubtful that / anyone could have stopped the *Creole*'s slaves from going free. The ship's crew was disabled, the captain was helpless, the black islanders outnumbered the whites at Nassau about four to one. The situation did not allow a choice.[22]

When the *Creole* finally arrived at New Orleans on 2 December, many people in the South, already sensitive about British interference with American maritime affairs, were demanding compensation for the √ slaves. The press in New Orleans, Washington, Nashville, and Jackson, Mississippi, denounced British actions, while the legislatures of Louisiana, Mississippi, and Virginia passed resolutions demanding restitution. Throughout the South, according to the Baltimore *Sun* and the Charleston *Courier*, the *Creole* incident had caused condemnation of Britain. In the Senate, Thomas Hart Benton criticized the British for encouraging mutiny and murder; Henry Clay warned of the danger to America's coasting trade; and John C. Calhoun appealed to national honor and property rights. If America's interstate slavers could not sail safely down the Atlantic seaboard, the South Carolinian warned, there would be no way to stop the British from interfering with its coastal trade in cotton as well.[23]

Southerners declared that earlier, in March 1841, the United States Supreme Court had handed down a decision in a remarkably similar case, which now could be used to support the *Creole* protests. The *Amistad*, a Spanish slaver, had been carrying fifty-three blacks (secured in Africa) from Havana to another Cuban port in 1839 when they mutinied and killed the captain and crew. Federal authorities in the United States eventually imprisoned the blacks, and the Spanish minister in Washington appealed to the treaties between Spain and the United States in 1795 (Pinckney's Treaty) and 1821 (Adams-Onís Treaty), which called for each nation to restore ships and property rescued from pirates and robbers on the high seas. President Martin Van Buren, perhaps wanting to avoid a major issue on the eve of a presidential election, would have complied with Spain's demand, but the United States Supreme Court refused. The blacks' counsel, former President John Quincy Adams, now representative from Massachusetts, argued for their freedom on the basis of humanity, but Justice Joseph Story ruled in favor of the blacks on other grounds: they were kidnapped Africans entitled to freedom because Spain had outlawed the African slave trade in 1820. In the *Creole* case, some Southerners argued that while there had been no reparation for the *Amistad* because its owners had been illegally engaged in the African slave trade, the *Creole*'s losses should be redressed because the blacks had belonged to a nation that recognized slavery.[24]

Other observers drew analogies between the *Creole* affair and earlier slave incidents involving the British Bahamas. Three American ships, the *Comet*, the *Encomium*, and the *Enterprise*, also had been driven into British islands by forces beyond their control (bad weather), and in all cases the colonial governor had freed the slaves on board. Less than a year before the *Creole* revolt, the *Formosa*, an American ship bound for Louisiana from Virginia with thirty-eight slaves on board, wrecked near Nassau, and British officials on the island set them free. The Louisiana Insurance Company of New Orleans made payment for the loss of the

Formosa's slaves and then sent the United States Congress a memorial asking for reimbursement from the federal government. After a brief debate in the Senate, Alexander Barrow of Louisiana declared that if the government would not defend Southern rights, the South should destroy Nassau. In the *Creole* case, for the first time in episodes concerning British violations of America's domestic slave trade, mutiny and loss of life were involved. The London government had made reparation for the *Comet* and the *Encomium* because the incidents had occurred before the British Emancipation Act of 1833, but refused to indemnify the *Enterprise* because this event had happened afterward. The *Formosa* affair remained unresolved, and there appeared little hope for the *Creole*.[25]

Southerners nonetheless continued to complain about the *Creole* case. The reader will recall that in the late 1830s, Minister Stevenson in London had followed the instructions of Secretary of State Forsyth in protesting British efforts to use visit-and-search tactics in suppressing the African slave trade. In addition to the usual praise given Stevenson by the Richmond *Enquirer*, two other papers, the Baltimore *Sun* and the *National Intelligencer*, acclaimed his defense of America's honor. In reply, the antislavery Portsmouth *Journal* of New Hampshire disgustedly denied that Stevenson's purpose was to protect America's integrity and declared that the South's only aim was to defend the slave trade. Now, in 1841 and 1842, spokesmen for the South resurrected warnings of infringements of America's freedom of the seas, including impressment, and proclaimed that Britain again was trying to dominate the ocean trade.[26]

The issue of national honor raised by the *Creole* affair obscured the fact that for social, political, and economic reasons, Britain's best interests lay in good relations with the United States. Clearly, impressment was no longer viable—if it ever had been. On the visit-and-search controversy, the British government many times had assured the United States that it could not trust the American flag as proof of a ship's nationality; its naval officers had to examine the ship's papers if they were to suppress the African slave trade. Lord Aberdeen even had assured Stevenson that if injury occurred during the visit, London would grant compensation.

Despite the arguments involving America's maritime rights, the central concern of at least some Southerners in the *Creole* controversy was the effect such British actions could have on encouraging slave rebellions and damaging the domestic slave trade. The Mobile *Register & Journal* warned that British interference with the coasting trade would result in the establishment of a place of refuge in neighboring islands for runaway slaves. The Baltimore *Sun* presented a similar argument, while the New Orleans *Picayune* at first argued questions of national honor, but finally declared that Britain was inducing the South's slaves to commit mutiny and murder in order to win freedom. Northern abolitionists warned the South not to use the argument of national honor to protect the trade. The Boston *Liberator* dared the United States to go to war with Britain over the "hellish slave trade," while the Worcester, Massachusetts, *Spy* could not believe the North would go to war to "DEFEND OUR AMERICAN SLAVE TRADE."[27]

Excitement continued to rise in the United States as abolitionists broadened their criticisms of the South's behavior to attack slavery itself. In early 1842 abolitionists from both the United States and Britain, including Theodore Weld, Joshua Leavitt of the *Emancipator*, and Lord Morpeth of the British and Foreign Anti-Slavery Society, had gathered in Washington to work with John Quincy Adams and other antislavery congressmen in presenting petitions denouncing slavery. James G. Birney, Liberty party candidate for the presidency in 1840 and 1844, wrote an article for the New York *American* calling for the slaves of the *Creole* to be freed. The renowned New England author, John Greenleaf Whittier, editor of the Pennsylvania *Freeman*, informed the chairman of the British and Foreign Anti-Slavery Society in London about the uproar in the United States caused by the *Creole* incident. In a letter to this British antislavery group, the corresponding secretary of the American and Foreign Anti-Slavery Society approved the British government's decision not to surrender the blacks, either as fugitives or as slaves. Abolitionist Lewis Tappan, instrumental with other members of the American society in securing legal counsel for the blacks of the *Amistad*, warned of trouble if either government granted compensation to the owners of the *Creole*'s slaves. The American society urged the British government to refuse to make reparation; otherwise London would become insurer of the American domestic slave trade against both shipwreck and revolt.[28]

The House of Representatives hosted some of the most bitter debates over the *Creole*. Abolitionist members rallied around resolutions written by Weld arguing that a state had exclusive authority only over slavery within its territory, but that on the high seas the Constitution did not require the federal government to seek redress for liberated slaves. They also used the revolt as an opportunity to launch another attack on the "gag rule," which barred antislavery discussions in the House. Southerners considered presenting resolutions on the *Creole* matter, but decided not to—probably because of the threat such action would present to the gag rule and perhaps because abolitionists could benefit from discussions about slavery. Some Southerners outside Congress warned that antislavery resolutions would ensure more slave revolts. The Baltimore *Sun* argued that passage of such resolutions would, in effect, place a knife in the hands of every slave and encourage him to commit murder.[29]

The *Creole* incident presented problems for both the American and the British governments. President Tyler, titular head of the Whig party, could not establish a convincing legal basis for demanding the surrender of the nineteen mutineers as fugitives, for the only Anglo-American extradition agreement (part of Jay's Treaty) had expired in 1807. The British minister in Washington, Henry Fox, quickly showed that in 1838 federal officials had intervened to prevent the state of New York from surrendering two British subjects accused of murder. Two years later the Supreme Court decided in *Holmes* v. *Jennison* that the American government should not surrender a murderer who had escaped from Canada. To be sure, legal opinion in both nations at this time held that when a matter affected peace and order there existed a right, independent of treaty, to surrender of fugitives, and a right of comity under international law, which called for a nation to assist a foreign vessel that involuntarily entered its port. Fox recognized these rights but declared that if his government delivered the blacks to the United States their status would revert to slavery. Though he did not say it, the truth was that no British ministry could do this or even make reparation for the freed slaves without causing a wrathful public outburst at home.[30]

Secretary of State Webster feared the outcome of the *Creole* case more than British seizures of American vessels illegally engaged in the African slave trade. Whether his conciliatory actions were motivated by a desire to placate the South and revive his waning chances for the presidency or simply by a wish to avoid trouble with Britain, he apparently hoped to tie the incident to legalities and to exchanges of diplomatic notes and thus allow time to calm emotions. He appealed to the principle of comity. British officials in Nassau, he decided, had not followed the understandings of hospitality; reparation was required, he explained in instructions to Minister Everett in London. The *Creole* had been passing from one American port to another on a lawful voyage and had carried a cargo of slaves whom the Constitution recognized as property in slaveholding states. Because the mutineers forced the vessel into Nassau, British authorities had a duty to help it resume its voyage. The secretary said that according to Palmerston's contention in 1837, claimants should receive compensation when officials interfered with another country's slaves, even if in British territory. British municipal law, Webster declared, had no bearing on a person who entered the Empire because of "disaster and distress."[31]

While Webster explained the Tyler administration's stand on the *Creole* incident to Everett, the Peel ministry was uncertain about a course of action and asked for an opinion from the crown's law officers. The latter unanimously opposed giving up the nineteen blacks accused of mutiny and murder because there were no municipal laws or treaty provisions establishing extradition. The legal advisers believed the case of the *Enterprise* furnished precedent for release of the blacks not involved in the revolt by island officials.[32]

Both abolitionists and nonabolitionists in Parliament agreed with the legal opinion. Abolitionist Lord Henry Brougham, after conferring with members of the British and Foreign Anti-Slavery Society, argued in the House of Lords that even if there were a treaty providing for extradition of criminals, a municipal law would be necessary to execute that treaty. Lord Thomas Denman, also an abolitionist, cited Sir Edward Coke's opinion that nations were sanctuaries for subjects fleeing for safety from one to another and pointed out that Justice Story of the United States Supreme Court, in a recent edition of his *Conflict of Laws* (1841), cited Coke as authority. Lord Campbell, mildly opposed to slavery, showed that the American minister in Berlin in 1842, the distinguished lawyer and publicist Henry Wheaton, had asserted in his book on international law that no nation had to surrender fugitives unless by special agreement. In the *Creole* affair, Campbell concluded, the United States government could not expect compensation, for the slaves had become free upon their arrival in British territory.[33]

This opinion, as well as approval of the London *Times*, stiffened the Peel ministry. To no one's surprise Foreign Secretary Aberdeen told the House of Lords that Britain would not try the mutineers of the *Creole* and would not turn over the other blacks to the United States government. In agreement with a petition from the Hibernian Anti-Slavery Society in Dublin and with a memorial presented to him a few days earlier by the British and Foreign Anti-Slavery Society, he told Everett that the colonial courts could not try the blacks accused of mutiny and murder because the acts had occurred outside British jurisdiction and that it was impossible to transfer them to the American courts because there was no extradition law. They had to go free. If the mutineers had been accused of piracy, he said, the colonial courts could have handled the case. In fact, the British government had offered its local tribunals to the American consul at Nassau if he had wanted to bring the nineteen blacks to trial for piracy. The consul, Aberdeen said, had shown no interest in the suggestion. Nassau's chief justice ruled soon after that the nineteen prisoners were free.[34]

Webster must have expected this decision, for he never instructed Everett to demand the return of the mutineers. The minister tried in vain to persuade Aberdeen to support reparation for the *Creole*'s blacks. After a long examination of the issues, he concluded in a note to the foreign secretary that Nassau officials should have brought the mutineers to justice and helped the ship resume its voyage. As for the attorney general's claim that the slaves' overseer on the brig gave "seeming consent" to their release, Everett maintained that the presence of numerous black islanders around the *Creole* had caused him to acquiesce. He added that it was incongruous for Britain to argue for the unconditional liberation of American slaves when it had only established conditional emancipation (with compensation) within its own territory.[35] Everett's protest was perfunctory, for the Peel ministry's decision was final.

The controversies over the African slave trade and the *Creole* affair were significant to Anglo-American relations because they directly affected the South, a section previously untouched by most arguments between the Atlantic nations. Southerners had not shown much interest in the northeastern boundary, nor had they closely followed the *Caroline* and McLeod issues because of their commercial ties with Britain and their geographical distance from the border disputes. But events involving the African slave trade and the *Creole* held great potential for trouble because they raised the issue of national honor and threatened to open the question of slavery to international debate. For different reasons, then, both Northerners and Southerners by 1842 believed that the national interest, as each group defined it, was at stake during the arguments with the United Kingdom. More than a few warned that these grievances, if not handled carefully, could lead to a third Anglo-American conflict.

6. Prologue to Compromise

By the time John Tyler became president of the United States, almost sixty years had passed since the country had established its independence and supposedly drawn the boundary between the Republic and British North America. Unfortunately, as preceding pages have shown, the line's location remained undetermined, and other problems had joined the border controversy to compile a veritable catalog of difficulties between Britain and the United States. Americans were also beginning to wonder whether the Oregon boundary should run as high as 54°40′, the southern tip of Alaska as drawn by the agreement with Russia in 1824. Britain and the United States had established joint occupation of Oregon in the treaties of 1818 and 1827; but as more Americans moved into the valleys of the Columbia and Willamette this policy appeared shortsighted, too favorable to the British. All of these questions, each in some way related to America's honor, had attached themselves to the northeastern boundary issue by the summer of 1842.

The obvious approach to these problems was to resolve the northeastern boundary first by negotiating a compromise. Before this could take place, however, both nations had to make a series of intricate arrangements with the people living in the areas directly concerned. The major obstacle was Maine. Its citizens distrusted the British, as did many Americans, and the New Englanders at times even questioned the motives of the government in Washington. The result was further delay. At last, in the summer of 1842, Secretary of State Webster and a special British emissary, Lord Ashburton, met in Washington to unravel all Anglo-American problems. Their conversations ranged over many issues, but the center of discussion was always the Maine boundary. Though the men could not foresee the explosive events of the latter part of the decade, the American nation would become involved in a crisis with Britain over Oregon and in war with Mexico. No sooner were these issues resolved than contentions rose over the future of slavery, which would lead straight into the Civil War. The year 1842 was a good time to settle the northeastern boundary dispute.

The political and economic problems facing the Tyler administration in mid-1841 were so immense that they mistakenly made the northeastern boundary seem unimportant. Yet those people who understood the ramifications of the border dispute knew a broader question was involved—the general direction of Anglo-American affairs. Over a half century had passed since the diplomats at Paris had worked out the details of the new Republic's independence, and yet Americans and Britons remained skeptical about each other's motives. In both countries there were severe complications for a person who wanted to be a patriot, as well as an advocate of closer political and economic ties between the Atlantic nations. Britons long had known this fundamental truth, but Americans became increasingly aware of its paradoxical nature during the decade of the 1840s. President Tyler, a Virginian, recognized the importance of the cotton trade to his home section, and Secretary Webster knew that his merchant friends in New England wanted amicable relations with Britain for obvious reasons, yet in both sections were Anglophobes and other opposition groups. And always there was the nagging belief that the British refused to recognize America's legitimacy. A British writer in London's *Edinburgh Review* understood these feelings. Though he denied that the Republic was "undervalued in England," he nonetheless conceded that "there is a nation by whom America is anxious to be esteemed—or, to speak more correctly, to be admired and feared—and that is England." This desire had become so intense, according to the writer, that America thinks that by adopting a "bold, or even a threatening tone towards England, she will obtain our respect." This was not so. England, he concluded, disliked America's "swagger or . . . bully" and feared its aggressive designs in Canada.[1]

The situation in the United States was so difficult that the Tyler administration was subject to attack no matter what course it adopted, yet it could not follow Van Buren's example of merely hoping that Anglo-American problems would take care of themselves. The government in Washington had to do something before the initiative passed into the hands of political opponents like Clay and Benton, and certainly before the problems with Britain combined with the economic plight of the United States to force the two countries into conflict.

Controversy over the northeastern boundary had continued to smolder after the Aroostook War in 1839, and leaders in London and Washington, disturbed by recurring trouble in the area, ordered longer, more involved surveys and countersurveys that confused everyone. When all appeared hopeless, each nation reverted to its original stand on the treaty line of 1783. Complexity after complexity dogged the question, and no one but a Philadelphia lawyer—one might say a Maine lawyer—could have hoped to understand the issues without months, perhaps years, of study. General Scott's stopgap arrangement of March 1839 had entrusted the Madawaska settlements to Britain and the Aroostook Valley to the United States, but a dispute quickly developed over the boundary between the areas. At stake was the fate of loyalists of both countries. More important, if Britain were to protect Canada by containing America's northern expansion, it had to construct a military road between the Maritime Provinces and Quebec. The natural boundary was the St. John River, but this line would divide British subjects at Madawaska. A compromise with equivalents was the logical solution. More than three additional years of serious unrest ensued before New Brunswick and Maine reluctantly considered the idea.

Though Washington's attention was on the effects of the Panic of 1837, its leaders were aware that by the end of 1840 Madawaska had become the focus of trouble along the New Brunswick–Maine border. Emotions grew in November when about a hundred Americans and a few French-Canadians, under protection of a posse from Maine, met near the mouth of the Fish River (north of the Aroostook River) to cast votes for a president of the United States. New Brunswick's warden of this disputed area had received directives to arrest anyone violating British jurisdiction, but when the province's justice of the peace protested the assembly, some Americans roughly escorted him and a fellow officer from the meeting and warned that their return meant imprisonment. The government in London argued that its dominion stretched to the St. Francis River and warned against further "encroachments" by armed posses, while Maine countered that Madawaska did not extend northward beyond the outlets of the Fish and Madawaska rivers and above the mouth of the Madawaska, which emptied into Lake Temiscouata in the north. Excitement again spread along the border. The New York *Herald* seemed to be reprinting editions of a year and a half before when it reported riotous activities in the area. And the federal government, as earlier, warned Britain to withdraw its troops.[2]

Like the events that led to the Aroostook War, local problems in late 1840 threatened to become national; but this time the outcome might not be as glorious—or as bloodless—as in the winter of 1839. The new governor of Maine, Edward Kent, warned that if New Brunswick refused to evacuate its soldiers he would urge the federal government to take the territory. In London, Colonial Secretary Lord Russell approved sending more regulars to Madawaska to show the United States nothing would be gained by delay, while Foreign Secretary Palmerston blasted the "cunning" Yankees for labeling British conciliation as fear and cynically remarked that the United States relied "very much upon bully." The head of the Foreign Office did not know it, but Maine's legislature was preparing resolutions calling on the governor to expel British troops and persuade the president of the United States to intervene. Eventually hearing of Maine's decision, some members of Parliament considered it a declaration of war and urged the ministry to assign a "strong fleet" outside American harbors and a "powerful army" along the disputed border, while others expected that as usual the state's belligerent stand would pass. But by late March, the states of Alabama, Indiana, and Maryland pledged support to Maine and urged the government in Washington to remove British soldiers from American soil.[3]

When Webster entered the State Department in the spring of 1841 the boundary controversy had become so entangled that compromise seemed unlikely. He immediately had his hands full with the Alexander McLeod case in New York, but somehow had to divert attention to the crisis building again in the Northeast. Questions of national honor had combined with Maine's almost natural inclination to distrust the British, and any hint of a financial settlement seemed an insult to all concerned. Maine denounced attempts to "barter her birthright" for money, while Britain refused at first even to consider a cash offer, realizing it probably would prejudice claims to the area by implying that the territory belonged to Maine. By midyear the New England state complained that its land had become a thoroughfare for British troops and warned that collision was likely unless they left the area. But their evacuation, the British realized, would allow Maine to take all of Madawaska. A Catholic priest in the settlements voiced the sentiments of many British subjects when he said war was preferable to union with the United States.[4]

Tyler and Webster knew the only solution to the boundary problem was compromise, and early in June the president tried to convert the issue into a purely national concern. He proposed to the British minister that small detachments of federal troops replace the state's posse at the mouth of the Fish River—to preserve peace, he added quickly, not to establish American control of the land. British soldiers, he declared, should remain only on the north bank of the St. John. Webster suggested that when federal forces replaced the posse at Fort Fairfield, Britain should station soldiers opposite the fort so as to give moral assurance to its people at Madawaska. The British government made note of Tyler's friendly intentions, but steadfastly reserved the right to quarter troops on either side of the St. John.[5]

At this point Webster received unexpected support for the administration's course from a relatively unknown figure—Francis Smith, a lawyer, newspaper publisher, and former congressman and senator from Maine. Something of a chameleon in both business and politics, Smith had lost heavily in a speculative banking venture in 1837 and later opposed President Van Buren's Independent Treasury. His fortunes soon improved. By the time he talked with Webster he was part owner of the Augusta *Age*, the Augusta *Patriot*, and the Portland *Eastern Argus* and had interests in the commerce and railroads of Portland. After buying a substantial share in Samuel Morse's patent for a magnetic telegraph, he eventually would make a fortune as contractor for the telegraph line constructed from Washington to Baltimore in 1843–44.[6] Smith clearly had much to gain from a peaceful resolution of the boundary.

In the spring of 1841, Smith outlined an intriguing program to Webster, which he guaranteed would bring about an amicable border settlement. The administration in Washington, he suggested, should quietly conduct a newspaper campaign in New England to convince that section's residents of the need for compromise. As early as the end of 1837, Smith had failed in an attempt to persuade President Van Buren to send a secret agent to New Brunswick and Maine to determine acceptable terms. He later explained to Webster that Van Buren's mistake had been to negotiate "at the wrong end of the dispute." The problem was to convince New Brunswick and Maine, not London and Washington, of the necessity for compromise. Now, in May, he assured Webster that Maine would support a compromise if someone could make the state's politicians and newspaper editors realize that a search for the treaty

√ line of 1783 would cost too much in money and time. Such agreement would be acceptable if Britain granted use of the St. John River and a "pecuniary indemnity."[7]

√ Smith's argument convinced Webster. The secretary knew the campaign would cost only a few thousand dollars as against hundreds of thousands for negotiations and surveys—and much more for a war. After Webster secured approval from the president, Smith offered to head the newspaper program. Compensation would be $3,500 a year, in addition to expenses. In the event of success, Smith said, he expected a "liberal commission" on whatever monetary exchanges took place during negotiations with Britain. Webster agreed to his terms. Tyler advanced Smith $500 from the president's secret-service fund, set aside for use in foreign relations. The agent eventually received $2,500 (including the $500) from the fund.[8]

√ Webster and Smith carefully proceeded with the plan. The secretary drew up a proposed boundary settlement and dispatched Smith to Maine to arrange to have it published in the Portland *Christian Mirror*, a politically neutral, religious journal with wide circulation in New England. Both men expected other newspapers to reprint their suggestions. Three editorials appeared in the *Mirror*, on 18 November and 2 December 1841 and on 3 February 1842. All signed by "Agricola" and entitled "NORTHEASTERN BOUNDARY—WHY NOT SETTLE IT?" they asserted that the most likely alternative to compromise was war. People in Maine, the articles urged, should petition their state government for the following terms: Maine's title to the disputed territory; Britain's ownership of land needed for a military road; America's free navigation of the St. John for fifty years; federal compensation to Maine for past defense of the disputed territory; British indemnity to Maine and Massachusetts for giving up claim to some of the land. Smith realized that Massachusetts, like Maine, had property interests involved in any settlement of the boundary. Under the act of separation of 1819, the state had reserved a half interest in Maine's public lands. The important goal was both states'
√ agreement to a compromise boundary in exchange for an equivalent.[9]

√ Webster believed the program would be a success. He had memorials circulated in Maine calling for legislative action and by mid-December was confident the state would accept the principle of compromise. Other newspapers—some outside the state—eventually reprinted the articles published in the *Mirror*. The Portland *Eastern Argus*, the most influential Democratic paper in Maine and the only one with substantial circulation outside the state, shifted from its original stand of opposition to full support of a boundary compromise by the spring of 1842. By August the articles had appeared in the Chicago *American*, the *Democratic Free Press* and the *Constitutional Democrat* of Detroit, and the Little Rock *Arkansas Times and Advocate*. The Richmond *Enquirer*, spokesman of Southern Democrats, quoted the *Eastern Argus* and advocated a settlement with Britain, despite the paper's dislike for Webster and the Whig party.[10]

When the secretary learned that the British government had appointed Lord Ashburton as special minister to the United States, he took an unusual step: he invited Maine and Massachusetts to send representatives to the negotiations. Their acquiescence, he knew, was vital to the Senate's acceptance of any treaty with the United Kingdom. In a private letter to Reuel Williams, Democratic senator from Maine and relentless critic of the Tyler administration, Webster emphasized the importance of a compromise line with compensation and at the president's suggestion asked if the state would consider sending delegates to the meetings with Britain. Williams thought that in exchange for equivalents Maine would surrender land for a British military road, but first London must withdraw its troops from the disputed area. The state's worry, he explained to the secretary, was that the British would refuse to accept the principle of compromise. Until they publicly conceded this point, Maine's legislature could not act on Webster's proposal.[11]

To inquire whether Maine's lawmakers were amenable to compromise, Webster sent two men to Augusta: Peleg Sprague, federal district judge in Boston and former senator from Maine who had moderated his earlier demands on the boundary, and Albert Smith, onetime federal marshal and now lame-duck congressman from the state. They learned that both Whigs and Democrats wanted a settlement but were unable to say so publicly for fear of political attack. Spokesmen in Maine apparently would surrender land north of the St. John above Grand Falls— north and east of Britain's desired communications line—in exchange for navigation rights on the St. John and for other territory that would create an equitable arrangement. The state also wanted the "narrow strip"— the land between the west side of the St. John and the due-north line and extending from the Eel River to Grand Falls. Leaders of both houses of the state legislature favored sending a commission to the negotiations, but were afraid the plan would not be acceptable in Maine because of Governor Fairfield's present unpopularity over other issues. For their efforts in Maine, Sprague received $250, though he reported an expense of only $30, while Smith received $600 for services of ninety days, which included trips to Boston, Portland, and Augusta. The reimbursements came from the president's contingency fund.[12]

Webster's steps probably were essential to the ultimate success of the settlement. His campaign no doubt influenced Maine's legislators to approve the principle of compromise; the newspaper articles reprinted in other parts of the country might have convinced people that Maine thought the terms acceptable; having state representatives at the negotiations surely was a factor in Maine's willingness to consider a treaty with Britain. Though historians have criticized the secretary for using the president's contingency fund illegally or improperly, Maine's behavior had such great effect on Anglo-American affairs that it justified his action. Because of the states' rights threat to international relations, and because of the explosiveness of the boundary situation, Webster's methods of persuading Maine to accept a compromise line were defensible. They did not comprise a mere program in propaganda, as some writers have asserted, for the steps outlined in the articles were fair, equitable, and above all practical. At this time the best way to contact masses of people, other than face-to-face, was through newspapers and pamphlets. Officeholders had resorted to the party press for many years (for example, Alexander Hamilton, Thomas Jefferson, John Marshall, John Adams), and the Tyler administration now used it to advantage on the northeastern boundary question. Tyler and Webster may have stretched the statute setting up the secret-service fund, but they did not act illegally. The law's provisions were open to interpretation. The fund was "for the contingent expenses of intercourse between the United States and foreign nations."[13]

As in America, the change in government in the United Kingdom combined with Britain's political and economic problems to encourage a move for better foreign relations. In the autumn of 1841, Peel and Aberdeen replaced Melbourne and Palmerston in the London government and joined Tyler and Webster in attempting to settle the boundary dispute. Two British journals urged peaceful resolution of Anglo-American issues. London's *Quarterly Review* pleaded for "a large and liberal spirit of conciliation and equity as well as of strict justice"; yet it demanded nothing less than the St. John River as the boundary. The *Foreign Quarterly Review* concluded that "the American question is not one of the greatest difficulties with which the [British] cabinet has to contend in its foreign policy"; but, curiously, it went on to warn that war with the United States would cost much in trade and could lead to the loss of parts of Canada. Palmerston, always wary of Yankee ingenuity, had added to the confusion by rejecting any American boundary proposals and substituting his own. Before leaving the Foreign Office in the fall of 1841, he again failed to show any understanding of the necessity for safeguarding Maine's prestige and simply urged the Washington government to withdraw the state's posse from the disputed territory. Peel, however, remembered his campaign promises to balance the budget and cut military expenditures. Both he and Aberdeen realized that Britain's financial stability depended in large part on relations with France and America. Consequently, they sought to relieve tension with France by emphasizing the broader question of good relations with the United States and worked to protect Canada by preventing local disagreements from interfering with a boundary settlement.[14]

The Peel ministry decided on a different approach toward improving Anglo-American relations—it would send a special minister to the United States to discuss all problems between the nations. The prime minister chose not to go through regular procedures of negotiation because the issues were many and he believed that the present British minister in Washington, Henry Fox, had fallen into disfavor with the American people because of his "feeling of hatred to the U. S. and it's [*sic*] Institutions." He and Aberdeen knew the step was risky, for failure through regular diplomatic channels was easier to keep quiet than failure through a publicized envoy. Yet a special mission, they thought, would impress Americans with Britain's sincerity. Besides, they might have recalled that the United States had furnished precedents for special commissioners during the 1790s when it sent John Jay to England and Thomas Pinckney to Spain. For the American post, Peel and Aberdeen in December 1841 chose Alexander Baring, Lord Ashburton, retired head of the banking

firm of Baring Brothers and Company, which then was working to resolve America's state-debts problems with British investors. His official
title would be "Commissioner Procurator and Plenipotentiary." With
"fear & trembling" the sixty-seven-year-old financial magnate accepted
the assignment. Absence from his family would be "painful," he said, but
he could afford a month. Ashburton then wrote his friend, John Croker,
that he wanted to talk with him about Anglo-American affairs. Later, on
Christmas Eve, Aberdeen informed Queen Victoria of the decision, and
she immediately approved.[15]

Two days after Christmas, Aberdeen told Minister Everett of the
special mission. The American was surprised, but indicated pleasure.
This news must have tested his composure. Since Everett hardly had
moved into the Court of St. James's, he must have felt dissatisfied to
realize that his role in resolving Anglo-American problems would be
diminished. Yet he could look forward to the social parties, the many
games of whist, the long walks and seemingly interminable discussions
—and these would help to establish a closeness between Everett and
Aberdeen that complemented the official negotiations in Washington.
The foreign secretary, following Ashburton's suggestion, explained to
Everett that he had wanted to reveal the decision to him before an
account arrived of Tyler's recent annual message to Congress. The mission was a gesture of goodwill, he assured the American minister, not
a reaction to grievances the president might have mentioned in his
message. Ashburton would have authority to settle all questions between the nations—even the right of search, which Aberdeen at the
time believed was the greatest problem. At the end of the conference he
asked Everett to keep news of the mission confidential until the official
announcement. On the last day of 1841 the London *Times*, evidently
with authorization, proclaimed the mission.[16]

Ashburton was an excellent choice for many reasons. He had close
ties with the United States. In 1795, as a young man of twenty, he had
bought more than a million acres in Maine (then part of Massachusetts)
from William Bingham, Federalist senator from Philadelphia who owned
almost a ninth of Maine, and from Henry Knox, former secretary of war.
None of this land, it is important to note, was part of the territory in dispute by the 1840s. After negotiating the purchase, Baring met Bingham's
sixteen-year-old daughter Anne Louisa and soon married her. Five years

Alexander Baring, Lord Ashburton

later, in 1803, Baring Brothers combined with Hope and Company of Amsterdam to finance America's Louisiana Purchase.[17]

Baring's business and political achievements also impressed Americans. His leadership of the banking house from 1810 until his retirement in 1832 was a huge success. The firm became so powerful in Europe that Lord Byron, in one of the cantos of *Don Juan*, asked in 1823,

> *Who hold the balance of the world? Who reign*
> *O'er Congress, whether royalist or liberal?*

Rothschild and Baring, he replied. When Baring retired he held a fortune of £3 million. From 1806 until he was made Lord Ashburton in 1835 he was a member of the House of Commons. In the years before the War of 1812 he opposed British restrictions on trade with the United States, albeit because of their detrimental effect on the British economy. He nonetheless appeared to be a spokesman for American interests. Respected in the Conservative party, Baring was president of the Board of Trade in Peel's short ministry of 1834–35 and declined an offer to sit in his cabinet in 1841. Many Americans considered Ashburton urbane, able, and respectable, a defender of American as well as of British interests. In a note to Webster, Lady Ashburton remarked that Englishmen considered her husband "most zealous" in the cause of America. "If you don't like him," she declared, "we can send you nothing better."[18]

Another factor in Ashburton's selection was his relationship with Webster. The two had been friends since meeting in England in 1839, but Webster had acted as legal adviser for the Baring firm since 1831 and continued to do so during the controversy over state bonds after the Panic of 1837. Shortly after his appointment Ashburton informed Webster of his mission to the United States. Two American members of the board of Baring Brothers privately agreed that both Ashburton and his banking firm had economic interests at stake. The special minister assured Webster that the best reason for good Anglo-American relations was the "moral improvement and the progressive civilization of the world."[19]

For the most part, British and American reactions to Ashburton's mission were favorable. The London *Morning Chronicle* remarked that commercial circles welcomed the news; the possibility of better relations with America had revived confidence in state stocks. The *Times* thought the move demonstrated Peel's intent to maintain peace, while the *Ex-*

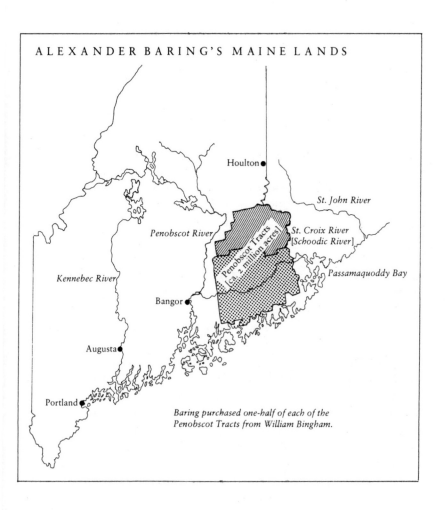

ALEXANDER BARING'S MAINE LANDS

Houlton

St. John River

Penobscot River

St. Croix River
[Schoodic River]

Penobscot Tracts
[ca. 2 million acres]

Kennebec River

Passamaquoddy Bay

Bangor

Augusta

Portland

Baring purchased one-half of each of the
Penobscot Tracts from William Bingham.

Prologue to Compromise / 99

aminer praised America's desire for harmony. The Halifax *Novascotian* agreed with both London papers. There were exceptions to this euphoric mood. The *Foreign Quarterly Review* worried that Americans were "not reasonable, wherever their pride is involved," while other skeptics expressed concern about Ashburton's "vacillation and irresolution" and about his age and long absence from public affairs. Most observers, however, seemed pleased with the appointment. In the United States several newspapers hailed the mission. Robert C. Winthrop in Massachusetts, Whig representative, later senator, and longtime friend of Webster's, noted that Ashburton's character will "disarm us of those suspicions and jealousies of the Mother Country which we inherited from our Fathers, & which have constituted hitherto, &, I suppose, will always continue to constitute, the greatest source of danger to the peace of the two Countries." Two Democratic papers, probably for political reasons, were hesitant. The Richmond *Enquirer* warned that Ashburton's goal would be to secure advantages for his country, and the Washington *Globe* reminded its readers that Webster recently had accepted an extraordinary fee of £1,000 from the Barings for a "sort of professional opinion." The Boston *Courier* and the Nashville *Union* also had reservations about chances for settlement, while Governor John Davis of Massachusetts warned Webster that Britain wanted part of Maine only "to enlarge her powers" against the United States. Senator Willie Mangum of North Carolina wrote a friend about the "strong proclivity" for war because of America's hatred for the British.[20]

The few doubts that existed in the United States quickly disappeared. Britain's decision to send a minister to the United States was important to Americans. The effect on the Republic's pride was predictable. Diarist Philip Hone noted that Ashburton's appointment was "an unusual piece of condescension" by our "haughty elder sister" and highly complimentary to the United States. President Tyler welcomed the mission, while Albert Gallatin, veteran of Anglo-American boundary negotiations and longtime friend of Ashburton's, believed the move indicative of the United Kingdom's desire to settle issues with America.[21]

While the special envoy made arrangements for the trip, Aberdeen hurriedly prepared instructions relating to all differences between the nations, the most immediate being the northeastern boundary. It was plain that a primary concern of the Peel ministry was to maintain the military security of British North America. Besides, a reasonable compromise with the United States, Aberdeen believed, would improve relations with France. The St. Lawrence River froze over in winter, he reminded Ashburton, and Britain had to secure a strip of land linking Montreal with the Atlantic seaboard. Though Ashburton could agree to any one of three alternative lines, he was to accept no less than the award limits of the king of the Netherlands in 1831. He could, however, leave unrectified the forty-fifth parallel from the Connecticut River to the St. Lawrence. Though such action would acknowledge American control of Rouse's Point, important to Britain's defense of Montreal, the foreign secretary knew the land contained Americans from New York, Vermont, and New Hampshire. He also apparently thought the military road would be adequate compensation for loss of the Point. Aberdeen added that he hoped to obtain the entire Madawaska settlement and all navigable portions of the St. John River, but admitted that his envoy might have to sacrifice these latter areas in the interests of compromise.[22]

Another sector of the North American border that was unclear but up to this time had aroused little interest was the northwestern boundary, or the line from Lake Huron through Lake Superior to the Lake of the Woods. This part of the contested frontier, the reader will remember, had been part of the King-Hawkesbury Convention that failed to pass the Senate in 1803. In the period thereafter, British and American commissioners under the Treaty of Ghent had not agreed on ownership of St. George's Island (Sugar Island) in the St. Mary's River between Lakes Huron and Superior and on the course of the boundary from Lake Superior to the Lake of the Woods. Aberdeen, however, thought this area was not of "paramount importance" and would grant the United States what it wanted. A factor possibly affecting his decision was the belief that British control of the upper lakes region would allow continued exploitation of the fur trade. But there was a more important point: a military road could halt suspected American expansion in the Northeast. Hence Ashburton's directives on the northwestern border were sweeping. He could yield even the rich soil of St. George's Island in exchange for an equivalent from the Oregon Territory or from any other debated boundary sector included in the instructions.[23]

In a private note Aberdeen enclosed a memorandum by the duke of Wellington that had the potential of disrupting settlement of the North

American boundary. The former military commander, now member of Peel's cabinet, was concerned about America's goals in Canada and wanted enough land to construct a military road directly from the eastern coast of the St. Lawrence to the waters off New Brunswick and around Prince Edward's Island. Britain, he argued, should not seek merely the award line of 1831, for it ran too near the St. Lawrence River. The Paris peace negotiators of 1783, Wellington insisted, could not have intended to place the American frontier along the St. John. The line had to be farther south. Aberdeen admitted that if Ashburton followed Wellington's recommendations, there would be little chance for success, but because of the duke's influence they deserved attention.[24]

In mid-February 1842, even before Aberdeen had completed the instructions, Ashburton left for the United States. There were several reasons for his hurried departure. The minister believed he could not wait until spring because if the negotiations took longer than expected and Congress adjourned before receiving the treaty, the settlement would be subject to a possible change in party power and to political infighting between the Tyler and Clay factions in the federal and state governments. Both Aberdeen and Ashburton feared that Whig control in the Senate, favorable to an Anglo-American agreement, might collapse. There also were advantages in leaving before Parliament met; a debate over the mission would mean delay. Since the Atlantic crossing would not improve much in late February or March, Ashburton wanted to leave immediately. He did not request special accommodations, but knew Aberdeen would ask the admiralty to make his entrance into the United States duly ceremonial.[25] Leaving his wife behind because of her poor health, he departed on the *Warspite*, an ominously entitled frigate of fifty-four guns and crew of five hundred.

At this point, February 1842, Providence or chance entered the mystery that had developed over the northeastern boundary. A series of events had begun that would pit Britain against the United States in what Ashburton in 1844 would call the "battle of the maps," a controversy still existing today in some quarters. How prophetic was his statement that it "may remain a vexed question to puzzle future historians."[26] The argument centers on which map of the disputed area contained the boundary line agreed to as final by the Paris negotiators in 1783. While more than one map used in Paris had what appeared to be definitive boundary markings, it is important to determine whether these were mere proposals or lines actually adopted as final. In short, a map has to be *authentic*—capable of proof that the Paris negotiators used it in drawing the boundary—and it has to be *valid*—clearly established that they adopted the lines on the map as final. Until a map meets *both* requirements, its inscriptions are not conclusive.

The tangle started innocently. The newspaper campaign in Maine hardly had gotten under way when Webster received a private letter from his friend, the eminent historian Jared Sparks, who was McLean Professor of History at Harvard, biographer of George Washington, and author and editor of many works. From Cambridge, Massachusetts, in early 1842, Sparks wrote the secretary that recently, while researching in the Paris archives of the French Foreign Office, he had discovered a letter of 6 December 1782 from Benjamin Franklin, one of America's delegates to the negotiations ending the Revolutionary War, to the Count de Vergennes, the French foreign minister. It indicated that Franklin had drawn on a map "a strong red line" showing the Canadian-American boundary established in the preliminary peace negotiations at Paris. Thinking this map would confirm America's title to the disputed territory, Sparks and the Keeper of the archives began an extensive search through the well-indexed and cataloged sixty thousand maps and charts relating to American affair.[27]

After a little looking Sparks came across a map of North America. It contained a red ink boundary of the northern part of the United States which he thought might have been the line Franklin described in the letter. Though this "red-line map" was a d'Anville of 1746, Sparks did not know then that Franklin, like all the Paris negotiators, had used a Mitchell. His only concern was that it supported *British* claims to the entire territory in dispute. Indeed, by showing a boundary south of the St. John and between its headwaters and those of the Penobscot and the Kennebec, it gave the United Kingdom more than its government leaders had claimed. The line extended north from the source of the St. Croix (Schoodic), as the British argued, but instead of proceeding to Mars Hill it abruptly turned west and left Britain all streams running into the St. John River. The United States apparently had no right to any of the disputed land, not even to the Aroostook Valley. Admitting there was "no positive proof" that this *was* Franklin's map, Sparks from memory and notes disconsolately reconstructed the boundary in black on a nineteenth-century map of Maine and sent it to Webster.[28]

The secretary was not surprised that the British claim appeared correct; more than three years earlier he had made a discovery "too much like this." In 1838 the British consul in New York had had opportunity to buy a Mitchell map of 1775 that had belonged to Baron Friedrich von Steuben of Revolutionary War fame. This map contained the same marking as Sparks's discovery, though no one knew who had drawn the line or how Steuben had acquired the map. The consul understandably refused to purchase it because he doubted the map's authenticity. That same year, 1838, Webster bought it from Steuben's legatee for $200. Perhaps to pressure Maine into a compromise, he sold the map, for the same price, to an agent of the state, Charles Daveis, who was working with Maine's congressional delegation in Washington to locate the treaty line of 1783. Daveis immediately concealed the map.[29]

In May 1842, over a month after Ashburton's arrival in the United States, Everett in London expressed concern that the British had withheld important maps from the United States. The American minister had asked Aberdeen if a new search should be made of the British archives for the original map of 1783, and the foreign secretary, Everett believed at the time, evaded the question. Aberdeen admitted that someone had said there was an old map in the archives; but because of the manner in which the foreign secretary spoke, Everett was convinced it was not the Mitchell used by the British negotiators at Paris in 1782–83, Richard Oswald and Henry Strachey.[30] The minister was sure there was another map in the archives of the Foreign Office.

Though Everett did not know it at the time, the map Aberdeen referred to probably was the one later uncovered in the State Paper Office (now called the Public Record Office) sometime in June 1842. A Mitchell map of 1755 of North America, it followed the British claim with a light red line. When the Foreign Office learned of its existence, it notified the cabinet, and after three cartographers confirmed its age the map was locked away. According to a close acquaintance of several members of the Peel ministry, diarist Charles Greville, British officials were sure it was the map used in Paris in 1782–83, and they so notified Ashburton. Yet it is unlikely that either Aberdeen or Ashburton believed the map con-

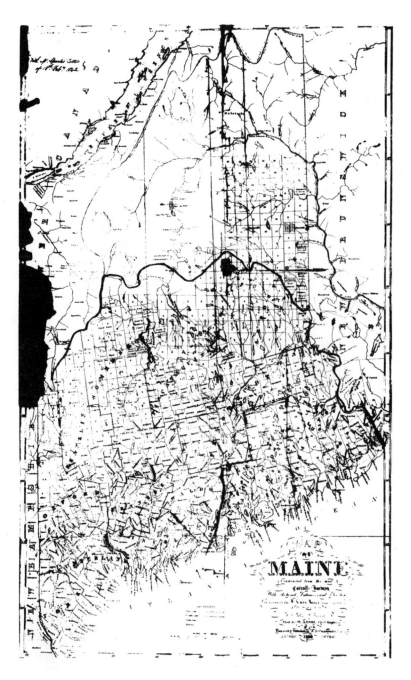

Jared Sparks's Map of Maine

vincingly supported British claims, for their correspondence, private and otherwise, mentions nothing about it. They no doubt realized the impossibility of proving that the map contained a boundary adopted as final. The London government probably felt the map so dubious that it never told Ashburton of its existence. Not until after the treaty negotiations did Aberdeen show this map to Everett—and then only because he apparently wanted to prove to the minister that the Peel government had not meant to hide anything. Though on rollers, soiled, and defaced, its marking clearly supported the British claim.[31]

Everett remained certain that the map used by Oswald in the negotiations was in the London archives, and this feeling has led some historians to maintain that both Everett and Sparks knew as early as 1838 or 1839 that the papers of the earl of Lansdowne (previously Lord Shelburne, British prime minister in 1782) in London contained evidence to substantiate the American claim to all of the disputed territory. This is unlikely. In a note to Everett in January 1843, Sparks declared that in his research he had seen nothing in the Lansdowne papers relating to the boundary; besides, Everett probably did not base his reasoning on any letter found there. He explained to Webster that the Paris commissioners of 1782–83 had used Mitchell maps ordered from London, that the American negotiators had sent their copy home whereas the British had not, and that British officials had been watching all people, including Sparks, who consulted the State Paper Office. For the last month, Everett told the secretary of state, four clerks had been searching through documents of the Revolutionary period. But even before receiving this note, Webster apparently believed that settlement of the northeastern boundary was within his grasp and that it might become impossible if the Oswald or any other map appeared. Consequently, without informing his minister of the Sparks or Steuben maps, Webster ordered Everett in mid-June to *"forbear to press the search after maps in England or elsewhere."*[32]

While it is clear now that the Sparks and Steuben maps were indefinitive, Webster could not have been certain in 1842. One fact was plain, however: he could not allow the British to see either of these redline maps until the boundary negotiations had ended. If Webster doubted their validity, he certainly understood the effects their release would have on the British public. And with Maine's adamant insistence on the entire area in dispute these questionable pieces of cartography could be a sufficient catalyst to set off the conflict Webster wanted to avert. Sparks himself must have had second thoughts about his discovery when he later found in the French archives at least four more d'Anville maps, each with a red boundary of the northern section of the United States. In truth, the only similarity between Sparks's map and Franklin's description was that the line was red. The boundary on Sparks's d'Anville probably was the southern edge of France's claims against Britain before the French and Indian War. Nor would a shrewd negotiator like Franklin have awarded so much land to the British. Rather than charging Sparks with irresponsibility for unearthing the red-line map, it seems fair to believe him when he said he forwarded the copy to Webster because it was important that the United States have all facts before attempting to settle the boundary with Britain. He did not expect the secretary to make the map public, he later remarked to a friend. The Harvard historian tried to establish the whole story of the boundary, even though he knew it might jeopardize his country's claims.[33]

The story of the "battle of the maps" still is not complete, for later, during Parliament's heated discussions of the Webster-Ashburton Treaty in early 1843, the Oswald map turned up—in London, as Everett had suspected. A Mitchell, it threw everything into a turmoil because it supported the *American* claim to all land in question. This map, used by Oswald at the Paris peace talks of 1782–83, showed a red line following the source of the St. Croix River (Schoodic) to its mouth and continuing northward to include in the American claim a piece of land above the St. John River as far north as the Metis. What seemed to make the map valid was that someone had written these words four times around its edges: "Boundary as described by Mr. Oswald." America's rights to the land in question seemed justified when the endorsement on the map appeared to be in the handwriting of George III himself. A diplomat likes to think he has all important and available information at hand when he begins negotiations. Yet in this case, not only had Ashburton been unaware of Webster's red-line maps, but the special minister had not known of the one in London. Further complications arose when the Peel ministry learned that its archcritic, Lord Palmerston, had discovered the map's existence in 1839 and had hidden it in the Foreign Office.[34]

Tracking down the history of the elusive Oswald or King George III map was an engaging experience. Someone apparently deposited it in the British Museum in 1828, where it remained until the 1830s. In Parliament during late March of 1839, several members, including Peel and Palmerston, were discussing the map problem and the northeastern boundary when Sir Charles Grey commented that a Mitchell map of 1755 was in the British Museum. Foreign Secretary Palmerston "understood" that he was "to make inquiry on the subject, and bring forward the map if it could conveniently be had." But one of the museum's keepers informed him that the trustees would not allow any article to leave the library without a warrant from the office of the secretary of state. The order came on 1 April. The map went from the museum to Palmerston in the Foreign Office, where he discovered that it supported the American claim to the disputed territory. He immediately put it out of sight.[35]

How the Oswald map made its way to the surface at such a critical time is an interesting question. Emotions were high in Parliament in February 1843, as some members debated the worth of the boundary compromise negotiated by Ashburton, while others merely used the halls as a forum to level more political attacks at the Peel ministry. Palmerston led the barrage by denouncing Webster's duplicity and Ashburton's stupidity. Minister Everett was perplexed at the map's sudden appearance and soon expressed his belief to Webster that Peel must have learned of its existence from George Featherstonhaugh, a British geologist once employed by the American government, who had resided in the United States for thirty-five years, but who had surveyed the disputed territory under Palmerston's commission in 1839. In a dispatch to the secretary in Washington, Everett wrote: "It [the Oswald map] was . . . brought from the British Museum to the Foreign Office in Lord Palmerston's time, and was known to him and to Mr. Featherstonhaugh. In whose custody it has been since the change of Ministry, so that it did not come to Lord Aberdeen's knowledge I was not told; very likely in that of Mr Featherstonhaugh himself, who has been employed till lately, as a sort of general Agent for the Boundary question."[36] The implication seemed to be that for some unexplained reason, Featherstonhaugh, party to the map's concealment in 1839, had decided to publicize the map.

Everett's suppositions no doubt were wrong; it is highly unlikely that Featherstonhaugh would have turned over the map to Peel. In the same month, February, Featherstonhaugh published a pamphlet and wrote an article for the London *Times*, both of which argued the British claim. In a letter to John Backhouse, longtime permanent undersecretary in the Foreign Office and now retired, he repeated his case and outrageously added that Ashburton deserved no honor for negotiating the treaty. If Peel rewarded him, Featherstonhaugh remarked, "it would be like Setting a fool's Cap on his head." Featherstonhaugh also had bitter comments about Americans. The "Set of Knaves" who deceived Ashburton during the negotiations (concealing the Sparks and Steuben maps) had succeeded because of the British emissary's "ignorance and indolence." Featherstonhaugh's hatred for his Atlantic cousins ran deep —too deep for him to reveal a map substantiating America's claims to the entire area in dispute. Though he might have done anything to embarrass Ashburton—such as releasing the Oswald map—he knew that such move had the counterbalancing evil of humiliating Palmerston. In the same letter of February, Featherstonhaugh warned that Palmerston's criticisms of the treaty lacked judgment, for "every ball that he Strikes will have a Ricochet movement upon himself."[37]

If Everett was wrong, then who did reveal the map to Peel at this propitious time? The supreme irony is that *Ashburton*—the target of Palmerston's verbal abuse—was the one who uncovered the Oswald map. In a letter of 1844 to William Rives, chairman of the Senate Foreign Relations Committee whose friendship he had gained during his mission in the United States, Ashburton wrote: "The facts are these. I returned home in September [1842] and went to town [London] the following February, and I myself discovered the existence of this map as enquiries at the Museum of which I am a Trustee between the time and the day of the Debate on the Treaty in Parliament. Neither Lord Aberdeen [,] Sir R. Peel [,] nor I had ever seen nor heard of the map before." It would have been easy for Ashburton, by then trustee of the British Museum, to ask a keeper or another trustee about the library's maps and eventually to locate the warrant authorizing the transfer of the Oswald to the Foreign Office in 1839. From here the rest of the story is obvious. Ashburton must have felt pleased to expose a map supporting the American claim; not only did the move make his diplomacy appear more adept, but it marked the total defeat of Palmerston's forces. The news that the former foreign secretary had concealed the Oswald map and that Peel had released it in Parliament was enough to deflate opposition to the treaty.[38]

In retrospect, the map controversy had taken on the qualities of a rich comedy; yet it was not amusing to the straitlaced Peel ministry. The opposing maps had the potential of undoing the work of Webster and Ashburton and leaving a bitterness that could have serious effects. As news of the Sparks map had threatened to convert the boundary compromise into a monument to the Peel ministry's ineptitude, even more important was the fact that discovery of the Oswald could endanger its credibility with the United States. Aberdeen immediately called Everett into his office and assured him that the Peel ministry had not known about the map during the negotiations of 1842 in Washington. Because of Aberdeen's unquestioned integrity, Everett believed him; but, as he wrote Webster, he considered the Oswald map authentic and the American claim valid.[39]

Webster's detractors have erroneously agreed with Everett that the Oswald map substantiated America's ownership to all disputed territory in the Northeast. There are several flaws in the minister's reasoning. During the Paris negotiations of 1782–83, one of the British representatives, Henry Strachey, had arrived late and probably revised the generous Oswald line to make it more advantageous to his country. British correspondence shows that after Prime Minister Lord Shelburne saw the boundary resulting from the preliminary negotiations of October 1782, he instructed Strachey to secure a new line more favorable to Nova Scotia. In a dispatch to Webster, Everett himself made this observation. The British argument seems correct that the Americans in Paris never suggested a boundary north of the St. John. Featherstonhaugh earlier had assured Palmerston that close examination of the negotiators' papers of 1782–83 revealed that the British spokesmen soundly defeated an American proposition to make even the St. John the boundary. Featherstonhaugh pointed out that Shelburne had informed his commissioners that the cabinet on 15 November 1782 formulated a new boundary article "for the Americans *to take or leave*." According to Featherstonhaugh, this article was "exactly the same as the 2nd Article of the treaty of 1783, word for word." Hence the British negotiators could *not* have agreed to the American claim outlined on the Oswald map; it was dated 8 October 1782. In addition, research has established that the endorsement on the map was not in George III's hand and that it is impossible to determine when the inscription occurred. As early as

1844, Ashburton himself expressed doubt that the king had signed it. ✓ Another Mitchell, owned by John Jay at Paris, contained the same line as Oswald's, and the words "Mr. Oswald's Line" appeared along the boundary in what Jay's son William asserted was his father's handwriting.[40] But, as with the Oswald map, there is no evidence that the Paris negotiators adopted this line as definitive.

The British government was relieved that the map controversy had not disrupted the negotiations. In Parliament, Peel brought attention to two additional maps supporting the American claim that had appeared in ✓ London during the 1780s. One, a Faden map, was published in 1783 and contained this inscription: "A map of the Boundary of the United States, as agreed to by the treaty of 1783; by Mr. [William] Faden, Geographer to the King." The other, a Bew map, was part of a publication of 1783 entitled *Political Magazine and Literary Journal* and edited by J. Bew. Although the prime minister admitted that the map found in the State Paper Office (mentioned earlier) corroborated the Sparks map (and thus the British claim), he argued that since the Oswald map deviated from both, the sensible conclusion was to accept the treaty of 1842 and ignore all of the maps. He might have added that neither the Faden nor the Bew map had made an impression on the king of the Netherlands in 1831 when Albert Gallatin had presented them (along with many others) during the arbitration hearings. Ashburton was pleased that the Sparks map had brought Maine to terms and that he had not known of its existence ∨ during the negotiations. Such knowledge, he told a trusted acquaintance, would have forced him to demand *all* the land in question; the British public never would have conceded what appeared to be a legitimate claim to the entire territory in dispute. And as for Maine, Ashburton wrote Aberdeen, "All the evidence of angels would not have moved the ✓ Maine lumberers." War seemed to be the alternative, he declared. He repeated his feelings to Webster. The most poignant comment came from Peel when he declared in Parliament that "nothing can be more fallacious than founding a claim upon contemporary maps, unless you can also prove that they were adopted by the negotiators."[41]

Many years later, in 1933, still another Mitchell map turned up— this one also containing a wide red line around the same areas designated ∨ on the Oswald map and hence favorable to the American claim. Located in the Spanish Foreign Office (after the Library of Congress of the United

States had requested a search), this map apparently had come from Count de Aranda, Spanish minister at Paris in 1783. A letter from him indicated that the line had been copied from the map marked for Vergennes by Franklin after completion of the preliminary peace articles of 30 November 1782. Some writers have argued that the Aranda map confirmed the American claim drawn on the Oswald and that Sparks's interference cost the United States a considerable amount of territory. But as with the Sparks, Oswald, and Jay maps, there is no evidence that the Paris negotiators adopted the Aranda as final. In addition, all maps in the Spanish archives had been disassociated from their covering dispatches for custody reasons, and one cannot say with certainty that the map described in Aranda's letter was the same one found in the archives. Aranda's map lacked the negotiators' signatures and was as dubious as the others.[42]

One can argue that the British and American negotiators had drawn a line on their Mitchell maps which they regarded as final and that the purpose of the postwar commission would have been to locate and mark *this* line. Yet their feeling that a commission was necessary implies that even *they* must have had doubts that the boundary was definitive. The diplomats in Paris likely intended the postwar commissioners to resolve the matter by compromise—as Webster and Ashburton did in the summer of 1842. In any case, the northeastern boundary was not the primary concern of the Paris negotiators in 1782–83, and their desire to postpone this problem until after the emotions of war had passed is easy to understand.

There can be one conclusion: all these red-line maps contained only *proposed* boundaries, not lines agreed to as final by the Paris diplomats. Since Oswald, Jay, and Franklin had wanted to defer the northeastern boundary to settlement by joint commission after the war, their red lines could only have been proposals. Franklin himself said his line was drawn during the *preliminary* peace negotiations. Shelburne's instruction to Strachey to revise the boundary of the Oswald map rules out its credibility. And since the Jay map contained the inscription, "Mr. Oswald's Line," it also is invalid. Prime Minister Shelburne's new boundary of November 1782, it seems, was identical to the one contained in the final treaty. The original intent of the negotiators to establish a postwar commission, though defeated, strongly suggests their belief that it would be difficult to execute the terms of any line described in the treaty. Thus none of the three maps constitutes the final word in the controversy. Though all *were* used in Paris in 1782–83, the negotiators did not accept their boundaries as final. To put it another way, the maps were authentic but not valid. Ashburton privately admitted to Aberdeen in January 1843, "Although Franklin's map seems quite conclusive as to the instructions of the Negotiators, it would not be Easy to maintain in argument that those intentions were Executed by the Words of the Treaty [of 1783]." He repeated these feelings to his close friend, John Croker, a month later. And in a private letter to Everett dated 25 April 1843, Webster gave his views on the map question. Neither the Oswald nor the Jay map should be considered definitive, he said, "because neither proves the line found upon it to have been drawn, in any part, *after* the Treaty was agreed to, and for the purpose of setting forth the Boundary, *as* agreed to. . . . [None of the maps is conclusive because] they bear no marked lines, which may not have been lines of proposal, merely. In other words, none of them shows a line, clearly purporting to be a line, drawn for the purpose of shewing on the map, a boundary which had been agreed on."[43] The reasoning found in the letters of Ashburton and Webster seems to apply to *any* of the controversial maps of the northeastern boundary.

Ironically, the historian who most vigorously criticized Webster on the northeastern boundary settlement—Samuel F. Bemis—once held the information that helps to clear the secretary of the charge of questionable conduct during the Washington negotiations of 1842. In his distinguished work, *The Diplomacy of the American Revolution*, Bemis showed that the Paris negotiators, in the preliminary articles, agreed to postpone the issue until after the war, when a joint Anglo-American commission would deal with it.[44]

Early on the morning of 4 April, Lord Ashburton, weary from a long, rugged voyage, arrived in the United States. He entered Annapolis after the wind had blown his ship off course from New York and was greeted royally by the state officials of Maryland. His entourage was impressive: three secretaries (including his son-in-law from the Foreign Office, Humphrey Mildmay), five servants, a carriage, three horses, and a huge quantity of baggage. In the meantime, Webster had arranged lodgings near his own residence, in a spacious, beautifully furnished

house on President Square (today, the parish house of St. John's Episcopal Church, its parlors maintained as they were in 1842), which the
Britisher leased for $1,000 a month. After meeting Tyler, Ashburton
delivered a short speech and presented his official letters. The president
expressed satisfaction that Britain wanted to preserve good understanding between the nations. The formalities over, Ashburton and Webster
visited the Capitol, the Senate, and the Library of Congress.[45]

To most Americans the arrival had been auspicious. The New York
Herald, normally critical of the British, thought Ashburton "republican"
in manner and appearance. He was about six feet tall, a little stooped
and heavyset, and had dark eyes, thick eyebrows, and white hair. Pale,
but with an "active step" and a "quick eye," the envoy appeared to be a
plain man who understood the American character. Even the longtime
antagonist of Britain, Thomas Hart Benton, admitted to Ashburton's
affability. *Niles' Register* was confident of success now that the queen's
representative had arrived. Some Americans, however, still were suspicious of British motives. In the House, Joshua Lowell of Maine warned
that Ashburton had come with olive branch in one hand and sword in the
other, emblematic of the choice offered the United States. The name of
the ship—the *Warspite*—was foreboding.[46] Though Lowell was trying to
justify appropriations for border defenses, many others shared his
attitude that the outcome of the negotiations depended upon whether
Ashburton's terms could establish a feeling of trust among people in
Maine.

When Ashburton indicated that he was authorized to compromise
the boundary dispute, Webster explained the necessity of having Maine
and Massachusetts participate in the border discussions. Though the
minister was skeptical about state involvement in international affairs, he
offered hesitant approval. Webster did not give Ashburton a chance to
change his mind and quickly notified Governor Fairfield of Maine and
Governor Davis of Massachusetts that it was in their interests to send
commissioners to Washington. The time required for exploration and
survey of the disputed area was three more years, the secretary warned,
for the American commission had worked two summers already and
much remained to be done. And if the nations established a joint commission with arbitration in case of disagreement, there would be exorbitant
expense and delay of seven or eight years.[47]

Webster now had to convince the legislatures in Maine and Massachusetts of the necessity for compromise and for sending delegations to Washington. Fairfield's Democratic party in Maine was divided, however, and many leaders urged him to call a special session of the legislature. The importance of such a move, they hoped, would override the popular opposition to compromise. At this point Francis Smith decided to write an article in the Portland *Advertiser* supporting the suggestion. In late April, Fairfield announced it for 18 May. Almost simultaneously, Webster learned that the governor of Massachusetts had received authority, with his council's advice, to appoint a commission. Although Davis, a Whig, publicly called Britain a thief and warned it to stop "bullying" the United States, he privately admitted to Webster that the state would agree to a settlement if the British granted equivalents for all advantages surrendered.[48] Once Webster persuaded Maine to send commissioners to Washington, there would be no problem with the Bay State.

The secretary of state now prepared his final strategem: use of the red-line maps to secure approval of the state commission idea. In mid-May, just before the special session of the Maine legislature, he secretly dispatched his trusted friend Jared Sparks to Augusta to inform Fairfield of the red-line maps (both the Sparks and the Steuben) supporting the British claim in hope that the governor might persuade political leaders to accept the principle of compromise before possibly losing the entire area in dispute. A few days earlier Webster himself had traveled to Massachusetts to inform Governor Davis of the Sparks map. While there he spent $300 from secret-service money to buy back the Steuben map from Maine's agent in Washington, Charles Daveis, who had converted to the idea of compromise and had brought the map to Boston for the secretary. Consequently, when Sparks went to Maine he took both maps. Though one may question the ethics of Webster's using maps that contained only proposed boundaries, no one has proved he knew this at the time. If he was aware of the maps' doubtful validity, he certainly realized the impact their publication would have in Britain. Maine could have a choice of giving up claim to all territory in dispute or of trying to force a reluctant United States into war with the United Kingdom. Governor Fairfield agreed that now was the time to settle the boundary dispute.[49]

Observers must have been surprised that the Maine legislature so readily approved appointment of the commission. When the special session convened on 18 May, Fairfield made his recommendation, and a joint committee unanimously approved. Webster had worried that if Maine restricted the bargaining power of its commissioners, other obstacles might arise to prevent a settlement. He realized that Ashburton already had conceded much by agreeing to the irregular procedure of state participation in international negotiations. If either Maine or Massachusetts set conditions, the British minister would have only the alternatives of accepting or rejecting them, for there could be little flexibility in the discussions. The result, Webster feared, would be failure. Peleg Sprague, Webster's earlier agent in Augusta, had warned that a few overly cautious members of the Maine legislature wanted a referendum on the question of instructions to the commissioners, but he considered this step unlikely. He was correct. The legislature soon approved the principle of compromise and, most important, imposed no restrictions on the commissioners' actions in the negotiations. It also announced opposition to acceptance of money from Britain because the sale of land would mar the state's honor. In exchange for giving up claim to any land, Maine wanted free navigation of the St. John and federal reimbursement for its past defense of the disputed area.[50]

In the end the Tyler administration got what it wanted, thanks no doubt to Webster's effective use of the Sparks and Steuben maps. By vote of 177 to 11 in the house and 29 to 0 in the senate, the legislature on 26 May authorized sending four commissioners to Washington, with provision that they must consent unanimously to any compromise line before it could go into effect. As commissioners the Maine legislature selected William Pitt Preble, erstwhile leader of the opposition to the Dutch award of 1831, Edward Kavanagh, former governor Edward Kent, and John Otis. The first two were Democrats, the others Whigs. That same month, Governor Davis of Massachusetts appointed a three-man delegation, all Whigs: Charles Allen, Abbott Lawrence, and John Mills.[51]

Webster asked the states' commissioners to be in Washington no later than 12 June. Maine's representatives arrived on time and notified the secretary that they were ready to begin work. The following day the men from Massachusetts appeared. After Webster met with both delegations in the State Department on 13 June, he was satisfied; even the irascible Preble did not seem to nurse old wounds.[52] The secretary now had to arrange a settlement satisfactory to the commissioners and to Ashburton. The task would not be easy. The British minister had been in the United States for over two months, and though he and Webster had discussed some of the other topics at hand, they had had no specific talks on the northeastern boundary. But the encouraging fact was that for the first time the outcome of the border dispute depended upon events in Washington.

7. The Peacemakers

Lord Ashburton was a veteran politician and businessman, perhaps even accustomed to dealing with what conservatives derisively called "radical" strains of thought, but he never overcame his dislike for the workings of America's democratic institutions. If anything, his disdain for the republican way of life increased during his visit in Washington. The Maine legislature, he confided to Aberdeen, was a "wild and uncertain Body." The United States Senate, he feared, would object to state participation in drawing a treaty as unconstitutional, and in any case he thought seven commissioners never could agree on anything. The minister also was apprehensive that the United States would collapse at any moment because of its poor financial condition, inept administration, and many conflicting interests. Tyler and Webster appeared to favor a settlement, but the chaotic condition of America's political system made them powerless. The government in Washington, Ashburton asserted, was influenced by a "lower description" of people than in any part of the world. The only discernible movements in the capital were the president vetoing bills and the Senate rejecting his appointments. Tyler was so vacillating, the minister believed, that it was difficult to predict what the "weak & conceited" man would do. By midsummer Ashburton would consider Webster helpless. The secretary promised everything, but was "so weak & timid & irresolute that he is frightened by Everybody and at last does nothing." The result of the political situation, Ashburton declared to Aberdeen, was that a "strange Confused state of Government moves on." Yet this "Mass of ungovernable and unmanageable anarchy" could unite in war and have immense power; it was wise to "humour the wild Beast."[1]

The problems of dealing with official Washington, and with the vagaries of life in rough-and-tumble America, were compounded for Ashburton by the apparently infinite complexities of the boundary issue in Maine and by a last-minute change in his instructions. The complexi-

FAIR ROSAMOND; OR, THE ASHBURTON TREATY.

From London Punch *3 (July–December 1842): 203.*

ties kept churning to the top, in an unpredictable but—taken as a whole—understandable manner. While Ashburton was en route to the United States, Aberdeen in London had asked military experts for advice on a boundary that would provide security for British North America, and the foreign secretary had altered his previously flexible instructions in line with these recommendations. Aberdeen did not expect real difficulty on the boundary, but if a quarrel developed he hoped Britain could take a stand for some principle of national policy or for humanity and justice—not for a few miles of "miserable pine Swamp." The new directives, stiffened by the duke of Wellington and his military colleagues, showed British concern over America's possible northward expansion into the Canadas. Though spokesmen for the military view did not agree on all particulars, they believed that Britain should have a military road between Quebec and Halifax. Aberdeen ultimately directed Ashburton to *improve* the Netherlands award of 1831 by acquiring more territory between the upper St. John and St. Lawrence rivers, running the boundary along the St. John from its source northeastward to its junction with the St. Francis. Though Ashburton's son-in-law and companion in Washington, Humphrey Mildmay, wrote Aberdeen that insistence on land north of the St. John would endanger the negotiations, the London government repeatedly instructed its special minister to make only moderate concessions in the lower St. John Valley.[2]

Perhaps inevitably, the question of money arose. If Maine was not satisfied with these territorial equivalents, Aberdeen said, the British government "would be disposed to indemnify" the state with an additional "pecuniary compensation." The payment, he pointed out in a private note to Ashburton, need not be extravagant in view of the poor financial condition of the United States. Britain might even grant Maine the right to float timber down the St. John River, but Aberdeen would not allow both concessions unless the payment was small. Peel agreed. The prime minister urged caution in mentioning money, for Maine might refuse to sell and interpret the United Kingdom's offer as recognition of the state's right to the territory.[3]

The issue of money was as complicated, in itself, as the issue of the boundary. In a private letter New Brunswick's lieutenant governor, Sir William Colebrooke, assured Ashburton that Maine would want money in the negotiations, despite its "bluster" about not selling American land.

If so, the British minister was determined that any monetary proposal would come from Maine. A friend of Tyler's, James Hamilton, had visited London in March and later told the president about a dinner party at which Aberdeen "plainly intimated" that Britain was ready to spend a half million dollars to acquire land for a military road. When Hamilton warned that New Englanders were "pretty sharp at a bargain," Aberdeen allegedly replied, "Where there is a will there is a way." Webster apparently passed this information to Ashburton. When the minister made an inquiry to Aberdeen, the foreign secretary denied having said anything to Hamilton about money, but reiterated that a moderate sum would be acceptable to Parliament as long as the expenditure improved the Netherlands award line and the proposal came from the American government. Ashburton remarked that Hamilton's story "set Governor Davis [of Massachusetts] dreaming about money" and that the governor undoubtedly "promoted the same Golden visions" throughout Maine and Massachusetts. In conversation with Webster the minister admitted that his government might pay something. But Webster was hesitant. He worried that a money payment would cause a nationwide outcry against selling part of the United States to the British. In any case, Webster agreed that Davis's expectations as to the amount were absurd. In the meantime Ashburton lightheartedly assured Aberdeen that he would defend the Exchequer.[4]

The money issue was now inextricably linked to the boundary. At least in this respect the discussions between Ashburton and Webster seemed open and forthright, as compared to the tortuosities of past negotiations. The boundary-money business, or perhaps the natures of the two diplomats, soon made it evident that if they were to negotiate anything in Washington during that humid summer of 1842 there would have to be some alteration in format in the procedure of negotiation.

During their first meeting about the boundary on 18 June, Webster and Ashburton decided to make their discussions simple, open, and friendly. They would dispense with formality and avoid detailed dialogues on geography. Ashburton claimed he was dealing with a person of "Penetration" and did not need the "tools of ordinary diplomacy." His only stipulation was a refusal to have regular communications with the state commissioners; they must go through Webster. Without protocol or minutes, the two diplomats informally discussed the issues and after reaching agreements wrote letters that received President Tyler's approval before their release to the public. Outside the conference room Webster and Ashburton took turns hosting elegant dinners and social functions for those concerned in the discussions. To balance Ashburton's furnishings of rare wines and exquisite desserts prepared by a French chef, Webster's rich table alternately included oysters, salmon from Maine, Virginia terrapin, crabs from Maryland, and Chesapeake duck. There never had been "a pair of more friendly negotiators" to "put their heads together," the secretary told a friend. The men would "smooth away all frowns and scowls" from government leaders and replace them with "most gracious smiles."[5]

The negotiations, however, soon took the familiar paths of diplomacy. Grand promises of open, candid discussions became only sounding boards when both negotiators resorted to private, secret arrangements. The inexperience of both men in the so-called art of diplomacy quickly became evident in the unorthodox methods they used in resolving the nations' problems. As already noted, Webster engineered an elaborate campaign in Maine to convince state legislators of the necessity for settlement before war resulted. Ashburton, too, tried his hand at being a crafty diplomat. As the British minister did not know about all of Webster's activities in New England, so was the secretary unaware that his counterpart privately sought advice on the boundary from Lieutenant Governor Colebrooke of New Brunswick. In fact, there is no evidence that either Peel or Aberdeen knew of their envoy's strategy—at least not until it was under way. The result was that a secret delegation from New Brunswick was sent to Washington to talk privately with Ashburton.

In answer to the British minister's written request for someone familiar with the local areas involved—perhaps the warden of the disputed territory, James MacLauchlan—Colebrooke sent three men: MacLauchlan, a private secretary from the lieutenant governor's office, and the speaker of the New Brunswick assembly, a wealthy merchant who owned land in the town of St. John and along its river. Also meeting privately with Ashburton was the owner of one of the largest sawmills in the area, Sir John Caldwell, who had talked with Maine legislators in Augusta during the Aroostook crisis of 1839. Though Webster surely knew of these men's presence in Washington, he doubtless was unaware of their recommendations forwarded to Ashburton. The British envoy learned that in exchange for an "equitable adjustment" New Brunswick approved of Maine's having duty-free use of the St. John (because of reciprocal advantages), but, not surprisingly, opposed giving up the Madawaska settlements. Such concession, the delegates declared, would alienate British settlers there, as well as close communications between Canada and Nova Scotia. In no case should there be Americans along the St. John.[6] Thus Ashburton's good intentions created new problems. His invitation to the lieutenant governor sharpened the well-known conflict between what the English and New Brunswick governments considered essential to a boundary settlement.

The initial optimism faded as Webster and Ashburton began discussing the boundary. Despite the British minister's professed flexibility he called for the entire Madawaska settlement—one of London's suggested proposals, but the point *insisted* on by Colebrooke. British subjects south of the St. John River, Ashburton argued with Webster, would be unhappy with American rule. French settlers from Acadia had helped to establish Madawaska and always had been under either French or British rule. Inhabitants recently had petitioned the queen to prevent their settlement from going to the United States. Furthermore, American control of the south bank of the St. John might endanger British communications. The two nations should not determine the boundary by merely splitting the acreage, he declared, for the southern portion—the Aroostook Valley— was much richer than the Madawaska in the north. If the United States recognized British rights to the river valley, Ashburton would allow Maine free use of the St. John for transporting produce into New Brunswick (an arrangement, it might be noted, that would benefit Britain as much as the United States). He also would yield the fertile area at the head of the Connecticut River and a sliver of land along the British side of the forty-fifth parallel, including the American fort at Rouse's Point— confirming the inaccurate American boundary survey of 1771–74 and giving the United States a belt of land containing American settlers. His only goal, he assured Webster, was to satisfy residents of all areas.[7]

There was little danger that the Peel ministry would risk war by rigidly supporting Ashburton's insistence on all of Madawaska; though Aberdeen understood New Brunswick's long-argued position, he had to think in terms of the Empire. Besides, such demand went beyond the

Netherlands award and called for more land than was sought by Britain's military experts. Aberdeen was concerned about the "ugly appearance" of allowing American settlements within sight of Quebec, even though he believed the territory between the upper St. John and St. Lawrence rivers was a "mere swamp." How could he go before Parliament with a treaty that failed to safeguard British North America from the United States? To keep Americans away from Quebec, he said, his envoy might grant Maine use of the St. John. Aberdeen was convinced that a settlement with the government in Washington would "greatly improve" relations with France, yet the probability is that the British position also had softened because the ministry feared another American war should the mission fail. Maine, Aberdeen realized, would not surrender the St. John Valley. A longer military communication between New Brunswick and Quebec was preferable to what he called the "manifold·Evils" of war with the United States.[8]

By late June, Webster expressed deep concern about the boundary negotiations. Differences existed between Britain and the United States, between Washington and the commissioners, and between the Maine and Massachusetts commissioners. Not knowing New Brunswick's demands, he guessed that Ashburton was under more restraint from London and sensed the Englishman's desire to return home. Webster, too, felt the strain. After he persuaded Ashburton to talk with the Maine commissioners, with no results, it appeared that the negotiations would end in frustration. Webster asked Tyler to meet with the minister. Though the president at the time was grief-stricken over his ailing wife (who would die within three months), he turned from personal affairs to help his secretary of state. Surely Ashburton would not have crossed the Atlantic on so arduous a mission, the Virginian said, unless he wanted to settle all Anglo-American problems. If "you cannot settle them, what man in England can?" The old man allegedly replied: "Well! Well! Mr. President, we must try again."[9]

A long note came from the Maine delegation on 29 June, confirming Webster's fears. Maine refused any line south of the St. John. When Britain asked for a strip of land between Halifax and Quebec for a military road, the state's commissioners allowed that the request was reasonable, but added that Ashburton's demand for all of Madawaska was not, especially since he refused to yield anything comparable in return. Had they known his aims in advance, they would not have taken part in the negotiations, and if the stipulations became a sine qua non, they would return to Maine. Use of the St. John alone was not satisfactory since it benefited New Brunswick *and* Maine. The commissioners required both the boundary at the St. John and free use of the river.[10]

Ashburton's unauthorized decision to support New Brunswick's insistence on Madawaska had brought this delay in the negotiations, but he blamed Maine. By July the heat was oppressive and his only goal was to "move out of this oven." To Aberdeen he wrote, "You My Dear Lord have not contributed much to get me out of it." Confusion in the United States caused by Mexican affairs and the president's opposition to Henry Clay's bank bill had made the minister realize he would be fortunate to settle the boundary—even at the sacrifice of Madawaska. In a humorous but pointed private note to Webster, Ashburton showed, somewhat plaintively perhaps, that much of his good nature and high expectations had evaporated in the Washington summer:

I must throw myself on your compassion to contrive somehow or other to get me released.—

I contrive to crawl about in this heat by day & to live my nights in a sleepless fever. In short I shall positively not outlive this affair if it is to be much prolonged. I had hoped that these Gentlemen from the North East would be Equally averse to this roasting. Could you not press them to come to the point and say whether we can or can not agree? I do not see why I should be kept waiting while Maine & Massachusetts settle their accounts with the General Government.

. . . Pray save me from these profound politicians for my nerves will not stand so much cunning wisdom.[11]

Ashburton's animosity soon focused on Maine's commissioner, William Pitt Preble, whom he considered the "very obstinate" leader of the malcontents. The delegate, the reader will recall, had been America's representative at The Hague who had worked against the arbitral award of 1831. Now, it appeared, he again was a key figure in determining Maine's feelings on the boundary. Ashburton had hoped that time and reflection had improved Preble's judgment. When the minister first had presented his proposal for all of Madawaska, Preble had retorted that his colleagues should walk out of the negotiations, return home, and dramatically inform the state that the United Kingdom insisted on crossing the St. John into Maine's territory.[12] To a Briton who only reluctantly had consented to the state's involvement in the Washington talks, this unexpected threat to success must have been exasperating.

Aberdeen then compounded his growing rift with Ashburton by accepting an outside offer of aid in the negotiations. The British consul in Boston, Thomas Grattan, was well acquainted with the boundary issue and with many of the people involved and claimed that the Maine commissioners had invited him to travel with them to Washington. He warned Aberdeen that since the vote of Maine's delegates had to be unanimous, Ashburton must humor them. In a move that no doubt irritated Ashburton, the foreign secretary suggested that since Grattan was in Washington at the time, he should try his hand at persuading Preble to accept a compromise line. But even though Grattan later declared that he had followed Ashburton's "repeated urgent request" to reconcile the negotiators' differences—even to the point of claiming to be the chief factor in keeping Preble from going home—the special minister privately expressed dislike for the consul's zeal and was happy to see him return to Boston.[13]

This apparent breakdown in the British diplomatic front must have encouraged Maine's commission to remain unyielding in its demands. Grattan wrote Aberdeen he had tried his best, but that Preble's room in Washington was full of maps, reports, and other documents relating to the boundary that showed his determination to exploit any loophole to outmaneuver Britain in the negotiations. Grattan's comment was unfair. Even though Maine had insisted on the St. John boundary, it was Ashburton's rigid and unsanctioned stand on Madawaska that had revived old controversies and hurt chances for compromise. The New Brunswick government had urged Ashburton to make this demand, but his London instructions did not; they even authorized him to change boundary proposals in case of serious opposition from the United States. Maine's position was understandable. Ashburton should not have been surprised that an informal memorandum written by Preble contained "some rather coarse insinuations" about British motives.[14]

These debates over the boundary do not comprise the entire story, for some historians have raised serious questions about Webster's motives in the negotiations—to the extent of charging him with accepting money from Ashburton to secure a settlement favorable to the United

Kingdom. Samuel F. Bemis has accused Ashburton of paying Webster (and Jared Sparks) to persuade Maine to give up its rightful claim to the entire area in dispute so that Webster could win favor in England and replace Edward Everett as minister at the Court of St. James's. Bemis's case rests upon the questionable character of the Sparks and Steuben maps, Webster's well-known desire for the London post, and a private note of 9 August 1842 from Ashburton to Aberdeen.[15]

The reader already is aware of the doubtful validity of the Sparks and Steuben maps, and no one has presented convincing evidence that Webster's motive in the negotiations was to conciliate the Peel ministry in preparation for his own appointment as minister to the Court of St. James's. One wonders how favor in Britain would get him the position anyway. Most important, a series of private letters between Webster and Everett indicates that by late summer of 1842 the secretary had about given up thoughts about the post, although he might have accepted a special mission to settle the Oregon question because it would have been more important than the regular position and of only limited duration.

The letters seem conclusive. They show that not only did the secretary believe Everett deserved the London position, but that Webster could not afford the expense, even for a year. Everett, a close friend of Webster's, offered to resign and assume the recently vacated post in Paris. Webster did not approve. He instead urged Everett to accept nomination as the first minister to China. Everett declined but still offered to leave London for Webster. The secretary privately admitted he did not want to go to England unless a "high sense of duty" forced him to do so, but indicated that if Everett went to China he might assume the post in London for a year. Yet Webster quickly assured Everett that the administration had not asked him to accept the China mission in order to open the English position for himself. Webster was not interested in the "ordinary routine of duties" and foresaw no "great objects" to accomplish. He finally asserted that even if the London position were vacant, he would not take it. Yet in one of his last communications to Everett on the subject, he seemed wistful, for he lamented that Aberdeen and Peel had not favored a special mission from the United States; it might have led to a commercial agreement and to settlement of the Oregon problem.[16] In any case, even though Webster had considered the

London post for years, it is highly unlikely he would have abandoned a good American claim to the disputed territory, especially one involving his native New England. How could he expect the Senate to approve such a treaty without a murmur? If complaints arose, how could he expect the maps and the whole deal to remain secret?

The argument concerning the letter of 9 August 1842 from Ashburton to Aberdeen is equally specious. In it the British minister said: "The money I wrote about went to compensate Sparkes [*sic*] & to send him, on my first arrival, to the Governors of Maine & Massachusetts. My informant thinks that without this stimulant Maine would never have yielded." Later in the same letter Ashburton wrote: "I have drawn on you a bill for £2998.1—90 days sight [about $14,500] for the purpose mentioned in my former private letter and you will find this put into proper form. I am not likely to want any thing more." This letter, according to Bemis, shows that Ashburton used British funds in shaping American opinion on the boundary question to suit his country's needs and that besides helping fill Webster's inexhaustible need for money, the payment brought about a treaty Webster hoped would make the British public receptive to him as American minister.[17]

The first two parts of Bemis's case clearly are faulty; the third, however, bears more careful consideration. In a private note to Aberdeen of 14 June 1842, Ashburton reported his suspicion that Webster had uncovered evidence favorable to the British boundary claim (the Sparks and Steuben maps?) and was using it in some way with the state commissioners. (Webster actually had shown at least the Sparks map to the Maine group the day before; these men also may have seen it during Sparks's trip to Augusta in February.) Aberdeen replied on 2 July that he had sent Ashburton's confidential postscript to the letter of 14 June to Peel, "under injunctions of the strictest secrecy." A search of the Peel papers in London did not lead to its discovery. And despite the likelihood that the prime minister returned Ashburton's letters to Aberdeen, as the foreign secretary said, it is not in the Aberdeen collection either. The following passage from Aberdeen's letter of 2 July is significant:

> But this incident [whatever was discussed in the missing postscript] has, I confess, quite taken me by surprise, and opens a new view of measures which perhaps may be followed up with advantage, should there yet be time for you to do so. In order to insure success, you need not be afraid of employing the same

means to a greater extent in any quarter where it may be necessary. In what you have done you have been perfectly right; and indeed I look upon the proposal made to you from such a quarter, as the most certain indication we could receive of a determination to bring the negotiation to a happy issue. In any further transactions of the same kind, I have only to desire that it may be made the means of leading to success, as the condition of having recourse to it. If you can command success you need not hesitate.[18]

Nowhere does Ashburton mention Webster's name. On the basis of this incomplete correspondence one can only conjecture that the British minister's unnamed confidant offered information for a price—possibly some or all of the £2998.1. Though the amount seems large, Ashburton may have acquired information more than once. If the informant was reliable, the sum was small compared to the expense of prolonging the boundary controversy and increasing the chances of war.

It is unlikely that Ashburton's informant was Webster, as Bemis has suspected, for the secretary of state surely would not have shown the Sparks and Steuben maps to *both* the Maine commissioners and Ashburton. Indeed, it is not clear that the British envoy realized that the information he sought *was* a map. The wording in his private letter to Aberdeen of 14 June indicates that he had not seen Webster's maps or anything else: "I have some reason to suspect that Webster has discovered some evidence, known at present to nobody, but favorable to our claim, and that he is using it with the Commissioners. I have some clue to this fact and hope to get at it." If Webster had shown the Sparks and Steuben maps to Ashburton early in the negotiations, he would have done so without guarantee that the envoy would compromise. In another letter to Aberdeen of 9 August, Ashburton wrote: "I should certainly, if I had known the secret earlier, have made my stand on the upper St. Johns & probably at the Madawaska settlements."[19] Had he seen the maps, Ashburton doubtless would not have surrendered *any* of the disputed territory. The full British claim would have been substantiated—in accord with New Brunswick's argument. The negotiators undoubtedly would have failed, for Maine adamantly refused to concede the southern half of the settlements. Webster's New England background, his experience with Maine, his awareness of the causes of the Aroostook War, and his interest in the northeastern boundary, at least since 1839, surely made this clear to him.

There are several reasons to doubt that Webster accepted money from Ashburton. No evidence shows that the secretary received a substantial amount of money from anyone at this time; in fact, from February through December of 1842 he was trying to borrow. Ashburton's remark, "The money I wrote about," did not necessarily mean *British* currency; he had learned about Sparks's trip to Augusta, and he likely referred to the money Webster took from Tyler's secret-service fund to finance the New England mission. Later in this same letter of 9 August, Ashburton mentioned the £2998.1 drawn on Aberdeen; yet there is no basis for connecting this amount with the compensation to Sparks. Ashburton moved to another matter in his letter and then returned to the subject of money. It is unlikely he was talking about the same sum both times. When Aberdeen told Ashburton to employ the "same means" where necessary, he probably referred to money paid by Ashburton to his informant. One does not have to "guess," as Bemis says he has done, that Ashburton gave £2998.1 to Webster "with only a general assurance that it would help out."[20]

There are other reasons to doubt Bemis's charge. Despite the apparently plain statements in Ashburton's letters of 9 August, it is unlikely that such an able businessman would have given £2998.1 to Sparks (by way of Webster) for a mission to Maine seemingly already completed and much less likely that he paid so much for evidence he did not see until late July or early August. Ashburton also wrote Aberdeen on the 9th: "Since I communicated to you the very extraordinary information about the Boundary, I have seen Sparkes's [*sic*] letter and the map to which he refers. . . . if I had known it before I agreed to sign [late July] I should have asked your orders, notwithstanding the manner of my becoming acquainted with it. At the same time the communication was strictly confidential and then communicated because I had agreed to sign." Ashburton added that this "very extraordinary information" (referred to above) was known to the president, his cabinet, the governors of Maine and Massachusetts, the seven state commissioners, and six senators, including William Rives, chairman of the Senate Foreign Relations Committee and staunch defender of the Tyler administration.[21] It seems unlikely that Webster would have leaked so "singular a Secret," as Ashburton called it, to at least twenty-one other persons. Nor is there any way to determine how many people besides Maine's boundary agent,

Charles Daveis, knew about the Steuben map he resold to Webster in May 1842. Instead of casting guilt at Webster, as Bemis does, it seems that there is as much reason to suspect one of the other men who knew about the maps—or anyone else in whom they might have confided the secret.

Perhaps Ashburton's suspicions, though unconfirmed, help to explain why he held out so long for all of Madawaska and, paradoxically, why he gave in. He did not realize until late July that Maine would not agree to the line he wanted, and despite assurances from his informant that Webster possessed something supporting the British claim, the fact remained that Ashburton had not seen this evidence. If he held out for more than the award of 1831 and the negotiations had ground to a halt, Britain's expansionist reputation would appear confirmed, and he would receive blame for the failure. Perhaps the vehemence of the Maine and Massachusetts commissioners combined with Webster's rigid insistence upon the St. John to convince Ashburton that his informant was wrong and that Webster had no evidence to substantiate the British line below the St. John. Even if there were a map that supported the British claim to all land in dispute, Ashburton realized that Maine would not surrender the Aroostook peacefully.[22]

Thus, although Webster felt justified in keeping the maps to himself, it no doubt would have made little difference if he had shown them to Ashburton during the negotiations. The British claim would have appeared just, but Maine probably would have denied the validity of the maps or refused to surrender an area occupied by Americans—the same argument Ashburton used for Madawaska. In either case Maine's prestige was at stake, and, as Ashburton well knew, disagreements about national honor had helped to bring on the War of 1812. He therefore found himself in the unenviable position of having to give up what seemed a legitimate British claim because he realized that another Anglo-American war was too high a price for several hundred square miles of woods and farmland.

No matter how much the United States benefited from the treaty, it still is surprising that after so many years, Maine should have accepted a compromise settlement of the northeastern boundary. Leadership in Maine had not changed radically; certainly the Anglophobes had not lost all influence. Perhaps Webster was correct when he declared that the "grand stroke" was his use of the maps to secure the prior consent of Maine and Massachusetts to a compromise.[23] Yet in assessing his effectiveness one cannot overlook the methods he employed to shape public opinion and to pressure Ashburton into giving up what appeared to be a just claim to all of the disputed territory.

Technically, perhaps, Webster gave up claim to over five thousand square miles of land to which the United States had an arguable right, both by possession and by the maps, however questionable they were. But one can say that the British case, for the same reasons, was defensible. There seemed no way for one side to convince the other that its claim was legitimate; sixty years of controversy was graphic illustration of this fact. Certainly there is no justification for Bemis's conclusion that "Webster achieved a diplomatic triumph—against his own country."[24] The land yielded to Britain was of little or no value to the United States. The map question was no longer relevant once the negotiations began. Webster and Ashburton had no choice but to work out a compromise.

Webster had outmaneuvered Ashburton in the northeastern boundary negotiations. Though the British claim seemed correct, the secretary knew that Ashburton could do nothing because of his fear of a third Anglo-American war. Webster realized that the British government wanted the military road and that Ashburton wanted peace, and he wisely kept the maps secret until the minister had agreed to sign the treaty. Surely no one should criticize Webster for acquiring only part of the area in dispute; compromise is the essence of diplomacy.

With this mutual subterfuge kept private in 1842, it appeared to the British and American publics that by a series of open compromises, Webster and Ashburton reached a congenial agreement on the northeastern boundary. In mid-July the secretary, influenced, he said, by the state commissioners, Congress, and public opinion, resorted to long discussions of the geography of the Northeast to show that the St. John boundary was the only solution. Experience, he asserted, proved that rivers and mountains were better national boundaries than arbitrary lines on land. When Ashburton was convinced that the commissioners would not yield southern Madawaska and that the Senate and others outside New England considered his demands extreme, he compromised.[25]

Webster now sought to convince the state commissioners that the boundary proposal was fair. In a note to the Maine delegation he showed that the proposed line would give the United States 7,015 square miles of land, while Britain would receive 5,012. Although the Dutch arbitration award had allotted 7,908 square miles to the United States and only 4,119 to the British, the additional 893 square miles given to the United Kingdom were unsuitable for farming or settlement. The United States would get all the good land south of the St. Francis and west of the St. John, so that, although its share would amount to only seven-twelfths of the disputed area, authorization for Maine to float its timber down the river toll free would enhance the value of the compromise. Retention of Rouse's Point would benefit the nation as well as the states involved, for it was the key to defending Lake Champlain. If the commissioners agreed to the proposed boundary, Webster explained, the government in Washington would pay Maine and Massachusetts $125,000 each and reimburse Maine for maintenance of the civil posse and for past surveys of the land in dispute.[26]

A little over a week later the commissioners from both states, at last, agreed to this boundary compromise. The Massachusetts representatives asked that navigation of the St. John include both grain and lumber and that the national government increase the compensation to $150,000, which it did, and when Ashburton and Webster agreed they nodded acceptance. Two days later the Maine commissioners joined them, issuing a statement praising their own "forbearance and patience" in the face of "unfounded pretensions, and unwarrantable delays, and irritating encroachments." Enclosed in their acceptance was a memorandum calling for New Brunswick to pay the United States the amount of the "disputed territory fund" (fines assessed by the province for timber cut illegally in the disputed territory), to be divided equally between Maine and Massachusetts. This provision also became part of the treaty. Ashburton, sitting with pen in one hand and fan in the other, wrote Aberdeen a few days later that the men of Maine had been most difficult to deal with and that when Preble yielded he "went off to his wilds in Maine as sulky as a Bear."[27]

After all these complicated dealings over the northeastern boundary, the other part of the international border that remained uncertain—the northwestern section from Lake Superior to the Lake of the Woods—seemed so inconsequential to the two diplomats that they resolved it in a nearly cavalier manner. Surveyors had reported the area as mountainous, with limitless rapids and streams, and of little agricultural value; the only people interested in the territory were fur traders and fishermen. But the boundary was important to the fur trade, for the Pigeon River linked Montreal with the Canadian heartland. In addition, St. George's Island in the St. Mary's River comprised about twenty-six thousand acres of excellent soil and was worth as much as most of the land between the Pigeon and Dog rivers. Islanders also derived a good revenue from the sale of sugar and syrup taken from the maple trees. At the outlet of Rainy Lake (Lac la Pluie), the country changed in character; river valleys became wider, timber more abundant, rich, and varied, and land more capable of cultivation.[28]

Britain already had control of the upper lakes region (mentioned earlier), and since the Peel ministry's primary concern was to halt American expansion above Maine, it was not concerned about this part of the international boundary. Ashburton easily gave up claim to St. George's Island and proposed that the line follow Pigeon River and the Grand Portage to Rainy Lake. The only condition was mutual navigation of waters in the adjoining area. Ashburton knew that British fur traders preferred a route farther north; but the proposed boundary had the counterbalancing advantage of enabling them to use the Grand Portage if they chose.[29] The United States thus acquired a tract of land almost 6,500 square miles in size.

The northwestern part of the boundary seemed unimportant in 1842, but it became significant by the last quarter of the century when Americans discovered that the area in present-day Minnesota contained the Vermilion iron deposits and part of the rich Mesabi Range. Some historians believe that Webster and Ashburton realized the territory was rich in minerals but that Ashburton gave up the British claim either because he knew the Peel ministry regarded it as inconsequential in comparison to the area around Maine or because he simply was anxious to return home. These writers base their argument on the message Tyler sent to the Senate with the treaty. The United States, the president declared, had received territory "considered valuable as a mineral region."[30] Tyler, of course, cited no authority for his statement, although rumor supported him. Most likely he was trying to promote ratification of the treaty by making the land sound more appealing.

Recent study shows that in 1842 neither Webster nor Ashburton was

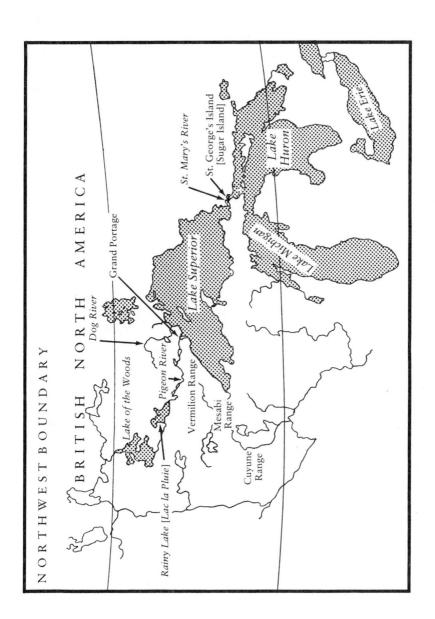

NORTHWEST BOUNDARY

BRITISH NORTH AMERICA

Dog River

Grand Portage

St. Mary's River

St. George's Island [Sugar Island]

Lake Huron

Lake Erie

Lake Michigan

Lake Superior

Lake of the Woods

Pigeon River

Vermilion Range

Mesabi Range

Cuyune Range

Rainy Lake [Lac la Pluie]

aware of the Minnesota iron deposits. In fact, the triangular area of land in dispute contained only the Vermilion Range; Britain did not claim the Mesabi. Even the American title to the Cuyune Range, farther southwest, was not in dispute. During the eighteenth century, fur traders and treaty explorers probably never entered the region. Though the Northwest Company and the American Fur Company traversed much of the Grand Portage between the head of Lake Superior and Rainy Lake, their route did not come closer than thirty miles from the nearest iron bed. Since the land was rough, swampy, or covered with heavy timber, the metal was not readily visible. Even the topographic survey team established by the Treaty of Ghent had found no iron. One might add to this argument that if the General Land Office of the United States suspected the existence of rich iron ore deposits in the region, it might have done a great deal of surveying there, especially as time for the boundary negotiations drew near. But the records show there was little interest, if any. Not until ten years after the Webster-Ashburton Treaty did anyone notice traces of iron ore in the Mesabi and Vermilion regions. The vast wealth of the Vermilion Range was not apparent until 1875 and that of the Mesabi not until about fifteen years later.[31] Part of the reason for the success of the treaty was that these discoveries came so late.

The boundary settlement outlined in the Webster-Ashburton Treaty of 1842 benefited both nations, although the United States received more land than Britain, both in quantity and quality. One of America's greatest gains, not recognized at the time, was the iron deposits in the 6,500 square miles of land Webster secured between Lake Superior and the Lake of the Woods. Also important were title to southern Madawaska, free navigation of the St. John, and ownership of St. George's Island. Ashburton's concession of Hall's Stream and Indian Stream gave the United States 150 square miles of land that the king of the Netherlands had awarded the British in 1831.[32] These particulars alone justify praise for the secretary of state.

Despite these obvious gains, the most far-reaching consequences of the agreement were military; they indicated a marked shift in strategic advantages along the international border that the Washington government believed could alter the existing balance of power in North America. Often underestimated in significance was America's retention of Rouse's Point. The secretary of war, John Spencer, had considered it militarily more valuable than all of Maine north of the St. John. Webster agreed. In fact, before the Senate in 1846, he would assert that this cession was more important than anything the British gained during the negotiations. The Point secured more than two hundred miles of lake coast in New York and Vermont, afforded a safe army headquarters, and opened resources along the borders of Lake Champlain. British control would have deprived the United States of the most important invasion route into Canada, Spencer asserted. Thus to the government in Washington, it did not matter that the British now had a communications line through the St. John Valley; an American force could break it by following the newly constructed military road from Bangor to Houlton. Another potential threat to the British was that the old Temiscouata road, one of their major communication routes north of the St. John River, now lay dangerously near what everyone knew would become American settlements.[33] Though the implications of these changes were not apparent to everyone in 1842, the United States had secured a position of strength along its new northern border.

On the other side of the ledger, the government in London believed it had won distinct advantages. The settlement had created a buffer zone below British North America of 5,000 square miles of pine forest along the Maine frontier, a thinly populated area even today; also important, it had relaxed tensions with the United States and thereby improved chances for better relations with France. Most of the territory lay above the St. John and St. Francis rivers; 893 square miles of it, a wasteland located west of the rivers, included enough land for Britain's long-sought military road from Quebec to the Bay of Fundy. Today the Canadian National Railroad and Highway No. 2 follow the route. The Peel ministry was satisfied with the arrangement, for by the arbitral award of 1831 the border of the United States would have come within thirty miles of Quebec and the St. Lawrence; the treaty line pushed it back to fifty miles.[34] The British also gained rich land along the north side of the St. John and by the Madawaska River and on the western bank of Lake Temiscouata. In addition, they received valuable timberland along the northern tributaries of the St. John. Perhaps the most incisive comment on the compromise nature of the treaty was that a vocal minority of politicians in each nation bitterly assailed it for the advantages awarded to the other side.

Resolution of the boundary, both Webster and Ashburton knew, was essential to agreement on the other matters threatening the Anglo-American relationship. The final treaty thus is capable of fair assessment only after observers recognize it for what it was—a package agreement. It would be unjust to judge each provision alone. The two diplomats were relieved that they had surpassed the most difficult obstacle. At a huge dinner later given in Ashburton's honor President Tyler looked at him and at Webster and offered the toast: "Blessed are the peacemakers."[35] Peel, Aberdeen, and Everett were not present, but should have been. The British leaders in London had originated the mission and ultimately guided it to an eventful conclusion, while Everett's repeated assurances that the United States wanted peace reinforced the Peel ministry's determination to settle all differences between the nations. Ashburton's willingness to compromise, even though such a step involved New Englanders he could barely tolerate, entitles him to share the acclaim of peacemaker with Webster and the others. Their work quite possibly prevented an Anglo-American conflict.

8. Completion of the Compromise

Settlement of the sixty-year-old North American boundary dispute by mid-July 1842 was the biggest step toward resolving all differences between Britain and the United States. Yet the two diplomats already had discussed many of the remaining Anglo-American problems—the African slave trade, right of search, impressment, the *Creole* and extradition, the *Caroline*, Oregon—and quickly discovered that some of them were almost as complicated as the boundary issue because they involved the touchy subjects of slavery and national honor. Burdened with the complexities of the boundary and mentally and physically drained by the heat in Washington, Webster and Ashburton became increasingly aware that the fundamental grievance between the nations since 1783 still existed: Americans were convinced that any British hesitation in resolving these disputes constituted an affront to their integrity. Ashburton thought the *Creole* incident of lesser importance than the northeastern boundary and the African slave trade, but he soon came to realize how deeply slavery was embedded in Southern thinking. The peculiar institution would prove a major obstacle to settling the maritime issues because it had worked its way into the question of America's honor. In fact, as Webster and Ashburton talked in Washington during that summer of 1842, they feared that the slavery question might combine with the issue of national honor to disrupt progress on all Anglo-American differences—even the Maine boundary.

In the minds of Americans at the time of the Webster-Ashburton negotiations the various problems connected with the African slave trade, including whether Britain had a right to search vessels flying the American flag, all were related to the grand problem of impressment—and any settlement of the difficulties over slavers first required satisfaction on that long-standing issue. Aberdeen agreed. The War of 1812 had been over for less than thirty years, and many adult Americans of the 1840s easily could remember the issues during the Jefferson and Madison administrations that had pushed the young nation into war on the side of Napoleon. Afterward, the Treaty of Ghent had not fully recognized America's sovereignty, for British refusal to renounce both the right of search and impressment implied that Britain might resort to these practices again. President Tyler naturally wanted the British government to renounce impressment and believed settlement of this issue would add "luster" to the negotiations then going on in Washington.[1]

Almost at the outset, the impressment issue was obfuscated by the American minister to Paris, Lewis Cass. The Michigan statesman had helped revive American feeling about impressment in early 1842 with publication of his pamphlet against the right of search, and, not content with having introduced this trouble into an already troubled negotiation, he now suggested a plan for getting around the hated practice of impressment. Each British cruiser hovering off the coast of Africa would carry an American citizen who, in case of sighting a suspicious vessel flying the American flag, would have authority to conduct a search and, if necessary, order capture of the ship.[2]

This foolish idea would have passed into the oblivion it richly deserved had not Lord Ashburton, wishing to arrive at almost any settlement of the issue, considered that perhaps it contained some merit. He knew the Royal Navy would object to having designated foreigners aboard, so he sought to make Cass's proposition acceptable by surrounding it with conditions. The American inspector might not belong to military or naval forces; he should act only when there was slaving under the American flag; the system should not affect the British right to determine the nationality of suspicious ships. When Aberdeen approached Peel with the plan, the prime minister flatly rejected it. Not only would the crew make life uncomfortable for the "Intruder," but no captain could maintain authority on his ship if his decisions were subject to an American's approval.[3]

Impressment should not have entered the Webster-Ashburton negotiations, and yet it became the key to resolving the search question. The principle behind both practices violated freedom of the seas, Americans long had argued, and Southerners worried that if British sailors could board alleged American slave ships in peacetime, the government in London soon might act against slavery itself. Others saw British search as a thinly disguised attempt to establish naval superiority. In conversation with Ashburton, Webster maintained that Britain's interest in enforcing its municipal laws on the high seas was an assertion of extraterritoriality. The United States had alleviated the island kingdom's problems of poverty and overpopulation by receiving its emigrants; to expect these same people to serve the crown in war was unjust. The English doctrine of "perpetual & indissoluble allegiance of the subject," Webster insisted, was wrong. After presenting other arguments against impressment, he warned that its most serious consequence was American resentment toward the United Kingdom. Since 1815 the British navy had shown marked reluctance to impress seamen, and for this and other reasons relations between the countries had improved. There was no better time to renounce the practice.[4]

Ashburton, of course, could not do this. Had the decision been his, he would have abandoned all claim to impressment, for he feared that the practice might lead to another Anglo-American war; it was, he wrote the foreign secretary, "the most serious cause of animosity and ill will." The minister had a suggestion: if Britain went to war and the United States declared neutrality, the crown should renounce impressment upon condition that the American government bar British subjects from the merchant marine until they had resided in the United States for at least five years. Ashburton argued realistically that the population and naval strength of the United States had increased greatly since 1815 and that impressment, therefore, was impractical. Would it not be wiser to surrender an unenforceable right? But Aberdeen declared just as realistically that any British concession endangered the crown's command over its subjects. Disavowal, he knew, might invite desertion from the British navy during the present period of intense maritime rivalry with France. Moreover, he later explained to Minister Everett in London, the British people were as sensitive about desertions as Americans were about search. Though Aberdeen privately assured him that British sailors would not impress Americans again, he could not renounce the practice publicly without causing adverse reaction in his country. There was a difference between not exercising a right Britain possessed and officially renouncing it. The distinction involved the nation's honor.[5]

Such debate threatened to raise issues vital to each side's integrity, and therefore the countries could not resolve the impressment question by treaty. Realizing this, Webster and Ashburton wisely decided not to incorporate any formal settlement involving the subject. Instead, they accepted Everett's suggestion to avert a public confrontation by merely recording their opinions on paper. The step, Ashburton agreed, might close the matter without causing popular excitement. Webster summarized American grievances against impressment in a diplomatic note in hopes of quieting Anglophobes and administration critics in general with a final statement against what he considered one of the most infamous acts the British navy ever had committed against the United States. Ashburton sought only cordial Anglo-American relations. If a mere exchange of notes furthered this goal, he favored it. Aberdeen concurred.[6] Webster's note on impressment finally removed the topic from discussion.

With the impressment issue on the way to resolution, Webster and Ashburton turned to the African slave-trade controversy. Before the negotiations the secretary had outlined a plan to end the practice which appealed to Ashburton. Webster called for a joint-cruising scheme whereby Britain and the United States would assign pairs of cruisers to patrol the West African coast. The idea was not new. In the early 1820s, John Quincy Adams, then secretary of state, had made a similar but futile recommendation to Congress. And in January 1839 the commissioners at Sierra Leone had suggested the measure to Palmerston; but when his minister in Washington passed it on to the State Department in October, no actions followed. Webster's plan was also an enlargement upon the short-lived Paine-Tucker agreement of March 1840, which had authorized mutual search. He apparently had followed the Navy Department's advice after it consulted Commander James Paine on how to suppress the African slave trade. Finally, President Tyler wrote his son years later that the cruising convention had become part of the treaty "upon my own suggestion." Ashburton believed that the joint-squadron plan would avert many problems over search, that naval cooperation would double the strength in African waters but at lower costs, and that American cruisers could act with more freedom than Britain's in stopping slavers bearing the American flag. The joint-cruising arrangement, he noted, would be the "very best fruit" of the mission.[7]

The United States had achieved much since winning independence and did not want to risk it all by becoming involved in European alliances. Washington's Farewell Address, Jefferson's first inaugural, and, of course, the Monroe Doctrine warned against entangling alliances that might drag the country into Continental affairs. By proposing an alternative to mutual search, Webster therefore fulfilled the American tradition of isolationism. A joint squadron established for a specified period, he explained, would allow the United States to stay clear of the Quintuple Treaty negotiated by Britain the previous December. America also would find it "more manly and elevated" to enforce its own laws than to depend upon other nations. Moreover, the arrangement might end controversy over British search and meet America's moral obligation under the Treaty of Ghent to halt the African slave trade.[8] There probably would not be much opposition in the United States to Webster's proposal, for it avoided European involvement, satisfied antislavery groups, cleared the consciences of those slaveowners who curiously condemned the African slave trade as inhuman, and afforded opportunity for proslavery men to cripple the joint squadron by providing inadequate enforcement.

Before Ashburton sent the draft of the cruising convention to London, Webster submitted it to Tyler for revisions. The president struck out a clause that read: "and should the traffic in slaves continue notwithstanding the efforts made for its suppression the contracting parties will hereafter confer together as to the most effective means of attaining an object so earnestly desired." One could interpret these words as approval of British search, he argued, should the joint-cruising plan fail. He also incorporated changes to clarify that the agreement pertained only to the African slave trade. After failing to bring about an increase in each naval force's guns from eighty to one hundred, he crossed out "protect and" from a section calling for the joint squadron to "protect and enforce, separately and respectively the laws, rights and obligations of the two countries, for the suppression of the said traffic"; such omission, he hoped, would prevent the British from expecting to enforce American laws. Tyler also eliminated another passage that had followed the above clause: "and any engagements which either may have entered into with other Governments." Though some critics thought the president was unduly careful, he wanted to preserve a semblance of isolationism by averting British interference with American affairs and by preventing United States involvement in treaties made by Britain with other countries.[9] Probably he also was trying to satisfy Southern interests.

Aberdeen did not insist upon a specific procedure as long as the agreement helped to end the slave traffic. He had indicated earlier that if Ashburton were unable to persuade the United States to join the league in Europe, the joint-squadron plan would be acceptable. Aberdeen approved Webster's proposal that London and Washington issue a joint remonstrance to Spain and Brazil to end importation of African slaves. By the end of June, Ashburton believed it impossible to reach a settlement on any matter other than the northeastern boundary and the African slave trade, the two principal objects of the mission. Because Webster's cruising plan seemed practical, the British minister agreed to it in early July. Article VIII of the treaty—the "African squadron clause"—stipulated that each nation maintain a naval force of at least eighty guns to patrol the West African coast. Each squadron would enforce its own government's laws, but would cooperate with the other when necessary, although remaining officially independent.[10] Webster probably had achieved the best alternative to a mutual search policy, for his plan did not require the nations either to revise their laws of 1808 against the traffic or to compromise their principles.

Though the joint-squadron plan sounded impressive, the story of its aftermath is one of failure—largely because the United States did not enforce its half of the agreement. In later years slaveholders feared that after ending the trade Britain might concentrate on the peculiar institution itself, and they pressured Congress to relax enforcement of the treaty article. The result was that after 1847 the United States generally failed to maintain eighty guns along the African coast. While Britain and France kept at least twenty-five ships in African waters, there rarely were more than five from the United States—partially because of the small number of vessels in its navy—but probably as important, because of Southern influence in Congress. To fulfill the treaty's requirements the American navy either overgunned a minimum number of ships or sent ones that were not seaworthy or were too slow and unsuited for chasing fast-moving slavers. Another sign of inadequate official concern is that sailors suffering from fever and other illnesses did not receive adequate food and medical supplies. Congressmen opposed to the squadron plan certainly managed to hamper its effectiveness. In 1853 they reduced the desired yearly appropriation from $20,000 to $8,000. The following year, Southern congressmen tried—and failed—to abrogate the entire treaty article and to substitute life imprisonment for the death penalty.[11]

Reasons for failure of the squadron idea are not difficult to discern. Commodore Matthew Perry, commander of the American ships in African waters and later to open Japan to Western trade, believed that a primary factor was the great profit of the slave trade itself. One writer has concluded, however, that the major reason was Southern leadership of the Navy Department. The secretaries of the navy, according to the argument, tried to change the squadron's goal from suppression of the slave trade to encouragement and protection of other commerce along the West African coast. Abel Upshur of Virginia, secretary from 1843 to 1844, was the first to follow this policy. It is perhaps coincidental, but of the nine secretaries of the navy from 1843 to 1861, six were from the South, and two others openly sympathized with that section's interests. Only one, George Bancroft of Massachusetts, openly opposed slavery. The Civil War brought the demise of the squadron plan, but effective action against the African slave trade finally began in 1863, the year of the Emancipation Proclamation.[12]

Problems stemming from the *Creole* affair also threatened the negotiations, for protests by the Tyler administration had brought no reparation from the British government. Ashburton regretted the incident but believed the British people so warmly approved Peel's anti-slavery policy that no compensation could be given for slaves freed from the vessel. As late as 9 February, Aberdeen had heard nothing from the United States government concerning the *Creole*, and as a result he was unprepared for Tyler's strong feelings on the matter. While the president's attitude reflected only a segment of American public opinion, Webster privately admitted that Britain's stand on the issue was sound and believed that lawyers, courts, and the South would agree. In early March, when the British Foreign Office received a claim from Everett relating to the *Creole*, Aberdeen already had decided that the government could not surrender the nineteen blacks accused of murder because such action would violate the British law barring slavery in the Empire; in addition, he said, no extradition agreement existed between the nations. Yet Ashburton had no instructions on the *Creole*, for Everett's formal request for reparation did not arrive until April—after the Britisher had departed for the United States. Even later Aberdeen told him only to do his best to eliminate hard feelings.[13]

Before Ashburton arrived in the United States, Webster privately asked his friend, Justice Joseph Story of the United States Supreme Court, for advice on the *Creole* incident. Webster often had turned to him on legal matters—most notably the McLeod case—and the judge usually had been helpful.[14] Story, a conservative from Massachusetts, was moderate in his antislavery beliefs and concurred with the secretary that protection of property, including slaves, was basic to society. Their common philosophy made it unlikely that there would be a confrontation with the British over the *Creole* affair.

Story agreed with Webster's original stand that the return of slaves who involuntarily entered a foreign port depended upon comity and not duty. The United States therefore could only appeal to the Peel government to turn over the mutineers; without an extradition treaty it had no legal argument. In addition, according to international law, persons committing offenses on the high seas could stand trial only in municipal courts of the country to which the ship belonged. The *Amistad* decision of 1841 supported his position, he thought, for in it he himself had stated the majority opinion of the United States Supreme Court that the ship's blacks had violated no law or treaty in winning freedom. But in the *Creole* case, Story surmised, laws had been violated.[15] The legalistic stand on extradition adopted by Webster and Story thus acknowledged the blacks' freedom.

Story's opinion coincided with that of the crown's lawyers, and Webster asked him to draft articles for incorporation into a treaty. One article stipulated that a ship driven involuntarily into a foreign port might repair damages and continue its voyage without molestation. A second related to extradition, while a third barred the judiciary from interfering with executive control over public acts (committed under government orders). Although Jay's Treaty was the basis of the extradition article, Story added a requirement that surrender should occur only through court action. He included the most common crimes on his list, omitting political offenses because many Americans opposed closing the United States as a haven for refugees. In the end, the treaty contained only Story's second suggestion on extradition, but the negotiators exchanged notes expressing their sentiments on the first one relating to ships in distress, and the third became part of the congressional law of August 1842 that authorized federal intervention in state court cases having international implications.[16]

In the *Creole* affair, as in other matters, Ashburton wanted to conciliate the United States by offering reparation, but lacked authorization. He was convinced that his government must promise some security from interference with America's coastal trade, for the reefs and bars between the Bahamas and Florida made the waters perilous so there likely would be other incidents like that of the *Creole*. Ashburton believed that London should instruct the governor of the Bahamas to disallow direct communication between islanders and those persons aboard American ships involuntarily driven into port. Violations like that of the *Creole*, he warned Aberdeen, might inflame the South. But the foreign secretary replied that it was impossible to guarantee security and adamantly repeated that slaves became free upon entering British territory. When Ashburton then suggested to Webster that perhaps the United States should convoy slave ships along the Atlantic coast, the secretary was astounded. It was ridiculous to convoy American ships in peacetime, he declared. Besides, how could the mere addition of ships prevent accidents at sea?[17]

Ashburton realized that the United States had not retreated from its stand of late 1841 and that this stubbornness might wreck negotiation of the other issues between the nations. By mid-July 1842, President Tyler had become so "sore and testy" about the *Creole* case that the British minister worried lest the president hold back on a convention to halt the African slave trade until Southerners were satisfied about the *Creole*.[18] Indeed, there was danger that Southern senators might seek revenge for British refusal to surrender the mutineers by defeating the entire treaty he was negotiating with Webster.

Aberdeen's initial misunderstanding of the Tyler administration's reaction to the *Creole* incident contributed to the confusion. The foreign secretary had wrongly assumed that Webster would demand surrender of the slaves as fugitives, and the result was that Parliament criticized the United States for a stand never adopted. Abolitionists were incensed at Webster's moderation and reliance upon the law of nations. Indemnification, they declared, would mark approval of slavery. The Boston *Liberator* denounced Webster, the Massachusetts Antislavery Society passed resolutions of condemnation, and the abolitionist, the Reverend William Ellery Channing of Massachusetts, criticized the secretary's instructions to Everett as "morally unsound" and a violation of the "law of humanity." Yet even though Webster never demanded the blacks' return, many Southern spokesmen surprisingly approved—perhaps because continuing excitement over such a divisive issue could disrupt trade with the British, or perhaps because they knew that the London government would refuse a demand for the blacks' release, thereby throwing questions of national honor or slavery—or both—into open debate. Tyler's attorney general, Hugh Legaré of South Carolina, believed Webster's actions would discourage fanatics in the United States and would avoid embarrassing the new and conciliatory Peel ministry in London. The Mobile *Register & Journal*, pleased that Webster had adopted the revised, moderate Southern view, nonetheless was apprehensive that his evasive stand could encourage more revolts. Webster, however, believed that a demand for the blacks' release was pointless. Either the British would free them in the Caribbean islands or, if they turned over the blacks to the United States, a fair trial would be impossible. Though even Tyler was doubtful about the secretary's position, Webster did not demand delivery of the blacks.[19]

By the end of July, Ashburton was so disgusted with the *Creole* affair that he decided to act on his own. Since the incident had caused so much public feeling and involved both national and international law, he thought he should refer it back to London, hoping the two governments might link an extradition convention with satisfaction on the *Creole* case. After Webster reiterated the administration's view in an elaborate note, Ashburton promised without authorization that the British government would instruct its island officials to observe hospitality and enforce municipal law in a way to "maintain good neighborhood" with the United States by avoiding "officious interference" (that is, unauthorized or unofficial) with ships driven by necessity into British ports. The basis for Ashburton's assurance may have lain in Aberdeen's private note of 26 May, where the foreign secretary claimed that Britain would "certainly do nothing to encourage mutiny either among slaves or Freemen."[20]

Tyler and Webster regretted that Ashburton was unable to settle the *Creole* affair by treaty and regarded the promise against officious interference as less than satisfactory, but they agreed to send the problem to London for consideration. The president wanted Ashburton's note to read that British officials would not interfere with vessels brought in by "any uncontrollable occurrence," rather than by "accident"; he believed officious interference was a poor term because that offense was "universally reprehended" and meant nothing special in this case. Yet the words remained, even though Tyler succeeded in having the British insert "or by violence" after "accident" in future instructions to colonial governors.[21]

Ashburton was relieved to dispose of the *Creole* affair; it had been his "great plague" during the negotiations. He had sought a dozen times to settle it, but Tyler's "garrulous" and "foolish" stand, the minister said, prevented an understanding until August. As it was, the president received Ashburton's proposal "sulkily." But for the popularity of the special mission in the United States, the Britisher believed, there would have been no agreement on the *Creole* case. Yet Article X of the Webster-Ashburton Treaty did not guarantee against future *Creole* cases. It provided only for the extradition of individuals accused of seven nonpolitical crimes: "murder, or assault with intent to commit murder, or Piracy, or arson, or robbery, or Forgery, or the utterance of forged paper." Without much argument, Webster had incorporated much of the extradition proviso of Jay's Treaty. When he had tried to add mutiny and revolt to the list of crimes, Ashburton had seemed amenable—until he understood the ramifications of the *Creole* case. Then he balked and agreed to the compromise settlement only with great reluctance. So did President Tyler. As late as two days before the negotiators signed the treaty, Tyler doubted the wisdom of an extradition article because he thought British authorities might not surrender a slave who had killed his master and escaped; a jury or court could call the act self-defense.[22]

Reaction to the *Creole* settlement varied. John C. Calhoun, perhaps voicing the feelings of many Southerners, was satisfied with the exchange of notes—probably because the procedure would bury the issue and allow peaceful continuation of trade with Britain. Though he would have preferred a treaty article, he was pleased that Ashburton had approved Webster's interpretation of the law of nations and that the British minister had promised that his government would send instructions to island officials. John Quincy Adams was furious with Calhoun and with the settlement in the negotiations. He called the South Carolinian the "embodied spirit of slavery" and denounced the treaty as a "ticklish truce" between freedom and slavery. Adams was disgusted with Calhoun's temperance as being obviously designed "to conciliate the Northern political sopranos, who abhor slavery and help to forge fetters for the slave."[23]

Abolitionists in both the United States and Britain would have misgivings about the possibility of having to extradite fugitive slaves. In September 1842, after the Senate had approved the treaty, a group of abolitionists met with Ashburton in Boston to express concern. The Britisher explained that in framing the extradition article, he had been careful, despite Webster's objections, that inferior officials in Canada would have no authority to surrender fugitives; in line with the Canadian government's wishes, the governor alone had extradition power. Ashburton also assured the men that the taking of articles considered necessary to a slave's escape into Canada would not be criminal and that if the extradition provision proved injurious to American blacks, the British government would terminate it. The delegation left, wholly satisfied. On the other side of the Atlantic, Parliament delayed approval of extradition, as Aberdeen predicted, for Ashburton was unable to offer adequate assurances to British abolitionists. The antislavery committee in Parliament, urged by abolitionists, tried to revise the extradition article to guarantee safety for fugitive slaves, but failed. Though still suspicious of the treaty, one member of the antislavery cause in Britain, the Reverend J. H. Hinton, eventually admitted that he and others were somewhat mollified by the provision that application for the surrender of alleged fugitives had to come from the United States government—not from the states involved. A year passed before extradition went into effect in Britain. In actual practice, however, British officials rarely enforced the treaty provision against runaway slaves.[24]

The two nations finally closed the *Creole* case in 1853 when an Anglo-American claims commission awarded $110,330 to owners of the liberated slaves, thereby vindicating the Southern position (and that of the Tyler administration) in the controversy. The umpire, Joshua Bates, Boston banker and partner in the House of Baring, declared that even though slavery was contrary to humanity, the law of nations did not prevent a country from establishing it by law. The *Creole* had been on a lawful voyage, he said. When "unavoidable necessity" drove the vessel into Nassau, its captain had the right to expect shelter from a friendly power. As for the other slaves, the governor should have helped officers of the *Creole* regain command. Bates ruled that the British Emancipation Act had no bearing on the case, inasmuch as no municipal law could authorize armed force in boarding the ship of another country. Since

Nassau officials had violated international law, the British government had to compensate owners of the *Creole*'s slaves.[25]

Controversy over the *Creole* affair thus disappeared into history. Despite its potential for trouble, it did not become a crisis between Britain and the United States for several reasons. The unsettled political situation in the United States was especially important. Even if the Tyler administration had been able to act forcefully, adoption of a policy toward London that might have satisfied Anglophobes without provoking abolitionists would have been almost impossible. President Tyler and Secretary of State Webster, the reader will recall, were without a party. A second reason was that the subject of slavery itself did not emerge as an issue. As one might have expected, Southern protests against interference with American shipping failed to arouse much sympathy north of the Potomac. Not only did many of the strongest antagonists of the British hesitate to help slavery interests indirectly, but many antislavery advocates apparently had not decided whether they hated Britain or slavery more and were cautious about criticizing one adversary and helping the other.[26] Perhaps the Peel ministry did not raise the question of slavery because the effect on Anglo-American relations might have been injurious. Even though Britain had moved strongly in an antislavery direction, it had become heavily dependent upon the South's cotton by the 1840s. Time also worked for a peaceful solution. News of the *Creole* incident arrived in the two capitals some weeks after its occurrence; the act of compensation did not occur until more than twelve years had passed. For these reasons, the *Creole* affair never achieved the prominence it might have had under different circumstances and at a different time.

Though historians have recorded the *Creole* affair as a minor incident in American history, it deserves more consideration because of its great potential for trouble. Besides raising maritime and legal questions that involved America's honor, the incident had three unexpected results: it appalled abolitionists in the United States, uniting them more in their opposition to slavery; it encouraged closer contact between abolitionists on both sides of the Atlantic; it threatened Anglo-American relations. That after their initial protests Southerners toned down their reactions to the *Creole* case and accepted the settlement by note may be significant in supporting the feeling that that section's most important desire was to prevent more slave insurrections. Much of the South's show of Anglophobia may have been sincere, its maritime grievances real, and its call for respect for national honor genuine. But if the South's spokesmen were politically astute—and there is good reason to believe they were—their actions raise several questions. Southerners like Calhoun must have realized that the British government valued its economic ties with the United States and that in peacetime it would not have risked alienating Americans by using outmoded and pointless practices like impressment or search. Aberdeen was antislavery and might have wanted to denounce slavery during the *Creole* controversy, but in 1842 he and Peel considered good relations with *both* North and South more important than an anti-slavery crusade. Domestic pressures in Britain encouraged the ministry to uphold its stand on the *Creole* affair—at least until the 1850s—but it did so on other than humanitarian grounds. Similarly, the South never got involved in a predicament that could have caused a confrontation with both Britain and Northern abolitionists on the question of slavery. For Southerners, as well as for those who agreed with Webster's stand during the *Creole* controversy, the most heralded goal was British respect for America's honor.

The *Caroline* matter remained. The British government still had not offered apology or made reparation for the invasion of American territory and destruction of the steamboat five years earlier. New Yorkers bitterly recalled that the government in Washington had not supported their demands for retaliation. Preservation of national honor required Britain to admit that the acts were wrong, but the Peel ministry saw political danger in apologizing, especially since the state of New York had tried a British subject who had obeyed government orders. Though the *Caroline* incident was no longer inflammatory, some American politicians hoped to capitalize on its emotional appeal, while others considered an apology essential to the nation's integrity. Shortly before the 1842 negotiations began in Washington, authorities in Rochester arrested a British subject, John Hogan, for the murder of Amos Durfee during the *Caroline* attack. Though they soon released him for lack of evidence, Webster realized that New Yorkers had not forgotten the incident at Schlosser.[27]

The Peel ministry would have preferred to ignore the *Caroline* issue, which might not have been a concern in 1842, Aberdeen believed, had the

Melbourne government in 1837–38 flatly refused the American demand for reparation. The steamboat's destruction, he said, was justified by self-defense, "however much to be lamented," and the trial of McLeod proved the true character of the vessel and ruled out any claim to compensation. In his instructions to Ashburton the foreign secretary repeated the arguments presented in 1838, but directed him to assure the United States that the act had not set a dangerous precedent in their relations. Ashburton agreed and thought an exchange of notes with Webster was advisable.[28]

As in the impressment and *Creole* controversies, questions much deeper than surface issues threatened the negotiations. Vital interests—matters of national honor and the sacred character of domestic institutions—again prevented Webster and Ashburton from considering a settlement by treaty provision. Destruction of the *Caroline*, the secretary emphasized, had compromised the "Sovereignty and the dignity of the United States." The issues at stake were America's "self-respect, the consciousness of independence and national equality." To avert a heated argument over principles, Ashburton skillfully proposed interweaving a "degree of apology" with a "decided justification" of the act. Though Tyler considered this note sufficiently apologetic, he sought an addition that might settle the question of remuneration to the steamboat's owner, William Wells. The note should acknowledge that Wells had accepted payment for innocently transporting passengers to Navy Island and that he had not intentionally taken part in the rebels' military effort. Wells therefore should receive reparation from the British government—but only after furnishing proof of his innocence. Though seemingly ingenious in concept, the suggestion lacked practicality. Tyler hoped that his stipulation might force Britain either to admit that war had existed in 1837 and refuse to make indemnification or to deny the existence of war and compensate Wells. If it chose the first alternative, the United States would have enjoyed neutrality status in 1837 and therefore now deserved an apology for the *Caroline*; if the second, Wells probably would fail to convince the British that he was innocent and the issue might be closed.[29] Ashburton wanted no part of this confusion and rejected Tyler's proposal.

The United States received something close to an apology from the British government for the *Caroline* incident. Though Ashburton admitted that Foreign Secretary Palmerston should have issued an explanation and apology immediately after the steamboat's destruction, it took Webster two days to persuade the minister to use the word "apology" in the note. Ashburton realized the importance to American honor of a settlement. Still, he could not ignore the danger of political reaction at home. Close perusal of the note reveals no actual apology by the Peel ministry—only a wishful statement that its predecessor had resolved the matter. The president dropped the subject after the British government offered assurances that it had intended no disrespect to the United States when its forces entered American waters and admitted that an apology—for the invasion—had been due at the time of occurrence. There could be no reparation for the *Caroline*, however; it had been engaged in illegal activities. The amenities concluded with Webster's expression of regret for McLeod's delayed release. When Congress in late August passed a law establishing federal jurisdiction over cases similar to McLeod's, the honor of both nations had been vindicated, and the *Caroline* matter at last was closed.[30]

The goodwill brought about by the Ashburton mission seemed conducive to settling all issues between Britain and the United States —perhaps even the question of Oregon. The northeastern boundary became a problem in Anglo-American relations partly because both nations had emphasized other matters for over a half century. It developed into a crisis when anti-British sentiment got entangled with the nationalistic aspirations of Americans in the troubled area. But, as in the early stages of the Maine controversy, the Atlantic nations postponed the Oregon matter because it seemed unimportant in 1842. Webster and Ashburton discussed the subject but after a few futile attempts they decided to leave it alone. Four years later the nations would resolve it—but not until after talk on both sides of the Atlantic of another Anglo-American conflict.[31]

Before 1846, Oregon territory comprised a wilderness forty times larger than the acreage involved in the northeastern boundary dispute. It extended north from the 42° parallel to 54°40′ and west from the continental divide to the Pacific Ocean. At various times in Oregon's history several nations contested ownership. Britain and Spain first laid claim until Spain retreated south of the forty-second parallel in 1819.

THE OREGON QUESTION
1818 - 1846

Russian-American Line—1824

54°40'

Vancouver Island

Juan de Fuca Strait

49°

enclave
offer

Puget Sound

Disputed Area

PACIFIC OCEAN

Columbia River

Fort Vancouver

Willamette River

Snake River

Adams-Onís Treaty Line—1819

42°

Spanish Mexican Possessions

San Francisco Bay

Then Britain, Russia, and the United States competed, until in 1824 and 1825, Russia withdrew north of latitude 54°40'. Thereafter, the rivalry was limited to Britain and the United States, although the former did not desire land as far south as the forty-second parallel, and the latter had been willing since 1818 to settle at the forty-ninth. The region in dispute, therefore, lay between the Columbia River and latitude 49° with control of the river believed vital to the interior fur trade. The two governments signed a convention in 1818 establishing joint occupation of Oregon for ten years; at the end of the period they renewed the policy indefinitely but provided for alteration of the agreement upon a year's notice.

Settlement of Oregon was sudden and almost overwhelming. There probably were no more than five hundred American settlers in the territory before 1841, but after that year emigration into the areas north and west of the Columbia River and south into the rich Willamette Valley caused ownership of the territory to become crucial. At stake was an empire in the Northwest spanning fertile farmland, dense timber forests, a fur trade still valuable though declining in importance, and opportunity for commercial expansion into Asia. Americans realized the importance of having a port near Puget Sound and Juan de Fuca Strait, for a sandbar blocked the mouth of the Columbia and made it unsuitable as a harbor. Many in the United States considered the forty-ninth parallel a satisfactory boundary, but the British government refused their suggestion in 1818, 1824, and 1826, and proposed an alternative line up the Columbia to the forty-ninth parallel. Oregon was not a pressing issue in the summer of 1842, but the Peel ministry thought that since it had authorized Ashburton to smooth all differences between the nations he might try this one as well.

As early as January 1842, the British government expected that in the negotiations Webster would propose abrogation of the convention of 1827 in favor of a definitive arrangement on the Oregon boundary. An equitable adjustment, according to a memorandum the ministry sent Ashburton, was a line beginning at the intersection of the Rockies and the forty-ninth parallel, dropping to the southeastern source of the Great Snake River, and trailing its waters to the mouth of the Columbia. There should be joint navigation of the Columbia and an understanding that neither country should support new settlements within territory given to the other. The Peel ministry thus expected to receive about three-fourths of the territory in question. Realizing this might not be acceptable to the United States, Aberdeen authorized Ashburton to resort to an alternative line if necessary. It started at the Rockies, ran along the forty-ninth parallel to the northeastern branch of the Columbia, and followed it to the sea. Under no conditions would the British accept a boundary along the forty-ninth parallel from the Rockies to the Pacific.[32]

Aberdeen's instructions showed that his government did not comprehend the immensity of the Oregon problem. Another member of Peel's cabinet, the duke of Wellington, admitted he knew little about the Columbia River area but thought Ashburton's instructions acceptable. Aberdeen, in fact, was unfamiliar with the question until a few days before Ashburton left for the United States. Even then, he was engrossed in the responsibilities of his new position and seemed unaware of Oregon's importance. He did not even know that in 1826—by the so-called "enclave offer"—the stern critic of America, Foreign Secretary George Canning, would have allowed the United States a piece of land north of the Columbia adjoining Juan de Fuca Strait. Albert Gallatin had turned down the offer because British territory or waters would have surrounded the American possession. The line Aberdeen wanted was determined by Henry Unwin Addington, veteran of the 1826 negotiations with Gallatin, nephew of a former prime minister, and no admirer of the United States. It resulted from a proposal made by the Hudson's Bay Company to the Foreign Office in 1825. Consequently, with hastily prepared, outdated, uninformed, and incomplete instructions on Oregon, Ashburton set out to secure a boundary that would deny the United States a harbor in the strait north of the Columbia River. There was little chance for success.[33]

A preliminary discussion on Oregon between Webster and Ashburton showed they would not reach a settlement. Ashburton believed the presence of Indians would temporarily prevent Americans from settling in great numbers on the Pacific coast and expressed doubt that the question was important at that time. He then stated that Britain could not allow Americans north of the Columbia, but would grant joint use of the river. Webster complained that the proposal left no port for the United States, yet "intimated" to Ashburton that it might be acceptable, if the British persuaded Mexico to sell San Francisco and its harbor to the United States. Ashburton, of course, could not commit his government to such a proposition. Though he agreed to pass the suggestion to Aberdeen, the minister explained that in the meantime the United States should try to make the arrangement by itself. The "tripartite plan" never materialized, however—partly because the negotiators moved to more pressing matters, but also because the British government refused to intervene in Mexican-American affairs. More important, growing friction between the United States and Mexico reduced all chances of a deal.[34] The Oregon negotiations came to an end.

The ministry in London later expressed disappointment over Ashburton's apparent willingness to defer the Oregon matter. If the United States expected to acquire San Francisco harbor, Aberdeen said, it should not object to Britain's receiving the north bank of the Columbia and the Strait of Juan de Fuca. Despite Ashburton's recommendation, however, the foreign secretary had refused to consider pressuring Mexico into the tripartite arrangement. Peel had hoped to settle the Oregon question before the area's population had increased materially, while Aberdeen simply told Minister Everett in London that Ashburton had failed his duty.[35]

Ashburton was surprised at his home government's attitude. Insistence upon an Oregon agreement in 1842, he told Aberdeen, might have impeded progress on the northeastern boundary question. Besides, an American exploring expedition led by Lieutenant Charles Wilkes of the navy recently had returned from the Pacific Northwest after an absence of four years and had stirred much public excitement about Oregon's rich future. Wilkes's report showed a dangerous bar at the entrance to the Columbia, but good harbors at Puget Sound. If the Tyler administration earlier had considered conceding British claim to the river in exchange for California, it no longer could do so. The United States *had* to have the line at the forty-ninth parallel. Ashburton understood. He believed that an agreement could have resulted had he been authorized to cede a strip of land north of the Columbia River. The United States, then, would have received a port within the Strait of Juan de Fuca. In what mistakenly appeared to be an effort to escape blame, he said the fault was partly Webster's for wanting to keep the issue open as an excuse for coming to London on a similar special mission. In addition, Ashburton later wrote Webster, negotiation on Oregon would have been aimless when the times were not conducive to settlement. Finally, the former envoy told his friend John Croker that a push for a northwest boundary during the Washington negotiations would have interfered with resolution of the other issues. Ashburton correctly concluded that the Oregon question must "sleep for the present."[36]

Neither Ashburton nor Webster was to blame for the inability to resolve the Oregon question in 1842; the source of difficulty lay in the unrealistic boundary proposals contained in Aberdeen's instructions to Ashburton. The offers ignored the magnitude of the problem and treated America as if it had no legitimate claim to the territory.[37] For a brief moment in the negotiations, the British government reverted to its imperialistic stand of the 1820s and reminded Americans of the treatment they had received from the mother country in the past. But to expect a commercial nation like the United States not to want—and get—at least one good port on the Pacific was unreasonable. The Peel ministry had burdened Ashburton with instructions impossible to fulfill.

Nor were the negotiators to blame that Oregon was a lesser consideration in the discussions. Though Britain and the United States should have dealt with the matter before it became a crisis in 1846, the priorities in the summer of 1842 were the northeastern boundary and the African slave trade. Even the *Creole*, the *Caroline*, impressment, and search were more urgent than Oregon. The London government had tossed in Oregon to take advantage of the good feeling brought about by the Ashburton mission. Americans were pleased with Britain's decision to send a special minister to Washington, but not to the extent of giving up claim to the Great Northwest. Even Webster and Ashburton thought the question might resolve itself if the nations allowed Oregon to become an independent republic like Texas.[38] The northwestern boundary question was not pressing in 1842 and could be postponed by the continuance of joint occupation.

Before the 1840s many Americans believed that Britain had refused to settle the controversies between the nations because it did not respect the United States. Violations of America's maritime rights showed British lack of concern for America's integrity; refusal to make reparation for the *Caroline* indicated that America's honor was not important to London; British hesitation in settling the northeastern and northwestern boundaries proved that Britain did not regard the United States government as legitimate. Since formation of the Republic in the late eighteenth century, the United Kingdom, Americans complained, had made few attempts to deal with their government on a reciprocal basis. But now, for one of the few times in their unsteady relationship, Britain openly treated the United States as an equal nation. The result was that the Webster-Ashburton Treaty affirmed the honor of the United States and encouraged the development of a better Anglo-American understanding.

9. The Maintenance of National Honor

The diplomacy of Daniel Webster and Lord Ashburton had achieved the optimum goal of sustaining both nations' honor. Their agreements were practical, perhaps brightened with tinges of idealism, but now, after a brief respite from the political world, the two negotiators had to get their treaty ratified. Popular reaction to the agreement was partisan in both countries. During a time of bitter warfare between the Tylers and the Clays, and between the Peels and the Palmerstons, it was predictable that an arrangement involving so many long-standing disputes would be subject to attack. Thomas Hart Benton relied upon the Senate chamber and the Washington *Globe*, while Lord Palmerston used Parliament and the London *Morning Chronicle* to criticize the treaty, each calling it a national betrayal. Newspapers in both countries followed their innermost inclinations—supporters of the "ins" considered the treaty an accomplishment that only the Tyler and Peel governments could have managed, while partisans of the "outs" called it a modest feat they could have surpassed if given the chance. Four years after the negotiations of 1842, Democrats in Congress accused Webster of illegal use of the president's secret-service fund and sought to impeach him retroactively. Charges lingered for generations, and more than a century later some historians believed that by drawing the treaty Webster sacrificed both his country's welfare and his own honor.

On 10 August 1842, Tyler and Webster, with Ashburton's approval, incorporated the northeastern boundary settlement, the cruising convention, and the extradition agreement into a single treaty. The day before, the two diplomats signed two treaties, one setting out the boundary, the other dealing with the remaining issues. Ashburton had objected to working everything into one treaty because he feared that Senate opposition to the slave-trade and extradition articles could defeat the whole pact; but he relented and with Webster affixed his signature to it. The new treaty canceled the previous ones and combined all articles into a single agreement, but kept the original date of 9 August. Ashburton might have changed his mind upon seeing the Sparks and Steuben maps, for he probably believed the Senate would be so anxious to approve the boundary that it would accept the other articles as well. In any case, the secretary sent two sealed packages, containing the Sparks map and other documents on the treaty, to Senator William Rives of Virginia, chairman of the Committee on Foreign Relations, who followed procedure by immediately moving for a secret session. Webster later expressed regret that in the process Rives informed the entire Senate of the Sparks map and thus opened the administration to attack. The secretary had wanted to convince the committee that the Senate should approve the treaty before the British learned of the map, but the damage had been done. The following day, 11 August, the president sent the treaty to the Senate, accompanied by the correspondence relating to the negotiations and by a supporting message written partly by Webster. The administration expected attack from the Democrats, but Webster was confident the treaty would receive the necessary two-thirds majority approval within a week.[1]

Benton's outspoken opposition to the treaty during the secret Senate debates illustrated how the politics of sectionalism was affecting Anglo-American relations. Though he and fellow Democrats said they attacked the settlement because it compromised the national interest and broke America's tradition against foreign alliances, many opponents obviously were Anglophobes who wanted to twist the lion's tail, while others either hated Webster or simply were politically motivated. Benton (supported primarily by James Buchanan) called on the Senate to reject the treaty because Webster and Ashburton had not settled all differences between the nations. Benton wanted to link the West's interests with those of the South—the dominating ambition of John C. Calhoun and others. By criticizing the *Creole* and African slave-trade agreements, the Missourian probably hoped to arouse Southern sentiment for Western causes. The same held true with his rebuke of America's newly gained right to navigate the St. John River, from which he complained that neither the South nor the West benefited. In regard to the *Creole* affair he warned that British liberation of slaves threatened both the Mississippi Valley and the South. Since slavery interests were shifting westward, the growing insecurity of the coasting trade between the Atlantic states and New Orleans would hurt the West as well as the South. Benton reminded his colleagues that the cruising convention violated Washington's Farewell Address and caused "astonishment, indignation, and shame." Only trouble could result from tying "our little ministers" to the "gorgeous representatives" of European monarchs. The United States, he declared, could not cut expenses at home if it assumed the responsibility of defending Africa from slave traders. "Has Don Quixote come to life, and placed himself at the head of our Government, and taken the negroes of Africa, instead of the damsels of Spain, for the objects of his chivalrous protection?"[2]

Benton then confounded the Senate proceedings by strongly condemning Webster's use of the red-line map. The treaty, he indignantly charged, was a "solemn bamboozlement." The day Webster announced to Ashburton that he could negotiate for a conventional line—17 June 1842—was "black Friday." Without instruction from the president and certainly without Senate approval, the secretary of state victimized Maine by bargaining away its territory. It would be appropriate, Benton sarcastically proclaimed, to construct a black monument to the treaty and mark the new boundary with black stones. Webster, the Missourian declared, had become "the champion of the British Government." He had dispensed with minutes and protocol during the negotiations and now used the "mysterious humbuggery" of Sparks's discovery—that "awful apparition of the disinterred map"—to scare the Senate into consenting to the treaty as the only alternative to war.[3]

Webster must have been disconcerted to see the map issue introduced again; but his old adversary from Missouri had seized upon it out of political expediency, and the secretary could only brace himself for the certain onslaught. Benton had an announcement. The Library of Congress, he told Senate colleagues, had a map in Thomas Jefferson's papers that supported the American claim to the disputed territory. Benjamin Franklin, the senator explained, had given it to Jefferson in 1790. A stir followed, and Benton had the map (published in Paris by Lattré in 1784) brought before the Senate. But to his surprise, as well as to that of others, a comparison of the Jefferson map's red line with that on the Sparks map showed they were identical. Both confirmed the *British* claim. In a remarkable attempt to regain composure, Benton abruptly reversed tactics. Webster's concealment of *any* map from Ashburton, he self-righteously concluded, was "a fraud upon the British if true." Even if the Sparks map invalidated the American claim, "honor requires us to show it to the British." Rives later commented in the Senate that the good Missourian "had been caught in his own trap, and fallen into the pit he laid."[4]

Most members of the Senate did not want to see old British issues raised again, and Benton's goal of a South-West political alliance fell through. The test came when Calhoun rose to speak on the treaty. The South Carolinian agreed that the Sparks and Jefferson maps appeared to justify the British claim, but he, along with Rives, did not want to reopen the boundary negotiations. Peace with Britain, Calhoun argued, was essential to the return of prosperity in the United States. He added that the African squadron clause did not recognize any British right to search American ships, for each nation was to execute its laws independently. As for the *Creole*, Ashburton's personal assurances were satisfactory safeguards of American shipping. The new northeastern boundary, Calhoun concluded, was more advantageous to the United States than the Dutch award of 1831. An observer who was neither a personal nor a political friend of Calhoun's said the senator had defended the treaty in a "most able, patriotic and majestic speech." His rebuke of the Bentonites was "most withering."[5]

Webster's private work contributed to Benton's downfall. During the negotiations in Washington, the secretary had published unsigned editorials that quieted opposition to the treaty and made it easier for the state commissioners to accept the proposed boundary line. The settlement, he argued, was vital to peace. Webster's personal friendship with a publisher of the widely read Washington *National Intelligencer* gave him access to a Whig newspaper that had the helpful reputation of being hostile to the administration. Besides carrying Webster's editorials, it reprinted articles from the Portland *Eastern Argus* favoring the treaty. To be sure, the Democratic Washington *Globe* did everything it could to undermine the agreement. It expressed Benton's bitter opposition to the treaty, printed Lewis Cass's letter criticizing the British stand on the right of search, accused Webster of accepting bribes from Ashburton and other British bankers to persuade the federal government to finance defaulted state bonds, and exposed the secretary's authorship of the newspaper editorials. Though it is difficult to determine whether Webster's efforts were directly responsible, numerous newspaper editors in the South and West, along with many other Americans, believed that the boundary settlement was honorable and just and popular in Maine.[6]

Fear of conflict with the United Kingdom no doubt was the Senate's guiding motive in approving the treaty, but Calhoun's support and Webster's editorials and use of the red-line map in the Senate also proved effective. After only four days, on Saturday, 20 August, at nine o'clock in the evening, the Senate consented to the treaty by vote of 39 to 9. All opponents except one were Democrats. Only two Southerners voted against the treaty. Even Webster confessed that he had not expected such a favorable margin. That evening he wrote an unsigned editorial for the *Intelligencer* proclaiming that "the National Honor has been maintained." A few days later when the New York *Courier and Enquirer*, supporter of Henry Clay, released the full text of the treaty without authorization, Webster at first was displeased, for he had wanted more time to prepare the public for its contents. But the timing was opportune, for the House of Representatives had passed a tariff bill, and Democratic editors turned from the treaty to denounce Northern protectionists.[7]

If newspapers and other public statements are accurate barometers of American public opinion, reaction in Maine to the Webster-Ashburton Treaty was generally favorable. As expected, the press divided along party lines. The Democratic Augusta *Age* thought the state had been "Most egregiously humbugged," while the Whig *Journal* of the same city exuberantly hailed the end of controversy. In Portland the Democratic *Eastern Argus*, partly owned by Francis Smith, praised the treaty and noted widespread approval throughout the state. The Bangor *Democrat*, however, warned that most of the profit brought by increased navigation of the St. John River would go to the British. Democratic Senator Reuel Williams, one of the nine who had voted against the treaty's approval, remarked to colleagues that "this is not the entertainment to which my State was invited" and vainly presented a resolution calling for President Tyler to order immediate military occupation of the disputed territory. Others in Maine condemned the treaty because of the loss of territory, and Governor Fairfield, careful to protect his political future, told the state legislature he was disappointed with the negotiations. When the Maine delegation submitted its report to the assembly, a joint committee concluded that the treaty contained unsatisfactory terms, and six of its twelve members voted to censure Webster. But Edward Kent, former governor of the state and one of the commissioners in Washington, considered the treaty honorable and thought most legislators in Augusta would agree. They did. Perhaps, as Webster would believe in 1846, there were not "fifty respectable persons in Maine" who wanted to revoke the treaty.[8]

Outside Maine, areas north of the nation's capital divided in their assessment. The Boston press considered the treaty the only alternative to war and quoted from "The Great Song" written in honor of the document:

> O'er the Lion and Eagle now hovers the Dove;
> To-day there's a banquet of national love.
> O, long live their glory, united and free!
> The Imperial West and the Queen of the Sea!

In Washington, the Whig businessman's source of news, *Niles' Register*, called the treaty a "harbinger of better times," while New Yorkers predicted good commercial relations. A shipping firm in New York constructed an elaborately designed vessel, the *Ashburton*, and proudly called it the "commercial queen of the seas." In the Midwest the Chicago *American* thanked Webster, while most others either did not comment or called the treaty an insult. The St. Louis *Republican* ignored the agreement and criticized Tyler's performance in office, while the Cincinnati *Enquirer* at first denounced both the treaty and the administration, then reluctantly admitted that the only other choice was war. Webster won one admirer's praise for the most outstanding service by an American since adoption of the Constitution, while the president of Harvard, Josiah Quincy, Jr., expressed gratitude for the greatest good done by any person in American history, excepting George Washington. In a move especially gratifying to Webster, Chancellor James Kent of New York and Joseph Story of the United States Supreme Court planned to add his arguments during the negotiations to their legal commentaries.[9]

In the South reaction to the treaty also was mixed. The Richmond *Enquirer*, spokesman of planter and commercial interests, approved the settlement, while the Baltimore *Sun* praised the British for finally recognizing the United States as an equal nation. Hugh Legaré, Tyler's attorney general from South Carolina, exalted the new, conciliatory approach to diplomacy introduced by Webster and Ashburton. Though the Charleston *Mercury* echoed Legaré's words, other Southern papers warned against trusting the British. The *Caroline* settlement, according to the Mobile *Register & Journal*, was unsatisfactory because the United States had admitted that the British interpretation of the incident was correct. In addition, the government in London had not renounced the right of search, and the boundary settlement was unfair to Maine. The only gain resulting from the negotiations, the *Journal* curiously remarked, was the probability of peace. Despite these criticisms, Mobile's chamber of commerce publicly expressed gratitude to Webster for the treaty.[10]

One can make several observations from America's reaction to the settlement. Not surprisingly, the pattern had developed that those Americans directly benefiting from the treaty considered it a vindication of national honor. Commercial areas supported the pact because it prevented a possible war, encouraged economic connections with the British, and aided recovery from the depression of 1837. Midwesterners had little to say, probably because the treaty did not affect them directly. Though Southerners believed it included inadequate assurances concerning the African slave-trade and *Creole* controversies, many gave more priority to the chance for expanded cotton markets in the United Kingdom. By fall of 1842 it appeared that most Americans—Democrats and Whigs—considered the settlement essential to peace and prosperity. To some Americans, a British observer noted, the treaty had "acknowledged the independence" of the United States. John Quincy Adams remarked that even Lewis Cass could not make great political headway in such a "popular gale."[11]

General reaction to the treaty in British North America likewise was favorable, with exceptions. Some observers believed that Ashburton had ignored his people's interests by sacrificing sole navigation of the St. John River and by giving up Rouse's Point and Madawaska, but such comments were rare. Most spokesmen were relieved that the treaty had prevented an Anglo-American war—especially since the antagonists probably would have fought on Canadian soil. New Brunswick papers were pleased that the boundary controversy was over and agreed with Lieutenant Governor William Colebrooke that there would be reciprocal advantages. A longtime critic of the United States, the governor general of Canada, Sir Charles Bagot, shared their optimism. Montreal and Toronto newspapers looked forward to economic advantages and regarded the treaty as the beginning of a new era in international affairs when disputes could be settled peacefully.[12]

To these choruses of praise were added the voices of spokesmen in England. Merchants called the treaty a total success, while the *Quarterly Review* believed that Ashburton had prevented war and secured Quebec. Both the *Edinburgh Review* and the usually anti-American London *Times* expressed the relief of many Englishmen that their emissary had settled the boundary and maintained peace. Though the British government had surrendered some rights, the *Times* argued that the overriding consideration was commercial. The Palmerston contingent had fumbled the border issue for ten years, it argued, and the only way out was compromise. Besides, Britain had acquired land for a military road between Fredericton and Quebec, as well as a buffer along the southern bank of the St. Lawrence River. The *Times* hesitated to approve free navigation of the St. John because the British government should have the "power to lock the door in case of emergency"; yet it hoped that Maine would not take advantage of its new right-of-way. In answer to critics, the *Times* asked: "Would they have settled the dispute on any other terms?"[13]

As Lord Ashburton contemplated the trip back to England, he might well have considered that the negotiations had been successful, that he had vindicated some of his country's rights, salvaged chances for better relations with France, and prevented contentions that might have cost more than any of his critics imagined. Meanwhile he enjoyed the praise of admirers in the United States. The American Peace Society made him an honorary member and awarded him a copy of its *Prize Essays on a Congress of Nations*, while several ornate occasions were held in his honor. At a dinner in Boston's Faneuil Hall he called the city the cradle of liberty. The Cambridge chapter of Phi Beta Kappa heard its president praise the negotiators in these words: "Peace had her victories as well as War." At the Astor House in New York, Whig businessmen sponsored an elaborate dinner in Ashburton's honor. After a series of speeches by dignitaries, including one by the emissary himself, a toast to President Tyler met total silence, while another to Queen Victoria brought a round of cheers.[14]

The last weeks of Ashburton's stay in the United States were pleasant enough. In New York the night before his ship sailed he attended a play at the Park Theater with a large group of British and American naval officers. As they entered the hall the band played "Rule Britannia," then "God Save the Queen," and concluded with "Yankee Doodle." Everyone rose and gave three cheers, while Ashburton, dressed in a plain, dark frock coat with white pants and vest, bowed gravely.[15]

The following day, 3 September, nearly eight hundred onlookers jammed the dock in New York harbor where a small boat waited to take the minister to the *Warspite*. As the boat brushed past the *North Carolina*, there were several exchanges of salutes. After Ashburton boarded the British warship, Commodore Matthew Perry left the *North Carolina* for the *Warspite* to join him and the ship's commanding officer in a farewell toast. Upon Perry's departure, the *Warspite* raised the stars and stripes, fired twenty-one guns, and began to pull out of the harbor, accompanied by a steamboat on each side.[16]

Almost three weeks later, Ashburton arrived in Portsmouth amid gun salutes from both the *Warspite* and batteries ashore and immediately departed for his country house at Anglesea, on the whole well pleased with himself.[17]

After the United States Senate consented to the treaty in August, Webster made arrangements for the exchange of ratifications and appointed a member of the State Department to take the document to London. There was a delay because of Ashburton's late departure from New York and because he visited his family before going to London; but on 13 October, in the Foreign Office, Aberdeen and Everett went through the formalities. Everett proudly noted that whereas the British wrote the ratification on parchment, the Americans placed it in a silver box bound in crimson velvet, with ribbons holding the covers. Several American cities greeted news of the exchange with public celebrations.[18]

It was one feat to obtain approval of the treaty in the Senate, ratification by President Tyler, and the exchange with Britain; it was another to contain Palmerston's wrath, which, however contrived, posed a touchy problem for the Peel ministry. Parliament was not in session when news of the treaty arrived in autumn of 1842, but Palmerston's barrage quickly got under way. The London *Times* carried a series of letters, signed by

"Tenax" and probably authorized by Palmerston, urging opposition to the treaty. The *Morning Chronicle* parroted his criticisms, the *Morning Herald* referred to the boundary article as "fear-prompted infatuation," and *Punch* ridiculed Ashburton in what it called "Unpublished Correspondence between Lord Ashburton and Mr. Webster, on the Boundary Question." The *Evening Star* claimed that Ashburton had returned to England "with his finger in his mouth," for he had been a "pigmy in the hands of a giant." Though Everett believed that most Britons welcomed news of the settlement, he noted that those people hurt by the failure of the Bank of the United States and by the depreciation of state stocks remained bitter toward Americans.[19]

According to one observer, Palmerston never had shown so much virulence. He attacked every part of the treaty. In a series of unsigned articles in the *Morning Chronicle* he assailed the new boundary as a *"wretchedly bad arrangement,"* a "needless, gratuitous, and imbecile surrender." On the slave-trade agreement he castigated Aberdeen for having to "go and beg" the United States to help Britain meet Christian obligations. Putting the boundary, slave-trade, and extradition conventions into one treaty was the "grand hoax" of Tyler and Webster, part of the "beautiful mystification" to "conceal the laugh in the sleeve" after Ashburton left the United States. "Jonathan enjoys making a dupe." The treaty was a "pitiful exhibition of imbecility." It was "Lord Ashburton's *capitulation.*"[20]

Though many contemporaries dismissed Palmerston's accusations as politically inspired, hindsight suggests that his indictment of the boundary bears careful consideration. The Peel ministry, he lamented to Lord Russell, had sacrificed the Empire's "future & permanent Interests" in securing peace. The United States should not have received land north of the St. John River, nor should Ashburton have discarded Rouse's Point. Palmerston assured Russell that the duke of Wellington agreed. The boundary provisions, Palmerston asserted, solidified "America's Means of attack." To former Prime Minister Melbourne, he pointed out the treaty's disadvantages in the event of war with the United States. Ashburton, Palmerston told two other English friends, had furnished Americans the "Instruments of future aggression" against British North America, and had cost the United Kingdom its "Character, . . . Moral Influence, and . . . military Security." The goals of the United

States in North America were military and political, not agricultural and commercial. The disputed territory extending between New Brunswick and the Canadas afforded a "Strong Military Position" for attack on the Empire. The United States, Palmerston concluded, had won a "Stepping Stone" toward its ultimate purpose: "Expulsion of British authority from the Continent of America."[21]

From the perspective of the nations' rivalry over North America, Palmerston's complaints were legitimate; yet the Foreign Office's view was that British relations with France were also important. Palmerston's assessment of the treaty showed his deep concern over the long-range military aspects of the Webster-Ashburton negotiations, while Aberdeen's stand emphasized European affairs as well. Though Palmerston admitted that he knew of no plans by the United States to attack Canada, he pointed out that Americans since the 1780s had talked openly about eliminating British influence from the continent. Peel and Aberdeen thought the risk that the United States would not invade Canada was worth taking. Palmerston warned, however, that the peace won by the negotiations was not an end for the Americans, but rather a means for the Washington government to continue its aggressive designs in North America and eventually to gain control of the continent. He maintained that the balance of power in North America threatened to shift in favor of the United States during the 1840s and that the treaty negotiated by Webster and Ashburton was vital to this change.

Most Britons, however, thought the treaty had preserved peace; and as the London *Times* once again entered the debate, it became apparent that Palmerston would be the loser. The *Times* felt ashamed of "being like a disputant who is boring a whole dinner-table" by a superfluous argument with an "obstinate and somewhat stupid opponent." Yet it understood Palmerston's frustration. When he moved out of the Foreign Office, Britain faced wars in China and Afghanistan and the likelihood of two more with the United States and France. How annoying that the Peel government had won the first two wars and resolved the other problems peacefully. Palmerston, said the *Times*, "has embroiled, Lord ELLENBOROUGH's troops have conquered, Lord ASHBURTON has pacified, and Sir ROBERT PEEL has all the credit." Surely the "noble Lord's cup of humiliation was full." The following quip must have caused even Palmerston's allies to hold back a smile: "Our contemporary [editor of the *Chronicle*] is, no doubt, wise in loading his guns heavily, but before he applies the match, he would be wiser if he would take care that Lord PALMERSTON is not standing before the muzzle."[22]

As criticisms of the treaty grew into personal attacks upon Ashburton—Palmerstonians spoke of him as "Lord Surrender"—the former minister lashed out at his enemies in a private note to his friend, John Croker. "Our Cousin Jonathan," he said, was an "offensive, arrogant fellow," and Britishers should be pleased that any agreement had resulted from the negotiations. The treaty prevented war, Ashburton declared. Whoever disliked the settlement might "kill the next Hotspur themselves." At that moment his patience was thin, for he was "suffering the torment" of posing for his picture to give to his "co-Capitulator," as he now called Webster in jest. They had agreed to exchange portraits with copies of the ratified treaty.[23]

The treaty therefore became a focus of party warfare in Britain as it had earlier in the United States. Palmerston's criticisms did not surprise Aberdeen; he expected hostility from someone out of office. "Viscount Chronicle," as some called Palmerston, would have condemned the treaty, no matter what articles it contained. But this time he went too far. Political allies began to fall away when they witnessed the treaty's popularity in Britain. Russell, a longtime friend, did not want to risk new problems with America and eventually gave reluctant approval, but probably out of deference to his party cohort he declared that the country could have gotten better terms with stronger leadership. More significant perhaps, George Featherstonhaugh, a Palmerstonian for years, praised the treaty before the Cornwall Polytechnic Society in Falmouth. Everett noted widespread British relief with the end of what had seemed a hopeless controversy.[24]

All in all the opening session of Parliament promised to be tumultuous. Not only did Palmerston plan to make it interesting, but news of the Sparks map had reached the British public in January 1843. His critics felt that Ashburton had sacrificed legitimate claim to the entire area between New Brunswick and Maine. The following month Featherstonhaugh revoked his earlier approval by publishing a pamphlet describing another map recently found in a London public office, which also substantiated Britain's original boundary claim. He criticized Webster for hiding the Sparks map and Ashburton for conceding the land so easily.

Even Aberdeen privately admitted that Webster's actions had constituted a "piece of concealment" that had caused an unfavorable impression in the United Kingdom and could lead to problems in Parliament.[25]

Ashburton planned to witness the political battle in the "Great Babylon" he called Parliament, but he was not worried about Palmerston's declaration that he had something that would "blow the Capitulation out of the water." If it were the Sparks and Steuben maps, the former foreign secretary would only expose himself to more ridicule. During his ten years in office, Ashburton argued, Palmerston could have discovered the red-line map in the Paris archives if he had not spent his time measuring mountains and surveying countrysides. As for Webster's clandestine use of the maps, Ashburton had asked experienced British diplomats if honor had bound the secretary of state to reveal them. Though receiving no straightforward answer, Ashburton believed they agreed with him that Webster had been under no obligation to do so. The former special minister knew that a diplomat, like a lawyer, is not expected to present evidence contrary to his case. Ashburton might not have known it at the time, but the Montreal *Transcript* concurred. And in London, the *Quarterly Review* defended Webster and dismissed a diplomat as "an honest man sent to *lie* abroad for the good of his country." Ashburton sarcastically commented to Croker that Palmerston *had* to criticize the administration; the treaty's success was embarrassing since he and Melbourne had not managed a settlement. Moreover, Ashburton believed that few Britons were concerned about the location of the boundary line at such remote places as Lake Pohenagamook. Certainly no one could label the treaty a "sharp bargain."[26]

The coup de grace to Palmerston's public stand against the treaty came when the Peel ministry revealed the King George III or Oswald map. As shown earlier (see chapter 6), it supported the American claim to the disputed territory. Palmerston had discovered the map in 1839 and had stored it out of sight in the Foreign Office. Now, after nearly four years, Ashburton tracked it down and made it available to Peel and Aberdeen. Its presentation in Parliament in late February 1843 signaled the end of Palmerston's active opposition to the treaty.

Though much of the uproar died down after Peel displayed the Oswald map, more trouble developed because of a message President Tyler delivered to the House of Representatives in late February. In it he carelessly intensified the controversy in both countries by expressing satisfaction that the British government, except in cases involving piracy, had renounced the right of visit and search in peacetime. His annual address to Congress of December 1842 already had drawn criticism from both Peel and Aberdeen for leaving the impression that they had made concessions. The ministry in London now had the support of the English and Canadian press. The president, the London *Times* adroitly declared, realized that the British had not renounced the right of search. His motive was to quiet administration critics by convincing Americans that this was the best treaty possible. In the meantime Webster explained to Minister Fox in Washington that the Peel government had misunderstood Tyler's statements. The cruising arrangement, he said, had removed the necessity of search *only* in African waters. Ashburton had a different view. He thought that Tyler, a "very weak and conceited man," was trying to win popularity at the expense of "common candour & honesty." In a note to Webster, the Britisher said he could not understand how the president had gotten so confused over the cruising article in such a short time. The agreement, he declared, did not rule out the right of search in non-African waters. Yet Ashburton recommended avoiding an encounter with the United States. The American government was "always more or less anarchical" and should be left alone.[27]

Opponents of the Tyler administration seized upon the search issue to denounce the treaty again. Everything, Benton proclaimed in the Senate, depended upon whether Britain had renounced visit and search. He quickly met stiff opposition from both Northerners and Southerners. In Congress, Calhoun again intervened. The senator from South Carolina convincingly explained that Peel and Tyler interpreted visit and search differently. While Peel used the term in a general sense, the president specifically referred to its use along the African coast. The British government, Calhoun rightfully observed, had abandoned the right in African waters by agreeing that each party in the joint-cruising arrangement could supervise only its own vessels.[28]

In Parliament on 21 March, a much-deflated Palmerston began his last attack on the treaty. The ensuing discussion lost the members' interests so quickly that the following day there were not enough present for a quorum. He nonetheless declared that the treaty was a "bad and very disadvantageous bargain" and that he would not stop his inquiries because of the "stale and hackneyed charge" that his actions might bring war with the United States. After stating that he would not waste the time of the House of Commons by relating the background of the northeastern boundary controversy, he delivered a speech on the subject covering about thirty pages in the journal of the Commons and containing several factual errors, some resulting from his reliance upon Featherstonhaugh's survey report of 1840.[29]

The cause of the concessions, Palmerston maintained, was the "pomp and parade" of the mission. With both the nation's prestige and his own reputation at stake, Ashburton sacrificed everything to bring a settlement. He later had the audacity, before an "assembly of foreigners" in Boston, to insult British honor by speaking of the city as that "hallowed spot," the "cradle of American Liberty and Independence." After berating the treaty for more than three hours, Palmerston surprised his few listeners when for some unexplained reason he conceded that the Peel ministry was wise in exchanging ratifications with the United States. He hoped his accusations were wrong and that friendship could develop between the nations.[30]

Peel then rose to defend the settlement. He answered Palmerston's charges by expressing amazement that anyone could brand a treaty worthless when it had settled so many long-standing disputes. After reminding the former foreign secretary that his decade in office had led to no comparable achievements on many of the same issues, Peel declared that no one could have expected Webster to reveal the Sparks map to Ashburton. There was no proof that the map found in Paris was the one Franklin described. Peel himself had seen the red-line map in the French archives in the late 1820s and was certain there was no connection between it and Franklin's letter. Britain's chief goal in the negotiations, the prime minister pointed out, was the security of British North America. The acquisition of land for the military road made the treaty a huge success. It had assured peace.[31]

Though Peel understandably focused his remarks on American affairs, his assessment of the pact was incomplete because he did not mention its broader impact. A primary concern of the ministry, as shown earlier, was France. In this regard the diplomacy of Peel, Aberdeen, and Ashburton was successful because it relieved tensions with the United States and thereby promoted Britain's chance for improved relations with the government in Paris. Aberdeen, with good reason, soon had serious doubts that successive administrations in Washington would carry out their commitments under the Webster-Ashburton Treaty. The period afterward, in fact, reveals numerous transgressions by Americans of the boundary provisions, the extradition agreement, and the slave-trade convention. Yet in 1843 the Peel ministry spoke optimistically about future Anglo-American relations.

Parliament's answer to Palmerston was a resolution of thanks to Ashburton for his public service. On 7 April the House of Lords unanimously adopted Lord Henry Brougham's motion: "That this House doth approve the conduct of late negotiation with the United States; doth rejoice in the terms, alike advantageous and honourable to both parties, upon which the treaty has been concluded; and doth express its high sense of the ability with which the Lord Ashburton, the Minister sent to treat with the United States, executed his commission, and its satisfaction at the restoration of a good understanding, which it is alike the duty and the interest of both countries to maintain unbroken." Almost a month later, in the House of Commons, Joseph Hume broke with Palmerston and made a similar motion, which his colleagues adopted by vote of 238 to 96. The London *Times* hoped these moves ended discussion of the treaty. It did not know who was the most pitiable—the ministry, which had become involved in an unexpected obligation to Hume; the public, which had seen too many newspaper columns devoted to the treaty; Palmerston, who must bear the "full dead weight" of censure by this deserter from his ranks; or the *Times*'s own editors, who had to take time to report this news about the treaty. It probably was no coincidence that at one time Palmerston had helped unseat Brougham from Parliament.[32]

Unrest over the treaty did not die easily, however, for four years after its ratification in the United States a few Democrats in Congress brought charges of misconduct in office against Webster. His old enemy, Charles Ingersoll of Pennsylvania, had failed to prove federal obstruction of justice in the trial of Alexander McLeod, and he now claimed to have new evidence that justified a House investigation of the former secretary's role in the treaty negotiations. When some members expressed concern about how Ingersoll had gained access to these documents, he explained that an unidentified subordinate of Secretary of State James Buchanan had granted him entry because of his position as chairman of the House

Committee on Foreign Affairs. Ignoring his friends who urged him not to pursue the matter, he called on the House to investigate three charges: unlawful use of the president's secret-service fund; improper deployment of the money to "corrupt party presses"; leaving the State Department in default of more than $2,000.[33]

Ingersoll's purpose clearly was the retroactive impeachment of Webster, the first, and as far as this writer can determine, the only time this has happened to a high official in the United States government. Asking Congress to censure Webster for "misconduct" while secretary of state, he urged a House resolution calling on President James K. Polk to furnish State Department materials that he said would prove "misdemeanors in office." The question was whether Webster's "malversation, corruption, and delinquency . . . will be deemed impeachable misdemeanors in office, and disqualify him to hold any office of honor, trust or profit, under the United States." That same day, the House moved by vote of 136 to 28 that the president furnish State Department documents relating to money drawn from the secret-service fund during Webster's tenure as secretary of state. On 27 April it passed the following resolution presented by John Pettit, Democrat from Indiana: ". . . a select committee of five be appointed, to inquire into the truth of the charges this day made in this House by Mr. C. J. Ingersoll against Mr. Daniel Webster, with a view to founding an impeachment against said Daniel Webster."[34]

Testimony before the committee was given privately, some of it later becoming public. It began with the appearance of the disbursing clerk of the State Department, Edward Stubbs, who underwent careful examination for almost ten days. His statements, all supported by documents he produced from State Department archives, conclusively defended Webster's conduct. All of the money Webster withdrew from the contingency fund, Stubbs showed, was approved by direct written order of either President Harrison or President Tyler. There was nothing outstanding against Webster when he left office, the clerk emphatically declared; the secretary had adjusted the account by reimbursing the department from personal funds.[35]

The committee investigation continued with the appearance of Francis Smith, whose four-day testimony reconstructed an elaborate tale of how the Tyler administration, through Webster, engineered Maine's assent to the boundary settlement by drawing finances from the president's secret-service fund. Smith concluded that there were no "sinister" motives in the government's efforts in New England. The campaign was a "worthy act" that did not involve bribery or "party purpose." Smith trusted that Ingersoll's allegations were "an error of temporary passion, and not of the heart," and that he would withdraw them.[36]

The decisive point in Webster's defense probably came with the testimony of former President Tyler. In addition to helping disprove Ingersoll's allegations, Tyler's presence—he was summoned officially—gave the prestige of the presidential office and might have had a psychological effect on members of the committee. He began with a long explanation of how dangerous Anglo-American relations had become by the time he took office in the spring of 1841. He then corroborated Stubbs's testimony by declaring that he had authorized Webster to draw upon the secret-service fund in hiring agents to gather information about the border dispute. Because there was no pro-Tyler newspaper in Maine, the president had followed Smith's suggestion to present the administration's view in the Portland *Christian Mirror*. Without the state's concurrence, he asserted, there could have been no boundary settlement. Use of the secret-service fund had had his approval, and employment of agents by the executive office had been accepted practice since the presidency of George Washington. As for the claim of default, Webster had deposited enough personal funds to balance the account, with the understanding that when he came up with the other vouchers the government would refund the money.[37]

There could be little doubt of the outcome. On 9 June 1846 the House committee, by vote of four to one, exonerated Webster of all charges. The chairman delivered the majority opinion: the law committed the secret-service fund to exclusive jurisdiction of the president, who could disburse the money himself or appoint an agent to do so. The committee found no evidence that Webster had used public money to "corrupt the party presses," a decision that suggests such claim was virtually unprovable. As for the president's use of confidential agents, the committee refused to "inquire into the propriety of employing agents for secret service" within the United States. On the final charge of default, there was little to debate after both Stubbs and Tyler testified that there was nothing outstanding in Webster's account by the time Tyler left office in 1845. The committee concluded that there was no evidence "to impeach Mr. Webster's integrity or the purity of his motives in the discharge of the duties of his office."[38]

A week later a motion was made in the House to print all testimony gathered in the investigation, but it was defeated (77 to 57) for the reason set forth in the majority report: the investigation had uncovered facts about America's foreign affairs that, if publicized, could endanger government policy. Members of the committee agreed with President Polk's recent congressional message that the only justification for turning over the documents was in the event of impeachment. Polk explained that if the House believed an inquiry necessary to determine whether public funds had been used improperly, "all the archives and papers of the Executive departments, public or private, would be subject to the inspection and control of a committee of their body, and every facility in the power of the Executive be afforded to enable them to prosecute the investigation." The committee concurred that government secrecy was secondary to punishing "great public delinquents." Webster admitted that a time might come when publication of secret government documents was necessary to bring "high handed offenders to justice," yet he could not foresee such case arising in America. The House accepted the committee's recommendation that the sections of Tyler's and Stubbs's testimonies dealing with secret agents should be sealed, labeled confidential, and deposited in the National Archives.[39]

Webster and Ashburton have not yet received satisfactory acclaim for their treaty, even though their work helped prevent a third Anglo-American conflict. Unfortunately, the charges against Webster in 1846 have left a heritage of suspicion about his motives in office. Some historians have found it difficult to separate his performance in the negotiations from the implications many have drawn from his almost insatiable drive for money. Ashburton's ordeal in England was similar. Palmerston's attacks kept him from receiving a public service award from the ministry. Peel later explained to Ashburton that he feared popular criticism if his government seemed overly favorable to the settlement with America.[40] In a negotiated compromise both sides always undergo criticism. Webster and Ashburton expected opposition, but they accepted the recriminations because they knew that the next important goal to winning a war is keeping the peace. Although the events prior to the treaty negotiations dictated much of their behavior during the summer of 1842, they managed to preserve each nation's honor.

The Webster-Ashburton Treaty, then, was significant because it temporarily reduced the danger of war by resolving several irritating disputes between the Atlantic nations and because it encouraged the prospects of better Franco-British relations. The Peel ministry had not ruled out conflict with the United States. In fact, several spokesmen did more than contemplate its possibility. Though public leaders often discuss the imminence of war to show that their tenure in office is vital, one cannot dismiss as solely a political maneuver the fact that noted moderates like Peel and Aberdeen followed the advice of Wellington and his military colleagues in devising secret contingency war plans. Both nations had grave interests at stake. Webster and Ashburton could not pretend to resolve their dilemma of having to find room in North America for two peoples so alike in their international goals that they almost inevitably became natural, bitter rivals. Though the two nations remained suspicious of each other, there was a saving factor: the settlement of 1842 proved that in a world ironically becoming increasingly intertwined yet more detached in its relationships, the strength of personal diplomacy still can override the seemingly irreversible elements of discord.

Appendix
The Webster-Ashburton Treaty*

A Treaty to settle and define the Boundaries between the Territories of the United States and the possessions of Her Britannic Majesty, in North America: For the final Suppression of the African Slave Trade: and For the giving up of Criminals fugitive from justice, in certain cases.

Whereas certain portions of the line of boundary between the United States of America and the British Dominions in North America, described in the second article of the Treaty of Peace of 1783, have not yet been ascertained and determined, notwithstanding the repeated attempts which have been heretofore made for that purpose, and whereas it is now thought to be for the interest of both Parties, that, avoiding further discussion of their respective rights, arising in this respect under the said Treaty, they should agree on a conventional line in said portions of the said boundary, such as may be convenient to both Parties, with such equivalents and compensations, as are deemed just and reasonable:—And whereas by the Treaty concluded at Ghent, on the 24th day of December, 1814, between the United States and His Britannic Majesty, an article was agreed to and inserted in the following tenor, viz "Art. 10.—whereas the Traffic in Slaves is irreconcilable with the principles of humanity and justice: And whereas both His Majesty and the United States are desirous of continuing their efforts to promote its entire abolition, it is hereby agreed that both the contracting Parties shall use their best endeavors to accomplish so desirable an object": and whereas, notwithstanding the laws which have at various times been passed by the two Governments, and the efforts made to suppress it, that criminal traffic is still prosecuted and carried on: And whereas the United States of America and Her Majesty the Queen of the United Kingdom of Great Britain and Ireland, are determined that, so far as may be in their power, it shall be effectually abolished:—And whereas it is found expedient for the better administration of justice and the prevention of crime within the Territories and jurisdiction of the two Parties, respectively, that persons committing the crimes hereinafter enumerated, and being fugitives from justice, should, under certain circumstances, be reciprocally delivered up: The United States of America and Her

*Text of treaty in Hunter Miller, ed., *Treaties and Other International Acts of the United States of America, 1776–1863,* 4:363–70.

Britannic Majesty, having resolved to treat on these several subjects, have for that purpose appointed their respective Plenipotentiaries to negotiate and conclude a Treaty, that is to say: the President of the United States has, on his part, furnished with full powers, Daniel Webster, Secretary of State of the United States; and Her Majesty the Queen of the United Kingdom of Great Britain and Ireland, has, on her part, appointed the Right honorable Alexander Lord Ashburton, a peer of the said United Kingdom, a member of Her Majesty's most honorable Privy Council, and Her Majesty's Minister Plenipotentiary on a Special Mission to the United States; who, after a reciprocal communication of their respective full powers, have agreed to and signed the following articles:

Article I.

It is hereby agreed and declared that the line of boundary shall be as follows: Beginning at the monument at the source of the river St. Croix, as designated and agreed to by the Commissioners under the fifth article of the Treaty of 1794, between the Governments of the United States and Great Britain; thence, north, following the exploring line run and marked by the Surveyors of the two Governments in the years 1817 and 1818, under the fifth article of the Treaty of Ghent, to its intersection with the river St. John, and to the middle of the channel thereof: thence, up the middle of the main channel of the said river St. John, to the mouth of the river St. Francis; thence up the middle of the channel of the said river St. Francis, and of the lakes through which it flows, to the outlet of the Lake Pohenagamook; thence, southwesterly, in a straight line to a point on the northwest branch of the river St. John, which point shall be ten miles distant from the main branch of the St. John, in a straight line, and in the nearest direction; but if the said point shall be found to be less than seven miles from the nearest point of the summit or crest of the highlands that divide those rivers which empty themselves into the river Saint Lawrence from those which fall into the river Saint John, then the said point shall be made to recede down the said northwest branch of the river St. John, to a point seven miles in a straight line from the said summit or crest; thence, in a straight line, in a course about south eight degrees west, to the point where the parallel of latitude of 46°25' north, intersects the southwest branch of the St. John's; thence, southerly, by the said branch, to the source thereof in the highlands at the Metjarmette Portage; thence, down along the said highlands which divide the waters which empty themselves into the river Saint Lawrence from those which fall into the Atlantic Ocean, to the head of Hall's Stream; thence, down the middle of said Stream, till the line thus run intersects the old line of boundary surveyed and marked by Valentine and Collins previously to the year 1774, as the 45th degree of north latitude, and which has been known and understood to be the line of actual division between the States of New York and Vermont on one side, and the British Province of Canada on the other; and, from said point of intersection, west along the said dividing line as heretofore known and understood, to the Iroquois or St. Lawrence river.

Article II.

It is moreover agreed, that from the place where the joint Commissioners terminated their labors under the sixth article of the Treaty of Ghent, to wit: at a point in the Neebish Channel, near Muddy Lake, the line shall run into and along the ship channel between Saint Joseph and St. Tammany Islands, to the division of the channel at or near the head of St. Joseph's Island; thence, turning eastwardly and northwardly, around the lower end of St. George's or Sugar Island, and following the middle of the channel which divides St. George's from St. Joseph's Island; thence, up the east Neebish channel, nearest to St. George's Island, through the middle of Lake George;—thence west of Jonas' Island, into St. Mary's river, to a point in the middle of that river, about one mile above St. George's or Sugar Island, so as to appropriate and assign the said Island to the United States; thence, adopting the line traced on the maps by the Commissioners, thro' the river St. Mary and Lake Superior, to a point north of Ile Royale in said Lake, one hundred yards to the north and east of Ile Chapeau, which last mentioned Island lies near the northeastern point of Ile Royale, where the line marked by the Commissioners terminates; and from the last mentioned point, southwesterly, through the middle of the Sound between Ile Royale and the northwestern mainland, to the mouth of Pigeon river, and up the said river to, and through, the north and south Fowl Lakes, to the Lakes of the height of land between Lake Superior and the Lake of the Woods; thence, along the water-communication to Lake Saisaginaga, and through that Lake; thence, to and through Cypress Lake, Lac du Bois Blanc, Lac la Croix, Little Vermilion Lake, and Lake Namecan, and through the several smaller lakes, straights, or streams, connecting the lakes here mentioned, to that point in Lac la Pluie, or Rainy Lake, at the Chaudière Falls, from which the Commissioners traced the line to the most northwestern point of the Lake of the Woods;—thence, along the said line to the said most northwestern point, being latitude 49°23′55″ north, and in longitude 95°14′38″ west from the Observatory at Greenwich; thence, according to existing treaties, due south to its intersection with the 49th parallel of north latitude, and along that parallel to the Rocky Mountains. It being understood that all the water-communications, and all the usual portages along the line from Lake Superior to the Lake of the Woods; and also Grand Portage, from the shore of Lake Superior to the Pigeon river, as now actually used, shall be free and open to the use of citizens and subjects of both countries.

Article III.

In order to promote the interests and encourage the industry of all the inhabitants of the countries watered by the river St. John and its tributaries, whether living within the State of Maine or the Province of New Brunswick, it is agreed that, where, by the provisions of the present treaty, the river St. John is declared to be the line of boundary, the navigation of the said river shall be free and open to both

Parties, and shall in no way be obstructed by either: That all the produce of the forest, in logs, lumber, timber, boards, staves, or shingles, or of agriculture not being manufactured, grown on any of those parts of the State of Maine watered by the river St. John, or by its tributaries, of which fact reasonable evidence shall, if required, be produced, shall have free access into and through the said river and its said tributaries, having their source within the State of Maine, to and from the seaport at the mouth of the said river St. John's, and to and round the Falls of said river, either by boats, rafts, or other conveyance: That when within the Province of New Brunswick, the said produce shall be dealt with as if it were the produce of the said province: That, in like manner, the inhabitants of the Territory of the Upper St. John determined by this Treaty to belong to her Britannic Majesty, shall have free access to and through the river for their produce, in those parts where the said river runs wholly through the State of Maine: provided always, that this agreement shall give no right to either party to interfere with any regulations not inconsistent with the terms of this treaty which the Governments, respectively, of Maine or of New Brunswick, may make respecting the navigation of the said river, where both banks thereof shall belong to the same Party.

Article IV.

All grants of land heretofore made by either Party, within the limits of the territory which by this Treaty fall within the dominions of the other Party, shall be held valid, ratified, and confirmed to the persons in possession under such grants, to the same extent as if such territory had by this Treaty fallen within the dominions of the party by whom such grants were made: And all equitable possessory claims, arising from a possession and improvement of any lot or parcel of land by the person actually in possession, or by those under whom such person claims, for more than six years before the date of this Treaty, shall, in like manner, be deemed valid, and be confirmed and quieted by a release to the person entitled thereto, of the title to such lot or parcel of land, so described as best to include the improvements made thereon; and in all other respects the two contracting Parties agree to deal upon the most liberal principles of equity with the settlers actually dwelling upon the Territory falling to them, respectively, which has heretofore been in dispute between them.

Article V.

Whereas, in the course of the controversy respecting the disputed Territory on the northeastern boundary, some moneys have been received by the authorities of Her Britannic Majesty's Province of New Brunswick, with the intention of preventing depredations on the forests of the said Territory, which moneys were to be carried to a fund called the "Disputed Territory Fund," the proceeds whereof, it was agreed, should be hereafter paid over to the Parties interested, in the proportions to be determined by a final settlement of boundaries: It is hereby agreed, that a correct account of all receipts and payments on the said fund, shall be delivered to the Government of the United States, within six months after the ratification of this Treaty; and the proportion of the amount due thereon to the States of Maine and Massachusetts, and any bonds or securities appertaining thereto, shall be paid and delivered over to the Government of the United States; and the Government of the United States agrees to receive for the use of, and pay over to the States of Maine and Massachusetts, their respective portions of said Fund: And further to pay and satisfy said States, respectively, for all claims for expenses incurred by them in protecting the said heretofore disputed Territory, and making a survey thereof, in 1838; the Government of the United States agreeing with the States of Maine and Massachusetts to pay them the further sum of three hundred thousand dollars, in equal moieties, on account of their assent to the line of boundary described in this Treaty, and in consideration of the conditions and equivalents received therefor, from the Government of Her Britannic Majesty.

Article VI.

It is furthermore understood and agreed, that for the purpose of running and tracing those parts of the line between the source of the St. Croix and the St. Lawrence river, which will require to be run and ascertained, and for marking the residue of said line by proper monuments on the land, two Commissioners shall be appointed, one by the President of the United States, by and with the advice and consent of the Senate thereof, and one by Her Britannic Majesty: and the said commissioners shall meet at Bangor, in the State of Maine, on the first day of May next, or as soon thereafter as may be, and shall proceed to mark the line above described, from the source of the St. Croix to the river St. John; and shall trace on proper maps the dividing line along said river, and along the river St. Francis, to the outlet of the Lake Pohenagamook; and from the outlet of said Lake, they shall ascertain, fix, and mark by proper and durable monuments on the land, the line described in the first article of this Treaty; and the said Commissioners shall make to each of their respective Governments a joint report or declaration, under their hands and seals, designating such line of boundary, and shall accompany such report or declaration with maps certified by them to be true maps of the new boundary.

Article VII.

It is further agreed, that the channels in the river St. Lawrence, on both sides of the Long Sault Islands and of Barnhart Island; the channels in the river Detroit, on both sides of the Island Bois Blanc, and between the Island and both the American and Canadian shores; and all the several channels and passages between the various Islands lying near the junction of the river St. Clair with the lake of that name, shall be equally free and open to the ships, vessels, and boats of both Parties.

Article VIII.

The Parties mutually stipulate that each shall prepare, equip, and maintain in service, on the coast of Africa, a sufficient and adequate squadron, or naval force of vessels, of suitable numbers and descriptions, to carry in all not less than eighty guns, to enforce, separately and respectively, the laws rights and obligations of each of the two countries, for the suppression of the Slave Trade, and said squadrons to be independent of each other, but the two Governments stipulating, nevertheless, to give such orders to the officers commanding their respective forces, as shall enable them most effectually to act in concert and cooperation, upon mutual consultation, as exigencies may arise, for the attainment of the true object of this article; copies of all such orders to be communicated by each Government to the other respectively.

Article IX.

Whereas, notwithstanding all efforts which may be made on the coast of Africa for Suppressing the Slave Trade, the facilities for carrying on that traffic and avoiding the vigilance of cruisers by the fraudulent use of flags, and other means, are so great, and the temptations for pursuing it, while a market can be found for Slaves, so strong, as that the desired result may be long delayed, unless all markets be shut against the purchase of African negroes, the Parties to this Treaty agree that they will unite in all becoming representations and remonstrances, with any and all Powers within whose dominions such markets are allowed to exist; and that they will urge upon all such Powers the propriety and duty of closing such markets effectually at once and forever.

Article X.

It is agreed that the United States and Her Britannic Majesty shall, upon mutual requisitions by them, or their Ministers, Officers, or authorities, respectively made, deliver up to justice, all persons who, being charged with the crime of murder, or assault with intent to commit murder, or Piracy, or arson, or robbery, or Forgery, or the utterance of forged paper, committed within the jurisdiction of either, shall seek an asylum, or shall be found, within the territories of the other: Provided, that this shall only be done upon such evidence of criminality as, according to the laws of the place where the fugitive or person so charged, shall be found, would justify his apprehension and commitment for trial, if the crime or offence had there been committed: And the respective Judges and other Magistrates of the two Governments, shall have power, jurisdiction, and authority, upon complaint made under oath, to issue a warrant for the apprehension of the fugitive or person so charged, that he may be brought before such Judges or other Magistrates, respectively, to the end that the evidence of criminality may be heard and considered; and if, on such hearing, the evidence be deemed sufficient to sustain the charge it shall be the duty of the examining Judge or Magistrate, to certify the same to the proper Executive Authority, that a warrant may issue for the surrender of such fugitive. The expense of such apprehension and delivery shall be borne and defrayed by the Party who makes the requisition, and receives the fugitive.

Article XI.

The eighth article of this Treaty shall be in force for five years from the date of the exchange of the ratifications, and afterwards until one or the other Party shall signify a wish to terminate it. The tenth article shall continue in force until one or the other of the Parties shall signify its wish to terminate it, and no longer.

Article XII.

The present Treaty shall be duly ratified, and the mutual exchange of ratifications shall take place in London, within six months from the date hereof, or earlier if possible.

In Faith whereof, we the respective Plenipotentiaries, have signed this Treaty, and have hereunto affixed our Seals.

Done, in duplicate, at Washington, the ninth day of August, Anno Domini one thousand eight hundred and forty-two.

DANL WEBSTER   ASHBURTON
[seal]   [seal]

Abbreviations

ASPFR	*American State Papers, Foreign Relations* (6 vols., Wash., 1832–59)
BFSP	*British and Foreign State Papers* (116 vols. London, 1812–)
CG	*Congressional Globe*
CO (PAC)	Colonial Office (Public Archives of Canada, Ottawa)
Disp., GB (NA)	Department of State, Diplomatic Dispatches, Great Britain (National Archives)
DL (NA)	Department of State, Domestic Letters (National Archives)
EP	Edward Everett Papers (Massachusetts Historical Society)
FO (PRO)	Great Britain, Foreign Office (Public Record Office, London)
HCSP	Great Britain, Parliament, *House of Commons, Sessional Papers,* 1801–1900
ML (NA)	Department of State, Miscellaneous Letters (National Archives)
N.B., Disp. (PAC)	New Brunswick, Dispatches (Public Archives of Canada, Ottawa)
NFBL (NA)	Department of State, Notes from the British Legation in the United States to the Department of State, 1791–1906 (National Archives)
NTFL, GB (NA)	Department of State, Notes to Foreign Legations in the United States from the Department of State, 1834–1906, Great Britain (National Archives)

Perry, Letter Books (NA)   Department of the Navy, The Letter Books
of Commander Matthew C. Perry (National
Archives)

WP   Charles M. Wiltse, ed., Daniel Webster Papers
(Dartmouth College)

Notes

Preface

1. Examples are: Samuel F. Bemis, *John Quincy Adams and the Foundations of American Foreign Policy*; Richard N. Current, "Webster's Propaganda and the Ashburton Treaty," pp. 187–200; Frederick Merk, *Fruits of Propaganda in the Tyler Administration*. A sound treatment of the British side of the Anglo-American questions is Wilbur D. Jones, *The American Problem in British Diplomacy, 1841–1861*.

2. Harry C. Allen has argued that "there was no deep, inherent antagonism" between the British and the Americans after the War of 1812 and that "Anglo-American cordiality" developed rapidly after 1814. See his *Great Britain and the United States*, pp. 50, 53, and his *Conflict and Concord*, ch. 3. On the theme of rapprochement, see Bradford Perkins's three works: *The First Rapprochement*, chs. 2, 8; *Prologue to War*, chs. 1, 3, 12; and *Castlereagh and Adams*, chs. 9, 10, 12. See also Charles S. Campbell, *From Revolution to Rapprochement*. For volumes placing emphasis on the problems between the nations, see Kenneth Bourne, *Britain and the Balance of Power in North America, 1815–1908*, chs. 1–4; Alfred L. Burt, *The United States, Great Britain and British North America from the Revolution to the Establishment of Peace after the War of 1812*, chs. 16, 17; George Dangerfield, *The Era of Good Feelings*, pt. 4; Allan Nevins, ed., *America Through British Eyes*, pp. 120–38. David M. Pletcher has examined the ambivalence in Anglo-American relations from 1815 to 1842 in chapter 1 of his *The Diplomacy of Annexation*. The quotation is from page 814 of an article entitled "The United States," which appeared in *Blackwood's Edinburgh Magazine* (author not identified).

3. For the social, political, and economic forces in the Atlantic nations' relationship, see Frank Thistlethwaite, *The Anglo-American Connection in the Early Nineteenth Century*, and his article, "Atlantic Partnership," pp. 1–17. A divisive factor, often overlooked, was the Anglo-American struggle for a copyright law (James J. Barnes, *Authors, Publishers and Politicians*).

4. Author not identified, "The United States," pp. 814–23; Myron F. Brightfield, *John Wilson Croker*, pp. 393–95.

5. Oliver P. Chitwood, *John Tyler*, chs. 14–21; Robert F. Dalzell, Jr., *Daniel Webster and the Trial of American Nationalism, 1843–1852*, ch. 2; Claude M. Fuess, *Daniel Webster*, 2: ch. 20; Robert Seager II, *And Tyler Too*, pp. 147–71; Glyndon G. Van Deusen, *The Jacksonian Era*, ch. 8.

6. The British government in 1841 had a total defense expenditure of $78 million, while America's was only $15 million. These figures do not reveal how much British money went to North America alone, but of the totals mentioned above, the British allotted $34 million for the navy, while the United States set aside only $6 million. The remainder from each nation's defense budget went to the army (Allen, *Great Britain and the United States*, p. 44, table).

7. Chitwood, *Tyler*, p. 113; Dalzell, *Webster*; Fuess, *Webster*, 2:416–17.

8. For Webster's alleged Anglophilia, see Charles M. Wiltse, "Daniel Webster and the British Experience," pp. 58–77.

Chapter 1.

1. Hunter Miller, ed., *Treaties and Other International Acts of the United States of America, 1776–1863*, 2:152.

2. The three principal American delegates at Paris were John Adams, Benjamin Franklin, and John Jay. The British representatives were Richard Oswald and Henry Strachey. Henry S. Burrage, *Maine in the Northeastern Boundary Controversy*, p. 96; John B. Moore, *History and Digest of the International Arbitrations to Which the United States Has Been a Party*, 1:66; John B. Moore, ed., *International Adjudications, Ancient and Modern*, 1:9; ASPFR, 1:92–93.

3. Alfred L. Burt, *The United States, Great Britain and British North America from the Revolution to the Establishment of Peace after the War of 1812*, p. 71; Adams's note cited in ibid., p. 79; ASPFR, 1:90–92, 94–98, 100; "Letter from Judge Sullivan Concerning the Eastern Boundary of Maine," 20 Oct. 1796, in *Collections and Proceedings of the Maine Historical Society*, 9:207–12; Miller, ed., *Treaties*, 2:152; Moore, ed., *Intern. Adjud.*, 1:6–8. Some time before these developments, the governor of New Brunswick (separated from Nova Scotia in 1784) asserted that the Treaty of Paris gave Britain all "such islands as now are or heretofore have been within limits of the province of Nova Scotia." The boundary problem thus encompassed some of the offshore islands as well (Burrage, *Maine*, pp. 37–38).

4. Samuel F. Bemis, *Jay's Treaty*, p. 320.

5. Bradford Perkins, *The First Rapprochement*, pp. 48–49; John B. Moore, *The Collected Papers of John Bassett Moore*, 1:108; Calvin D. Davis, *The United States and the Second Hague Peace Conference*, p. 16.

6. Moore, ed., *Intern. Adjud.*, 1 and 2, summarizes the St. Croix commission's proceedings. Henry S. Burrage, "St. Croix Commission," paper read before Maine Historical Society, 6 Feb. 1895; Burrage, *Maine*, pp. 46, 47; Adams's letter cited in ibid., p. 48; George L. Rives, ed., *Selections from the Correspondence of Thomas Barclay* [British commissioner on St. Croix commission], pp. 43–94; Perkins, *First Rapp.*, p. 49; Moore, *Intern. Arbit.*, 1:7, 14, 18, 19, 21, 22; Franklin's letter cited in ibid., p. 22; Moore, ed., *Intern. Adjud.*, 1:15, 22, 63, 65, 66; Burt, *United States, Great Britain*, p. 163; Thomas C. Amory, *The Life of James Sullivan* [American lawyer on St. Croix commission], 1:315, 321–22, 328; ASPFR, 1:91.

7. Amory, *Sullivan*, 1:330; Moore, ed., *Intern. Adjud.*, 2:371; Burt, *United States, Great Britain*, p. 165.

8. Moore, ed., *Intern. Adjud.*, 1:80; Robert Ernst, *Rufus King*, p. 245; Madison to King, 28 July 1801, 8 June 1802, ASPFR, 2:585; Perkins, *First Rapp.*, p. 144; Samuel F. Bemis, *John Quincy Adams and the Foundations of American Foreign Policy*, p. 473.

9. ASPFR, 2:584, 586–87; Christopher Gore [American chargé] to Madison, 6 Oct. 1802, ibid., p. 587; King to Madison, 28 Feb. 1803, ibid., p. 590; Burt, *United States, Great Britain*, pp. 188, 191; Perkins, *First Rapp.*, p. 147.

10. Jefferson's message to Congress, 17 Oct. 1803, ASPFR, 1:62.

11. King to Madison, 9 Dec. 1803, ibid., 2:591; Perkins, *First Rapp.*, pp. 146–48; Samuel F. Bemis, "Jay's Treaty and the Northwest Boundary Gap," pp. 465–84; Burt, *United States, Great Britain*, pp. 193, 195; Bemis, *Adams and Foundations*, p. 126.

12. Monroe and Pinkney to Madison, 22, 25 Apr. 1807, ASPFR, 3:160, 163; Anthony Steel, "Impressment in the Monroe-Pinkney Negotiations, 1806–1807," pp. 352–69; Burt, *United States, Great Britain*, p. 206.

13. Bradford Perkins, *Castlereagh and Adams*, p. 103; Kenneth Bourne, *Britain and the Balance of Power in North America, 1815–1908*, pp. 44, 54, 57. It was not until 1867 that the British North America Act established the Dominion of Canada, a federal union consisting of the four provinces of Nova Scotia, New Brunswick, Quebec, and Ontario. Other provinces joined the Confederation later.

14. George Dangerfield, *The Era of Good Feelings*, pp. 64–65; Perkins, *Castlereagh and Adams*, p. 104, n. 4; Bemis, *Adams and Foundations*, p. 215; Moore, *Collected Papers*, 1:110.

15. Moore, ed., *Intern. Adjud.*, 6:30–34; Rives, *Corresp. of Barclay*, pp. 353–404; Fred L. Engelman, *The Peace of Christmas Eve*, pp. 231, 246, 262, 263, 266–79, 299; Burt, *United States, Great Britain*, pp. 423–26; Moore, *Intern. Arbit.*, 1:74, 76, 78–80; ASPFR, 5:50–51; Robert McElroy and Thomas Riggs, eds., *The Unfortified Boundary*; Burrage, *Maine*, pp. 108, 111; Bourne, *Britain*, pp. 59, 60; Dangerfield, *Era of Good Feelings*, p. 368; Moore, *Collected Papers*, 1:110–11.

16. Bemis, *Adams and Foundations*, pp. 471–72. Perhaps part of the explanation for the faulty survey in 1771–74 lies in the team's bill for "sundrys." Totaling £146 6s. 6½d., it included wages of only £51 3s. Most of the rest went for madeira, rum, wine, and brandy (John T. Faris, *The Romance of the Boundaries*, p. 48). See also Moore, *Intern. Arbit.*, 1:80–82, 112; Bourne, *Britain*, p. 60.

17. Bemis, *Adams and Foundations*, pp. 474–76.

18. Ibid., pp. 476–77; ASPFR, 6:643; Moore, *Intern. Arbit.*, 1:87; Richard Rush, *Memoranda of a Residence at the Court of London, . . . ,* p. 398.

19. Bemis, *Adams and Foundations*, pp. 472, 475, 477; Rush, *Memoranda*, p. 485.

20. Raymond Walters, Jr., *Albert Gallatin*, pp. 339, 340; ASPFR, 6:644; Moore, *Intern. Arbit.*, 1:85–86, 88, 100–103, 106–9; Davis, *U. S. and Second Hague Peace Conference*, p. 16. King William worked with another map. "Map A," as the Treaty of Ghent labeled it, was published in 1830 by S. L. Dashiell and was entitled, "Map of the Northern Part of the State of Maine and of the adjacent British Provinces" (Moore, *Intern. Arbit.*, 1: map insert opposite p. 85; Hunter Miller, "An Annotated Dashiell's Map," pp. 70–73).

21. Gallatin's booklet was entitled *Definitive Statement on the Part of the United States*.

22. Bemis, *Adams and Foundations*, p. 478; Frederick Merk, *Fruits of Propaganda in the Tyler Administration*, p. 48.

23. Walters, *Gallatin*, p. 343; Merk, *Fruits of Propaganda*, p. 48; Miller, ed., *Treaties*, 4:407–10.

24. Moore, *Intern. Arbit.*, 1:132–36; Miller, ed., *Treaties*, 3:359–69.

25. Burrage, *Maine*, p. 174; Gallatin to Henry Clay, 30 Oct. 1826, ASPFR, 6:649; Davis, *U. S. and Second Hague Peace Conference*, p. 16.

26. Burrage, *Maine*, pp. 170, 171; Edgar W. McInnis, *The Unguarded Frontier*, p. 161; George T. Curtis, *Life of Daniel Webster*, 2:139; Jesse S. Reeves, *American Diplomacy under Tyler and Polk*, p. 10; Bemis, *Adams and Foundations*, p. 478; James D. Richardson, ed., *A Compilation of the Messages and Papers of the Presidents*, 2:547; Merk, *Fruits of Propaganda*, pp. 49–50; Edward Everett [the acquaintance] to Daniel Webster, 21 Jan. 1842, WP (F16/21355).

27. Moore, *Intern. Arbit.*, 1:138; Burrage, *Maine*, pp. 195–96, 198.

28. Burrage, *Maine*, pp. 199, 201, 204, 206; Merk, *Fruits of Propaganda*, pp. 50–51; Moore, *Intern. Arbit.*, 1:138–39. Though the commissioners again changed their minds and accepted the president's proposal, the new agreement did not become public until long after the controversy had passed.

29. Burrage, *Maine*, pp. 210–11, 215; Merk, *Fruits of Propaganda*, p. 51.

30. Burrage, *Maine*, p. 218; Herbert C. F. Bell, *Lord Palmerston*, 1:245–46; Merk, *Fruits of Propaganda*, pp. 53–54; Henry S. Burrage, "The Attitude of Maine in the Northeastern Boundary Controversy," pp. 353–68; William F. Ganong, "A Monograph of the Evolution of the Boundaries of the Province of New Brunswick," pp. 139–449; John Forsyth [sec. of state] to Vaughan, 28 Apr. 1835, NTFL, GB (NA).

31. Perkins, *Castlereagh and Adams*, pp. 135–38, 150, 154–55, 282; Bourne, *Britain*, p. 7; Burt, *United States, Great Britain*, p. 373.

32. Jackson also acted in the interests of states' righters in Georgia during the Indian problems of the early 1830s.

Chapter 2

1. *North American Review* cited in Albert B. Corey, *The Crisis of 1830–1842 in Canadian-American Relations*, pp. 15, 16.

2. R. A. Mackay, "The Political Ideals of William Lyon Mackenzie," pp. 1–22; Augustus N. Hand, "Local Incidents of the Papineau Rebellion," pp. 376–87.

3. Edgar W. McInnis, *The Unguarded Frontier*, p. 150; Orrin E. Tiffany, *The Relations of the United States to the Canadian Rebellion of 1837–38*, pp. 1–147; Chester W. New, "The Rebellion of 1837 in Its Larger Setting," pp. 5–17; D. G. Creighton, "The Economic Background of the Rebellions of Eighteen Thirty-Seven," pp. 322–34; Wilson P. Shortridge, "The Canadian-American Frontier during the Rebellion of 1837–38," pp. 13–26; Corey, *Crisis*, pp. 34–35; R. S. Longley, "Emigration and the Crisis of 1837 in Upper Canada," pp. 29–40.

4. Albany *Argus*, 9 Dec. 1837; *Nat. Intell.*, 11 Apr., 5, 7 Dec. 1837.

5. James D. Richardson, ed., *A Compilation of the Messages and Papers of the Presidents*, 3:485–87; James C. Curtis, *The Fox at Bay*, p. 171; C. P. Stacey, ed., "A Private Report of General Winfield Scott on the Border Situation in 1839," pp. 407–14; John K. Mahon, *History of the Second Seminole War, 1835–1842*, pp. 225–26; CG, 25 Cong., 2 sess., pp. 77, 78, 83, 248–49.

6. Head to Brit. Min. Henry Fox, 23 Dec. 1837, CO 537/139 (PAC); Head to Fox, 8 Jan. 1838, FO 881/9 (PRO, confidential). Another confidential print, FO 881/8 (PRO), related to the Alexander McLeod case (see ch. 4), but could not be located. Depos. of John Elmsley, 27 Nov. 1841, Disp., GB (NA); Head to MacNab, 21 Dec. 1837, Sir Allan MacNab Papers; *Niles' Reg.* 53 (27 Jan. 1838): 337.

7. McCormack to MacNab, [?] 1838, MacNab Papers; Forsyth to Stevenson, 12 Mar. 1838, William R. Manning, ed., *Diplomatic Correspondence of the United States*, 3:48; Head to Fox, 8, 10 Jan. 1838, FO 881/9 and FO 5/328A (PRO); MacNab to H. W. Rogers, 29 Dec. 1837, FO 5/328A (PRO); Depos. of William Merritt, 19 Apr. 1838, encl. in Palm. to Stevenson, 27 Aug. 1841, Disp., GB (NA); Depos. of Wells, 30 Dec. 1837, U.S., Congress, *House Executive Documents*, 25 Cong., 2 sess., vol. 9, no. 302, p. 46. See my article, "The *Caroline* Affair," pp. 485–502.

8. Elmsley to MacNab, 29 Dec. 1837, Manning, ed., *Dipl. Corresp.*, 3:421; MacNab to Drew, 29 Dec. 1837, ibid.; MacNab to Rogers, 29 Dec. 1837, FO 881/9 (PRO).

9. Drew's Report to MacNab, 30 Dec. 1837, FO 881/9 (PRO). There was only one hotel in the area, and twenty-three New Yorkers had secured permission to sleep on board the *Caroline* with its officer and nine crew members.

10. Depos. of McCormack, 11 Dec. 1838, in Palm. to Stevenson, 27 Aug. 1841, Disp., GB (NA).

11. John C. Dent, *The Story of the Upper Canadian Rebellion*, 2:214; Drew to Sir John Barrow, 1 Jan. 1838, FO 5/328A (PRO); statement of claims for losses of *Caroline*, 30 Dec. 1837, *House Exec. Docs.*, 25 Cong., 2 sess., vol. 9, no. 302, p. 61; Milledge L. Bonham, Jr., "Alexander McLeod," pp. 189–217; Edwin C. Guillet, *The Lives and Times of the Patriots*, pp. 71–87. A participant recalled four years later that he was the last person to leave the boat before it was burned and that no one was left on board (W. Wright [?] to MacNab, 17 Nov. 1841, MacNab Papers).

12. Depos. of Samuel Longley, 30 Dec. 1837, *House Exec. Docs.*, 25 Cong., 2 sess., vol. 9, no. 302, p. 19; Appleby to N.Y. grand jury, ibid., p. 34; other depositions encl. in Palm. to Stevenson, 27 Aug. 1841, Disp., GB (NA); Forsyth to Stevenson, 12 Mar. 1838, Manning, ed., *Dipl. Corresp.*, 3:49. There is belief that Durfee was black, which would substantiate a witness's account that he had seen a black man lying on the wharf after the attack (Bonham, "McLeod," p. 190, n. 6).

13. *Niles' Reg.* 53 (20 Jan. 1838): 323; *Nat. Intell.*, 5 Jan. 1838; Rochester *Republican*, 2 Jan. 1838; Albany *Argus*, 3 Jan. 1838; Buffalo *Star Extra* (n.d.), quoted in N.Y. *Herald*, 4 Jan. 1838; N.Y. *Herald*, 4, 5, 6 Jan. 1838; William Kilbourn, *The Firebrand*, p. 202.

14. "Minutes of the Niagara Sessions relative to the murder on board the *Caroline*," 25 Jan. 1838, FO 881/9 (PRO); Rogers to Van Buren, 30 Dec. 1837, Manning, ed., *Dipl. Corresp.*, 3:456; poem in Robert H. Ferrell, *American Diplomacy*, p. 207; N.Y. *Herald*, 9, 16 Jan. 1838; *Nat. Intell.*, 19 Jan. 1838; Head to MacNab, 1 Jan. 1838, MacNab Papers.

15. Jacob Gould to Van Buren, 8 Jan. 1838, Martin Van Buren Papers; N.Y. *Herald*, 5, 8 Jan. 1838.

16. N.Y. *Herald*, 4, 5, 16 Jan. 1838.

17. Winfield Scott, *Memoirs of Lieut.-General Scott, LL.D.*, 1: 307.

18. Thomas Hart Benton, *Thirty Years' View*, 2:280–81, 293; MacNab to Col. J. M. Strachan, 1 Jan. 1838, FO 881/9 (PRO); CG, 25 Cong., 2 sess., pp. 76–78, 82–83, 87, 248–49.

19. Forsyth to Fox, 5 Jan. 1838, NTFL, GB (NA).

20. Fox to Forsyth, 6 Feb. 1838, NFBL (NA); Law officers' opinion, 21 Feb. 1838, in FO 881/9 (PRO); Fox to Palm., 25 Feb. 1838, 26 Jan. 1841, FO 5/322 and FO 115/69 (PRO); Forsyth to Fox, 13 Feb. 1838, NTFL, GB (NA); Forsyth to Stevenson, 12 Mar. 1838, Manning, ed., *Dipl. Corresp.*, 3:50–51; Palm. to Stevenson, 6 June 1838, ibid., p. 469; Aberdeen to Fox, 18 Apr. 1842, ibid., vol. 79; C. A. Nayerman [?] to MacNab, 31 Dec. 1837, MacNab Papers.

21. Stevenson to Palm., 22 May 1838, Manning, ed., *Dipl. Corresp.*, 3:449–56.

22. Lord Glenelg to Palm., [June?] 1838, CO 537/139 (PAC); Sir George Arthur to Glenelg, 17 Dec. 1838, FO 5/339 (PRO); Head to MacNab, 1 Jan. 1838, MacNab Papers. Palmerston had instructed Fox to say that "the attack upon the *Caroline* was the publick Act of persons in Her Majesty's Service, and, according to the usages of nations, that proceeding can only be the subject of negotiations between the two governments, and cannot be made the ground of proceedings against individuals" (Palm. to Fox, 6 Nov. 1838, FO 5/321 [PRO]). Fox to Forsyth, 6 Feb. 1838, 13 Dec. 1840, NFBL (NA); Fox to Palm., 10 Jan. 1841, FO 115/69 (PRO); Fox to Aberdeen, 20 Nov. 1841, ibid., vol. 76 (disp. 124); Palm. to Stevenson, 25 Feb. 1841, John Rutherfoord Papers; J. [James?] Hamilton to Stevenson, 3 Mar. 1841, ibid.; Stevenson to Rutherfoord, 3 Mar. 1841, ibid.; Stevenson to Palm., 31 Aug. 1841, ibid.

23. N.Y. *Herald*, 11 Jan. 1838; Scott, *Memoirs*, 1:308–17; Stacey, ed., "Private Report of Scott," p. 408; Curtis, *Fox at Bay*, pp. 174–75; Charles W. Elliott, *Winfield Scott, the Soldier and the Man*, pp. 338–57.

24. Buffalo resident quoted in Elliott, *Scott*, p. 340; ibid., pp. 338–57; Scott, *Memoirs*, 1:308–17.

25. McInnis, *Unguarded Frontier*, p. 154; Charles Grey to his father, 11 June 1838, William G. Ormsby, ed., *The Grey Journals and Letters*, p. 32; Sir John Colborne to Marquis of Normanby, 28 July 1839, HCSP 31 (1840): 92; Corey, *Crisis*, pp. 82–90; Melbourne to Queen Victoria, 22 Nov., 3 Dec. 1838, Arthur C. Benson and Viscount Esher, eds., *The Letters of Queen Victoria*, 1:133, 135; John G. Palfrey, "British American Politics," pp. 373–431.

26. Chester W. New, *Lord Durham*, pp. 378–80; C. P. Stacey, "The Myth of the Unguarded Frontier, 1815–1871," pp. 1–18. A recent study questions the effect of the Durham Report on British colonial policy: Ged Martin, *The Durham Report and British Policy*.

27. CG, 25 Cong., 2 sess., pp. 77, 78, 83, 248–49; Fox to Palm., 13, 21 Jan., 26 Feb. 1838, FO 5/322 (PRO); Richmond *Enq.*, 13 Jan. 1838; Wash. *Globe*, 6 Jan. 1838; *Nat. Intell.*, 19 Jan. 1838; Palm. to Fox, 13 Jan., 10 Mar. 1838, Lord Palmerston's

Letter-Books, vol. 79; Palm. to Fox, 13 Jan. 1838, FO 5/321 (PRO); John C. Fitzpatrick, ed., *The Autobiography of Martin Van Buren*, 2:466; Kenneth Bourne, *Britain and the Balance of Power in North America, 1815–1908*, pp. 76–79.

Chapter 3

1. Thomas LeDuc, "The Maine Frontier and the Northeastern Boundary Controversy," pp. 30–41; *Hansard's Parliamentary Debates*, 3d ser., 38 (24 Apr. 1837): 251.

2. Stevenson to Forsyth, 22 Feb. 1837, William R. Manning, ed., *Diplomatic Correspondence of the United States*, 3:382; *Parl. Debates* 38 (24 Apr. 1837): 251; Fox to Palm., 7 Mar. 1839, *HCSP* 32 (1840): 21; Palm. to Stevenson, 3 Apr. 1839, ibid., p. 65; Fox to Palm., 23 Feb. 1839, FO 115/69 (PRO).

3. Robert Dunlap [gov. of Maine] to Forsyth, 3 July 1837, Manning, ed., *Dipl. Corresp.*, 3: 29, n. 3; MacLauchlan to Sir John Harvey [lt. gov. of New Brunswick], 10 June 1837, ibid., pp. 27–28, n. 3; Harvey to Dunlap, 12 June 1837, ibid., p. 28, n. 3; Charles Peters [New Brunswick dist. atty.] to Harvey, 5 June 1837, *HCSP* 39 (1837–38): 57; New Brunswick solicitor gen. to Harvey, 5 Sept. 1837, ibid., p. 68.

4. Dunlap to Harvey, 26 June 1837, *HCSP* 39 (1837–38): 60; Dunlap to Forsyth, 3 July 1837, Manning, ed., *Dipl. Corresp.*, 3: 29, n. 3; Forsyth to Stevenson, 12 July 1837, ibid., pp. 27–30; Stevenson to Palm., 10 Aug., 18 Nov. 1837, ibid., pp. 398–99, 403; Stevenson to Forsyth, 6, 26 Mar. 1838, ibid., pp. 427, 435; Palm. to Stevenson, 16 Apr. 1838, ibid., pp. 438–39; Harvey to Fox, 29 Aug. 1837, *BFSP* 27 (1838–39): 945; Henry S. Burrage, *Maine in the Northeastern Boundary Controversy*, pp. 225, 228–29; Palm. to Fox, 19 Nov. 1837, Lord Palmerston Papers, GC/FO/166/1–3, by permission of the Trustees of the Broadlands Archives.

5. Stevenson to Forsyth, 4, 20 May 1837, Manning, ed., *Dipl. Corresp.*, 3: 393, 394–95; Palm. to Fox, 19 Nov. 1837, Palmerston Papers, GC/FO/166/1–3.

6. Fox to Forsyth, 10 Jan. 1838, Manning, ed., *Dipl. Corresp.*, 3: 412–14; Forsyth to Fox, 7 Feb. 1838, NTFL, GB (NA); Alvin L. Duckett, *John Forsyth, Political Tactician*, pp. 204–5.

7. Kent's message to assembly, 14 Mar. 1838, HCSP 32 (1840): 16; Burrage, *Maine*, pp. 228, 248–58; Forsyth to Fox, 27 Apr. 1838, NTFL, GB (NA); Kent to Van Buren, 28 Apr. [28 Mar.?] 1838, *BFSP* 27 (1838–39): 825; James D. Richardson, ed., *A Compilation of the Messages and Papers of the Presidents*, 3: 474–75.

8. Report to Maine's land agent, 7 May 1838, *HCSP* 32 (1840): 49–50; Burrage, *Maine*, pp. 258–62; Elijah Hamlin [land agent] to Fairfield and council, 22 Jan. 1839, ibid., pp. 132–34; Kent's message to assembly, 2 Jan. 1839, William S. Jenkins, ed., *Records of the States of the United States, 1836–41. Maine: Legislative Records, Journal of the State of Maine, Appendix* (joint meeting of House and Senate), 19 Legis., pp. 1–33; Fairfield's message to assembly, 4 Jan. 1839, ibid., pp. 35–53; Fairfield's confidential message to assembly, 23 Jan. 1839, ibid., pp. 56–58. Maine elected its governors for one-year terms. Fairfield won in 1838, 1839, 1841, and 1842.

9. Harvey to Fox, 13 Feb. 1839, FO 5/331 (PRO); Procl. by Harvey, 13 Feb. 1839, ibid.; MacLauchlan to Harvey, 17 Jan. 1839, N.B., Disp. (PAC); Burrage, *Maine*, pp. 259–60; Bangor *Whig* (n.d.) cited in David Lowenthal, "The Maine Press and the Aroostook War," pp. 315–36; John F. Sprague, "The North Eastern Boundary Controversy and the Aroostook War," pp. 216–81.

10. Harvey to Fairfield, 13 Feb. 1839, *HCSP* 32 (1840): 38; Sprague, "North Eastern Boundary," p. 274; Bangor *Whig*, 17 Feb. 1839, cited in ibid., n.*; Portland *Adv.* (n.d.) [Democratic] quoted in Augusta *J.*, 9 Apr. 1839 [Democratic]; Burrage, *Maine*, pp. 260–63; Jarvis to Harvey, 19 Feb. 1839, N.B., Disp. (PAC).

11. Fairfield's special message to house, 15 Feb. 1839, Jenkins, ed.,

Records . . . *Maine: J. of Sen., Append.,* 19 Legis., pp. 61–63; Fairfield's message to assembly, 18 Feb. 1839, ibid., pp. 63–67; N.Y. *Herald,* 20 Feb. 1839; Fairfield to Everett, 18 Feb. 1839, Jenkins, ed., *Records . . . Maine: Executive Records,* pp. 104–5; Fairfield to Van Buren, 18, 19 Feb. 1839, ibid., pp. 115–19; Fairfield to Harvey, 19 Feb. 1839, ibid., pp. 106–10. Both houses unanimously moved for the military defense of the state. Jenkins, ed., *Records . . . Maine: J. of Lower House,* 19 Legis., p. 265 (18 Feb. 1839); ibid., *J. of Sen.,* 19 Legis., pp. 273–74 (19 Feb. 1839). Harvey's proclamation charged law officers to "adopt all necessary measures" in resisting invasion (FO 5/331 [PRO]). For the long roster of men called to military duty, see *Aroostook War.*

12. New Brunswick *Royal Gazette,* 6 Mar. 1839; St. John *Observer,* 19 Feb. 1839, cited in *Gleaner* (Miramichi, N. B.), 26 Feb. 1839; St. John *Herald,* 13 Mar. 1839, cited in *Gleaner,* 19 Mar. 1839; Col. A. Maxwell's address to New Brunswick militia, cited in *Gleaner,* 5 Mar. 1839; Fredericton *Sent.,* 16 Feb. 1839, quoted in *Gleaner,* 26 Feb. 1839; London *Times,* 20 Mar. 1839; London *Morning Herald,* 21 Mar. 1839, cited in *Gleaner,* 30 Apr. 1839; Depos. of Nicholas Cunliffe, 16 Feb. 1839, N.B., Disp. (PAC).

13. Sir John Colborne, [lt. gov. of Lower Canada] to Harvey, 18, 22 Feb. 1839, N.B., Disp. (PAC); Sir Colin Campbell, [lt. gov. of Nova Scotia] to Harvey, 27 Feb. 1839, ibid.; Maxwell to Harvey, 7 Mar. 1839, ibid.; MacLauchlan to Harvey, 27 Feb. 1839, ibid.; Joseph Sherwood [British consulate at Portland] to Harvey, 18, 26 Feb., 2 Mar. 1839, ibid.; Colborne to Campbell, 27 Feb. 1839, FO 5/331 (PRO); Colborne to Harvey, 27 Feb. 1839, ibid.; Sprague, "North Eastern Boundary," pp. 275–76; Fairfield to Van Buren, 19 Feb. 1839, Jenkins, ed., *Records . . . Maine: Exec. Records,* pp. 118–19; Fairfield to Harvey, 21 Feb. 1839, ibid., pp. 114–15; Albert B. Corey, *The Crisis of 1830–1842 in Canadian-American Relations,* pp. 114–15; Harvey to Fairfield, 18 Feb. 1839, *HCSP* 32 (1840): 43; Fairfield's message to house, 21 Feb. 1839, ibid., p. 42; Harvey to Glenelg, 24 Feb. 1839, ibid., p. 161. Under a "parole of honor," the accused is released on his word that he will appear on his trial date.

14. Pittsfield *Sun* (Mass.), 28 Mar. 1839; letter of 26 Feb. 1839, cited in Lowenthal, "Maine Press," p. 321; Leonard B. Chapman, ed., "Rev. Caleb Bradley on the Madawaska War," pp. 418–25.

15. Bangor *Whig* (n.d.) cited in Sprague, "North Eastern Boundary," p. 275; Belfast *Repub.* (n.d.) cited in Lowenthal, "Maine Press," p. 323; *Southwick's Family Paper,* 17 Mar. 1839, cited in ibid., p. 329; Augusta *J.,* 19, 26 Feb. 1839; Fairfield's speech in ibid., 5 Mar. 1839; Augusta *Age* (n.d.) cited in ibid.; Northampton *Cour.,* 27 Feb. 1839; "Maine Battle Song" in "Documentary History of the North Eastern Boundary Controversy," pp. 282–327; Pittsfield *Sun,* 7, 28 Mar. 1839. See my article, "Anglophobia and the Aroostook War," pp. 519–39.

16. *CG,* 25 Cong., 3 sess., pp. 216–19; J. C. Bennett of Ill. militia to Fairfield, [?] 1839, Arthur G. Staples, ed., *The Letters of John Fairfield,* p. 253; S. T. Carr of N.Y. to Fairfield, [?] 1839, ibid.

17. Boston *Adv.,* 21 Feb. 1839; N.Y. *Albion,* 23 Feb. 1839; N.Y. *Comm. Adv.,* 21, 22 Feb. 1839, all cited in New Brunswick *Royal Gazette,* 6 Mar. 1839. N. Y. *Gazette,* 5 Mar. 1839, cited in New Brunswick *Royal Gazette,* 27 Mar. 1839; Richmond *Enq.,* 2 Mar. 1839; Northampton *Cour.,* 20 Mar. 1839; Boston *Adv.* (n.d.) cited in *Gleaner,* 26 Mar. 1839; Boston *Patriot,* 16 Mar. 1839, cited in Lowenthal, "Maine Press," p. 329; *Nat. Intell.,* 24 Feb. 1839; N.Y. *Herald,* 25 Feb., 1 Mar. 1839.

18. Lowenthal, "Maine Press," pp. 327ff.; Fairfield to Van Buren, 22 Feb. 1839, Martin Van Buren Papers; James C. Curtis, *The Fox at Bay,* pp. 184–85; Forsyth to Fox, 25 Feb. 1839, NTFL, GB (NA); Forsyth to Fairfield, 26 Feb. 1839, *HCSP* 32 (1840): 41; Richardson, ed., *Messages and Papers,* 3: 517, 518. The gubernatorial election of 1840 in Maine reveals how evenly balanced party politics was. The Whig, Edward Kent, received 45,574 votes, while Fairfield, the Democratic incumbent, got 45,507.

19. Burrage, *Maine,* pp. 265–66; *CG, Append.,* 25 Cong., 3 sess., pp. 211, 213, 260,

312, 315, 316; CG., 25 Cong., 3 sess., pp. 229, 231, 233, 239, 242; Claude M. Fuess, *Daniel Webster*, 2:72; Fox to Palm., 7 Mar., 10 Aug. 1839, FO 115/69 (PRO).

20. *CG*, 25 Cong., 3 sess., pp. 229, 232.

21. Burrage, *Maine*, pp. 266–67; Fox to Palm., 23 Feb., 7 Mar. 1839, FO 115/69 (PRO); Palm. to Fox, 1 May 1839, *HCSP* 32 (1840): 80.

22. *CG*, 25 Cong., 3 sess., pp. 232, 238, 242; Poinsett quoted in Fuess, *Webster*, 2:72; ibid., p. 73; "Memorandum on northeastern boundary, 9 Mar. 1839," by Webster, in WP (F12/15393). On Van Buren's political decision not to send a special minister to England, see Reuel Williams et al. to Van Buren, 9, 18 Mar. 1839, Van Buren Papers; George Evans of Maine to Van Buren, 20 Mar. 1839, ibid.; Fairfield to Van Buren, 22 Mar. 1839, ibid.; Isaac Hill on Webster for English mission, 21 Mar. 1839, ibid.; memo by Van Buren, [?] Mar. 1839, ibid.; H. J. Anderson to Van Buren, 6 Apr. 1839, ibid.; Fox to Palm., 7 Mar., 16 May 1839, FO 115/69 (PRO).

23. Richardson, ed., *Messages and Papers*, 3:526, 527; memo by Fox and Forsyth, 27 Feb. 1839, in Dept. of State, folder marked "NE. Bdry. Negot.," E89 (NA); Fox to Harvey, 27 Feb. 1839, FO 5/331 (PRO); Palm. to Fox, 6 Apr. 1839, Palmerston Papers, GC/FO/168/1–2; Fox to Palm., 7 Mar. 1839, FO 115/69 (PRO); Lowenthal, "Maine Press," p. 329.

24. Poinsett to Scott, 28 Feb. 1839, Manning, ed., *Dipl. Corresp.*, 3:108; Winfield Scott, *Memoirs of Lieut.-General Scott, LL.D.*, 2: 333–34.

25. Maxwell to Harvey, 26 Feb. 1839, N.B., Disp. (PAC); "Statement of Melvin House" [deserter from Maine's militia and native of New Brunswick], [1839], ibid.; Lowenthal, "Maine Press," pp. 323, 333.

26. Scott, *Memoirs*, 2:334, 336–40; Maine senator's speech quoted in Charles W. Elliott, *Winfield Scott, the Soldier and the Man*, p. 360.

27. Burrage, *Maine*, pp. 271–72. Fairfield was confident there would be no war (Fairfield to wife Anna, 15 Mar. 1839, Staples, ed., *Letters*, p. 271).

28. Curtis, *Fox at Bay*, p. 186; Burrage, *Maine*, pp. 273–74; Scott, *Memoirs*, 2:336–45; Elliott, *Scott*, pp. 362–65. One of Harvey's emissaries to Augusta, John Caldwell, noted Fairfield's desire for peace (Caldwell to Harvey, 12, 18 Mar. 1839, N.B., Disp. [PAC]).

29. Scott to Harvey, 21 Mar. 1839, *HCSP* 32 (1840): 164; "Doc. Hist.," pp. 322–23; Fairfield's message to assembly, 12 Mar. 1839, Jenkins, ed., *Records . . . Maine: J. of Sen., Append.*, 19 Legis., pp. 70–86; Harvey to Fox, 6 Mar. 1839, FO 5/331 (PRO); Marcus T. Wright, *General Scott*, pp. 143–44. Maxwell complained in late February that he still had not received arms and ammunition (Maxwell to Harvey, 26 Feb. 1839, N.B., Disp. [PAC]).

30. Francis P. Wayland, *Andrew Stevenson*, p. 144; Fox to Palm., 7 Mar., 20 Apr., 10 Aug., 28 Sept. 1839, FO 115/69 (PRO); Richard Rush to Van Buren, 14 Apr. 1840, Van Buren Papers; Benjamin Rush [sec. of U.S. legation in London] to Forsyth, 16 Oct. 1839, Manning, ed., *Dipl. Corresp.*, 3:540–41; Herbert C. F. Bell, *Lord Palmerston*, 1:251, 252.

31. Forsyth to Fox, 29 July, 24 Dec. 1839, 25 Mar. 1840, NTFL, GB (NA); Aaron Vail [acting sec. of state] to Fox, 19 Aug. 1839, ibid.; Jenkins, ed., *Records . . . Maine: J. of Sen.*, 19 Legis., pp. 433–36 (21 Mar. 1839); Kenneth Bourne, *Britain and the Balance of Power in North America, 1815–1908*, pp. 84 (n. 2), 85; Bell, *Palm.*, 1:251; Harvey memo for warden of disp. territ., 30 Aug. 1839, *HCSP* 32 (1840): 95; Palm. to Fox, 14 Oct. 1839, ibid., p. 94; Fairfield to Vail, 21 Nov. 1839, ibid., pp. 141–43; instructions to Brit. survey team in Palm. to Fox, 9 July 1839, ibid., p. 85; Brit. surveyors' report, 16 Apr. 1840, ibid., pp. 56–57; Palm. to Melbourne, 22 Apr. 1840, ibid., 61 (1843): 18; Fox to Forsyth, 26 Jan., 7 Mar., 28 July 1840, Manning, ed., *Dipl. Corresp.*, 3:553–55, 559–61, 582–87; Fox to Vail, 30 July 1839, ibid., pp. 519–20; James Stephen to Lord Teveson, 30 Aug. 1841, FO 5/374 (PRO); Williams, C. S. Daveis, Fairfield, and Kent to

Forsyth, 19 June 1839, in Dept. of State, folder marked "NE Bdry. Negot.," E89 (NA); Forsyth to Van Buren, 20 June 1839, ibid.; Duckett, *Forsyth*, p. 205; Fox to Palm., 20 Apr., 28 Sept. 1839, FO 115/69 (PRO); Fairfield to Van Buren, 23 Dec. 1839, Jenkins, ed., *Records . . . Maine: Exec. Records*, pp. 141–43.

32. MacLauchlan to officer in charge of Amer. armed posse on Fish River, 21 Apr. 1839, N.B., Disp. (PAC); Lord Sydenham [gov. gen. of Canada] to Russell, 13 Mar., 24 Nov., 20 Dec. 1840, Paul Knaplund, ed., *Letters from Lord Sydenham, Governor-General of Canada, 1839–1841, to Lord John Russell*, pp. 52–53, 102, 108; Palm. to Russell, 19 Jan. 1841, Lord John Russell Papers. Sir William Colebrooke replaced Harvey.

Chapter 4

1. N.Y. *Herald*, 23 Mar. 1841; McLeod's memorial of 2 May 1842 to Sir Charles Bagot [gov. of Upper Canada], and his open letter of 4 Jan. 1845 to Sir Allan MacNab, both cited in Alastair Watt, "The Case of Alexander McLeod," pp. 145–67.

2. Watt, "McLeod," p. 164, n. 1; Fox to Forsyth, 13 Dec. 1840, NFBL (NA); account of Manchester incident in McLeod's letter reprinted in London *Examiner*, 30 Oct. 1841.

3. Watt, "McLeod," p. 153; Fox to Forsyth, 13 Dec. 1840, NFBL (NA); Fox to Palm., 27 Dec. 1840, 10, 26 Jan. 1841, FO 115/69 (PRO).

4. Bradley to Forsyth, 15 Dec. 1840, ML (NA); Forsyth to Bradley, 30 Dec. 1840, DL (NA); Forsyth to Fox, 26 Dec. 1840, NTFL, GB (NA).

5. CG, 26 Cong., 2 sess., pp. 74, 80–81; Thomas Hart Benton, *Thirty Years' View*, 2:294; Fox to Palm., 27 Dec. 1840, 10 Jan. 1841, FO 115/69 (PRO).

6. Phil. *Public Ledger and Daily Transcript*, 21 Dec. 1840.

7. Russell to Stevenson, 2 Feb. 1841, cited in Albert B. Corey, *The Crisis of 1830–1842 in Canadian-American Relations*, p. 137; *Hansard's Parliamentary Debates*, 3d ser., 66 (8 Feb. 1841): 364–66; Palm. to Fox, 19 Jan. 1841, Lord Palmerston's Letter-Books, vol. 79; Henry Goulburn to John Croker, 8 Feb. 1841, John Croker Papers (Duke U.); Stevenson to Van Buren, 9 Feb. 1841, Martin Van Buren Papers; Stevenson to Webster, 3 Mar. 1841, John Rutherfoord Papers; Stevenson to Rutherfoord, 3 Mar. 1841, ibid.; Palm. to Fox, 9 Feb. 1841, FO 5/358 (PRO); Palm. to Fox, 9 Feb. 1841, Lord Palmerston Papers, GC/FO/170, by permission of the Trustees of the Broadlands Archives; Fox to Palm., 15 Mar. 1841, FO 115/69 (PRO).

8. James Hudson to John Backhouse, 29 Mar. 1841, John Backhouse Papers.

9. N.Y. *Herald*, 4, 10 Feb. 1841; Marcus T. C. Gould, *Gould's Stenographic Reporter*, 2:17–18 (hereafter cited as Gould).

10. George E. Baker, ed., *The Works of William H. Seward*, 2:552–53.

11. U.S., Congress, *House Reports*, 26 Cong., 2 sess., no. 162, pp. 2–3, 5; CG, 26 Cong., 2 sess., pp. 171–75; CG, *Append.*, 26 Cong., 2 sess., pp. 374–75; Lord Sydenham to Russell, 10 Apr. 1841, Paul Knaplund, ed., *Letters from Lord Sydenham, Governor-General of Canada, 1839–1841, to Lord John Russell*, p. 128; Fox to Palm., 7 Feb. 1841, FO 115/69 (PRO).

12. Webster's 1846 speech before Congress in James M. McIntyre, ed., *The Writings and Speeches of Daniel Webster*, 9:123; Webster to Crittenden, 15 Mar. 1841, ibid., 11:264–66; Seward's message to N.Y. legis., 4 Jan. 1842, Baker, ed., *Works of Seward*, 2:302; Harrison to Crittenden, 15 Mar. 1841, DL (NA). A nolle prosequi is a formal notice by the prosecutor that prosecution in a criminal case will be ended.

13. Palm. to Queen Victoria, 15 June 1839, quoted in Herbert C. F. Bell, *Lord Palmerston*, 1:247; Webster to Thomas Ward of Baring Bros. of London, 29 Feb. 1840, Baring Papers (PAC); Webster to Joshua Bates of Baring Bros., 26 Mar. 1840, ibid.; Fox to Palm., 7 Mar. 1841, FO 115/69 (PRO); Ralph W. Hidy, *The House of Baring in American Trade and Finance*, pp. 100, 283–84, 293, 316, 320–21, 327.

14. London *Times, Morning Chronicle,* and *Morning Herald* cited in Corey, *Crisis,* pp. 138–39. For Peel's speech, see Russell to Queen Victoria, 6 Mar. 1841, Arthur C. Benson and Viscount Esher, eds., *The Letters of Queen Victoria,* 1:260. John Powell to Hull, 11 Mar. 1841, U.S., Congress, *Senate Documents,* 27 Cong., 1 sess., no. 33, pp. 4–5; Cass to Webster, 5 Mar. 1841, quoted in George T. Curtis, *Life of Daniel Webster,* 2:62; E. Vernon Harcourt [friend] to Webster, 12 Mar. 1841, cited in ibid., n. 1; Joseph H. Parks, *John Bell of Tennessee,* p. 190; Stevenson to Hull, 8, 12 Mar. 1841, Disp., GB (NA); Stevenson to Webster, 9, 18 Mar., 7 Apr. 1841, ibid.

15. Webster to Spencer, 11 Mar. 1841, DL (NA); Webster's 1846 speech before Congress in McIntyre, ed., *Writings and Speeches of Webster,* 9:134. Webster carefully worded his statements, however, and since the British government actually paid Spencer's fee, one could interpret the secretary's denial as truthful. Webster's words were: "The government of the United States had no more to do than the government of France with the employment of Mr. Spencer for the defence of McLeod. They never interfered with his appointment in the slightest degree" (ibid.). Fox to Palm., 12 Mar., 28 Apr., 12 May 1841, FO 115/69 (PRO); Spencer to Hiram Gardner [one of McLeod's defense attorneys], 31 Jan. 1842, ibid., vol. 79; Gardner to W. H. Draper [atty. gen., Upper Canada], 21 Feb. 1842, ibid.; Bagot to Lord Stanley, 16 Mar. 1842, ibid.; C. E. Trevelyan to Viscount Canning, 4 May 1842, ibid.; Aberdeen to Fox, 18 May 1842, ibid.; Fox to Aberdeen, 28 June 1842, ibid.

16. Seward to Webster, 22 Mar. 1841, Baker, ed., *Works of Seward,* 2:558; Albert D. Kirwan, *John J. Crittenden,* p. 145; Glyndon G. Van Deusen, *William Henry Seward,* p. 77; Charles W. Elliott, *Winfield Scott, the Soldier and the Man,* p. 398; Samuel F. Bemis, ed., *American Secretaries of State and Their Diplomacy,* 5:16; Seward to Richard Blatchford, 23 Mar. 1846, WP (F20/26798).

17. McIntyre, ed., *Writings and Speeches of Webster,* 9:133.

18. Bell to Scott, 12 Mar. 1841, *Military Book No. 23, War Office,* No. 210, p. 266 (NA); Robert Anderson to Bell, 17 Mar. 1841, Dept. of War (NA); Anderson to Lt. Col. J. B. Crane, 17 Mar. 1841, ibid.; Scott to Bell, 26 Mar., 6 Apr. 1841, ibid.; Sec. of War Spencer to Pres. John Tyler, 29 Apr. 1842, Dept. of War (NA).

19. Tyler's Inaug. Address, 9 Apr. 1841, James D. Richardson, ed., *A Compilation of the Messages and Papers of the Presidents,* 4:37; Tyler to Judge N. Beverley Tucker, 25 Apr. 1841, John Tyler Papers; Tyler to Alexander Gardiner, 6 May 1845, ibid.; Webster to Fox, 24 Apr. 1841, McIntyre, ed., *Writings and Speeches of Webster,* 11:251–52; Fox to Palm., 13 Sept. 1841, FO 115/76 (PRO); Fox to Aberdeen, 26 Oct., 20 Nov. 1841, ibid.

20. Claude M. Fuess, *Daniel Webster,* 2: 96–100; Oliver P. Chitwood, *John Tyler,* pp. 272–73, 278; Robert F. Dalzell, Jr., *Daniel Webster and the Trial of American Nationalism, 1843–1852,* pp. 37–39, 85.

21. See note 48 for evidence that the British paid Spencer's $5,000 fee.

22. Seward to Lovell Mickles, 23 Aug. 1841, Baker, ed., *Works of Seward,* 3:452; Seward to Tyler, 4, 10, 20 May 1841, ibid., pp. 558, 562–66, and 2:560; Tyler to Seward, 7, 25 May 1841, ML (NA); Webster to Spencer, 19 Apr. 1841, DL (NA); Tyler to Seward, 15 May 1841, Lyon Gardiner Tyler, *The Letters and Times of the Tylers,* 2:208–9; Fox to Aberdeen, 23 Sept. 1841, FO 115/76 (PRO).

23. Seward to Crittenden, 31 May 1841, John J. Crittenden Papers; Seward to Thomas Ewing, 17 May 1841, Thomas Ewing Papers; Tyler to Seward, 25 May 1841, ML (NA); Van Deusen, *Seward,* pp. 77–78.

24. CG, 27 Cong., 1 sess., p. 115; *CG, Append.,* 27 Cong., 1 sess., pp. 77, 79.

25. CG, *Append.,* 27 Cong., 1 sess., pp. 15, 44–46, 66–69, 82–83; Benton, *Thirty Years' View,* 2:293.

26. *The People* v. *Alexander McLeod,* 6 May 1841, Nicholas Hill, Jr., *New York Common Law Reports, Vol. 15,* 1:164–84. Detailed account of prosecution and defense is in John L. Wendell, *Reports of Cases Argued and Determined in the Supreme Court of . . . New York, Vol. 25,* pp. 917–60.

27. N.Y. *Herald*, 13, 24 July 1841; Montreal *Cour.* (n.d.) cited in *Niles' Reg.* 60 (7 Aug. 1841): 368; Fox to Palm., 27 July 1841, cited in Watt, "McLeod," p. 155; London *Times*, 11, 18 Aug. 1841; Liverpool *Mail* (n.d.) cited in Corey, *Crisis*, p. 140; Stevenson to Webster, 18 Aug. 1841, Disp., GB (NA); Fox to Palm., 5, 8 Aug. 1841, FO 5/362 (PRO). Americans disagreeing with Cowen included Daniel Tallmadge of the Superior Court of New York City, Chancellor James Kent of New York, Roger Sherman of the Supreme Court of Connecticut, and Simon Greenleaf, professor of law at Harvard (Wendell, *Reports*, pp. 1205–18; Kent to Webster, 21 Dec. 1842, WP [F18/23932]).

28. Fox to Palm., 28 Aug. 1841, FO 5/362 (PRO); Samuel S. Nicholas [the Washington judge] to Crittenden, 13 June 1841, Crittenden Papers; Gardner and Alvin Bradley [McLeod's defense attorneys] to Draper, 19 July 1841, FO 5/374 (PRO); Sydenham to Fox, 3 Aug. 1841, ibid.; Webster to Spencer, 6 Aug. 1841, DL (NA); Webster to Fox, 20 Sept. 1841, NTFL, GB (NA).

29. Wellington to Peel, 17 May 1841, Sir Robert Peel Papers (BM, 40459); Sydenham to Russell, 10, 12 Apr. 1841, Knaplund, ed., *Letters from Lord Sydenham*, pp. 129, 133; Sydenham to Russell, 27 July 1841, Lord Russell Papers.

30. Russell to Palm., 22 Apr. 1841, Palmerston Papers, GC/RU/57; Stevenson to Webster, 18 Aug. 1841, Disp., GB (NA); Palm. to Fox, 29 June, 18 Aug. 1841, Palmerston's Letter-Books, vol. 79; Corey, *Crisis*, p. 139.

31. Fox to Webster, 5 Sept. 1841, NFBL (NA); Tyler to Webster, ca. 8 Sept. 1841, WP (F16/20183); N.Y. *Herald*, 17 Sept. 1841. For the Peel ministry's emphasis on French relations, see Wilbur D. Jones, *The American Problem in British Diplomacy, 1841–1861*, pp. 8, 18.

32. Everett to Webster, 30 Mar. 1842, WP (F17/22011); Aberdeen to Queen Victoria, 20 Oct. 1841, Lord Aberdeen Papers (BM, 43041); Queen Victoria to Aberdeen, 20 Oct. 1841, ibid.; Webster to Everett, 20 Nov. 1841, Dipl. Instr., GB (NA).

33. Fletcher Webster [acting sec. of state] to Fox, 28 Sept. 1841, NTFL, GB (NA); Fox to Fletcher Webster, 21 Oct. 1841, NFBL (NA); Fox to Daniel Webster, 26 Nov. 1841, ibid.; Daniel Webster to Fox, 27 Nov. 1841, NTFL, GB (NA); Wash. *Globe*, 29 Sept. 1841; Frederick W. Seward, ed., *William H. Seward*, 1:551, 556–57; Albert B. Corey, "Public Opinion and the McLeod Case," pp. 53–64; Wellington to Peel, 19 Oct. 1841, Peel Papers (BM, 40459); Peel to Stanley, 20 Oct. 1841, ibid. (40467); Peel to Wellington, 20 Oct. 1841, ibid. (40459); Aberdeen to Fox, 3 Nov. 1841, FO 5/358) (PRO).

34. Webster to Spencer, 24 Aug. 1841, DL (NA); Webster to Spencer, 9 Sept. 1841, WP (F16/20190); Seward, ed., *Seward*, 1:566; Seward to Webster, 3, 11, 16, 17, 21, 22 Sept. 1841, WP (F16/20103, 20205, 20268, 20281, 20334, 20346); Webster to Seward, 14 Sept. 1841, DL (NA); Seward to Webster, 23 Sept. 1841, Baker, ed., *Works of Seward*, 2:579–83; Seward to Oneida sheriff, 24 Sept. 1841, ibid., pp. 585–86; Seth Hawley to Seward, 17, 20 Sept. 1841, WP (F16/20381); Seward to Rev. Eliphalet Nott, 17 Sept. 1841, Baker, ed., *Works of Seward*, 3:453; Webster to Seward, 23 Sept. 1841, WP (F16/20353); Tyler to Webster, [?] 1841, WP (F16/02178); N.Y. *Herald*, 22 Sept. 1841; Procl. by Pres. Tyler, 25 Sept. 1841, Richardson, ed., *Messages and Papers*, 4:73; Wool to Scott, 24, 29 Sept. 1841, Dept. of War (NA); Scott to H. Underwood, 27 Sept. 1841, ibid.; Scott to Lt. Horace Brooks, 29 Sept. 1841, ibid.; Wool to Judge F. C. White, 30 Sept. 1841, ibid.; Wool to Brooks, 1 Oct. 1841, ibid.

35. Aberdeen to Fox, 14 Sept. 1841, FO 5/358 (PRO); Christopher Hughes to Webster, 18 Sept. 1841, WP (F16/20300); "McLeod Resolutions" to Aberdeen, 20 Aug. 1841, FO 5/374 (PRO); Aberdeen to Colonial Society, 31 Aug. 1841, ibid.; *Parl. Debates* 59 (5 Oct. 1841): 1129; Peel's Memo to Lords Aberdeen, Haddington, and Stanley, 17 Oct. 1841, Charles S. Parker, ed., *Sir Robert Peel, From His Private Papers*, 3:387–88; Peel to Wellington, 18 Oct. 1841, Peel Papers (BM, 40459); Peel to Stanley, 20 Sept. 1841, ibid. (40467).

36. Fox to Aberdeen, 30 Sept. 1841, cited in Watt, "McLeod," p. 157; Aberdeen to

Fox, 18 Nov. 1841, FO 5/358 (PRO); Peel to Queen Victoria, 28 Oct. 1841, Benson and Esher, eds., *Letters of Victoria*, 1:355–56; Fox to Aberdeen, 1, 12 Oct. 1841, FO 115/76 (PRO).

37. Spencer to Webster, 24, 27, 29 Sept., 1 Oct. 1841, WP (F16/20389, 20421, 20441, 20477).

38. For the most complete account of the trial, see *Gould*, vol. 2. See also N.Y. *Sun's* booklet, *Trial of Alexander M'Leod for the Murder of Amos Durfee and as an Accomplice in the Burning of the Steamer Caroline in the Niagara River, during the Canadian Rebellion[s] in 1837–8*, and *Niles' Reg.* 61 (16 Oct. 1841): 104–8, 120–25, and (23 Oct. 1841): 120–25.

39. *Gould*, 2:6, 11, 41, 145, 191.

40. N.Y. *Herald*, 13, 21 Sept. 1841; *Gould*, 2:11, 40–41, 66; N.Y. *Sun*, *Trial*, p. 3; Utica *Observer*, 11 May 1841, cited in Milledge L. Bonham, Jr., "Alexander McLeod," p. 201.

41. Prosecution's case in *Gould*, 2:21–82.

42. Ibid., p. 77; defense argument in ibid., pp. 85–205, 232–84.

43. Ibid., p. 233; N.Y. *Sun*, *Trial*, p. 26.

44. Seward to Moulton, 24 Sept. 1841, Baker, ed., *Works of Seward*, 2:585–86; Wool to Scott, 11, 18 Oct. 1841, Dept. of War (NA); Bonham, "McLeod," p. 215.

45. Fox to Sir Richard Jackson [acting lt. gov. of Upper Canada], 11, 25 Oct. 1841, cited in Watt, "McLeod," p. 158; Fox to Palm., 28 Mar. 1841, FO 115/69 (PRO); Fox to Aberdeen, 28 Sept., 28 Oct. 1841, ibid., vol. 76; Seward's message to N.Y. assembly, 10 May 1841, in Baker, ed., *Works of Seward*, 2:407; Charles Z. Lincoln, ed., *Messages from the Governors . . .*, 3:932–33.

46. Van Deusen, *Seward*, p. 78.

47. Tyler's message to Congress, 7 Dec. 1841, Richardson, ed., *Messages and Papers*, 4:75; Everett to Webster, 15 Dec. 1841, WP (F16/20851); Berrien to Webster, 14 Jan. 1842, WP (F16/21309); *U.S. Statutes at Large*, 5:539; Fox to Aberdeen, 28 Nov. 1841, FO 115/76 (PRO).

48. CG, 29 Cong., 1 sess., pp. 344, 419, 422. Seward told Ingersoll, as he had told "a thousand others," that the Tyler administration tried to prevent McLeod's trial. He added, however, that he had not expected Ingersoll to use this knowledge in any way (Seward to Blatchford, 23 Mar. 1846, WP [F20/26798]). McIntyre, ed., *Writings and Speeches of Webster*, 9:130–31; Watt, "McLeod," p. 158. The following letters show that the British hired Spencer for $5,000: Aberdeen to Fox, 18 May 1842, Aberdeen Papers (BM, 43154); Fox to Aberdeen, 28 June 1842, FO 115/79 (PRO). Sydenham said the money came from the "Military Chest" of Canada (Sydenham to Russell, 25 May 1841, Knaplund, ed., *Letters from Lord Sydenham*, p. 138). See also Frederick Merk, *Fruits of Propaganda in the Tyler Administration*, pp. 14–15; "Statements of Thomas Butler King & Robert Cumming Schenck re Ingersoll charges," Apr. 1846, WP (F20/26877); Webster to Edward Curtis, 15 Apr. 1846, WP (F20/26842).

49. Aberdeen to Fox, 18 Nov. 1841, FO 5/358 (PRO); Everett to Webster, 15 Dec. 1841, WP (F16/20851); Watt, "McLeod," pp. 160–61; Edwin C. Guillet, *The Lives and Times of the Patriots*, p. 189, n. 13; "Draft Note in Colonial Office" by Aberdeen, 2 June 1842, FO 5/388 (PRO); John B. Moore, *History and Digest of the International Arbitrations, to Which the United States Has Been a Party*, 1:391–425, and 3:2419–28; William M. Malloy et al., eds., *Treaties, Conventions, International Acts, Protocols, and Agreements Between the United States and Other Powers, 1776–1937*, 1:664–68; John B. Moore, *A Digest of International Law*, 6:1014.

Chapter 5

1. Sec. of State Adams to Gallatin and Richard Rush, 2 Nov. 1818, ASPFR, 5:73; Adams to Stratford Canning, 29 June 1822, Charles F. Adams, ed., *Memoirs of John*

Quincy Adams, Comprising Portions of His Diary from 1795 to 1848, 6:37.

2. Adams, ed., *Memoirs of JQA*, 3:557.

3. Bradford Perkins, *Castlereagh and Adams*, pp. 275, 276; Philip D. Curtin, *The Atlantic Slave Trade*, p. 250.

4. *U.S. Statutes at Large*, 3:532–34; Adams to Stratford Canning, 30 Dec. 1820, *ASPFR*, 5:76, 90–93, 140–41; Adams to Rush, 24 June 1823, ibid., pp. 333–35; Adams to Stratford Canning, 15 Aug. 1821, Worthington C. Ford, ed., *Writings of John Quincy Adams*, 7:171.

5. Adams, ed., *Memoirs of JQA*, 6:328.

6. Alvin L. Duckett, *John Forsyth, Political Tactician*, pp. 182–83, 192. Forsyth repeated these arguments six years later (Forsyth to Fox, 12 Feb. 1840, NTFL, GB [NA]).

7. Hugh G. Soulsby, *The Right of Search and the Slave Trade in Anglo-American Relations, 1814–1862*, pp. 42, 49.

8. Paine-Tucker agreement encl. in Fox to Forsyth, 15 Aug. 1840, NFBL (NA). Stevenson to Webster, 3 Mar. 1841, John Rutherfoord Papers; *BFSP* 30 (1841–42): 1138, 1145; Palm. to Stevenson, 5 Aug. 1841, Disp., GB (NA); Everett to Aberdeen, 21 Feb. 1842, ibid. Fox sent Forsyth a list of forty-two slave ships flying the American flag which had left Havana for Africa in 1838–39 (Fox to Forsyth, 19 Aug. 1840, NFBL [NA]).

9. Stevenson to Webster, 18 May 1841, Disp., GB (NA); Palm. to Stevenson, 27 Aug. 1841, ibid.; Stevenson to Palm., 16 Apr. 1841, ibid.; Stevenson to Aberdeen, 10 Sept., 21 Oct. 1841, ibid.

10. Peel to Aberdeen, 25 Oct. 1841, Sir Robert Peel Papers (BM, 40453); Aberdeen to Stevenson, 13 Oct. 1841, Disp., GB (NA).

11. Croker to Peel, 26 Oct. 1841, Lord Aberdeen Papers (BM, 43061); Peel to Croker, 29 Oct. 1841, ibid.; Peel to Aberdeen, 1 Nov. 1841, ibid.

12. Wilbur D. Jones, *Lord Aberdeen and the Americas*, p. 15; Aberdeen to Everett, 20, 31 Dec. 1841, Disp., GB (NA); Everett to Webster, 28 Dec. 1841, ibid.; Everett to Aberdeen, 27 Dec. 1841, ibid.

13. Everett to Webster, 3 Jan. 1842, WP (F16/20984); Everett to Webster, 1 Mar. 1842, Disp., GB (NA).

14. Cass to François P. G. Guizot [French for. min.], 13 Feb. 1842, Disp., France (NA); Cass to Webster, 15, 25 Feb., 29 Apr., 11 Dec. 1842, 7 Mar. 1843, ibid.; Cass to Webster, 14 Mar. 1842, Lewis Cass Papers; Varina (Howell) Davis, *Jefferson Davis, Ex-President of the Confederate States of America*, 1:277; Brit. Consul William Peter [observer] to Aberdeen, 20 Apr. 1842, Aberdeen Papers (BM, 43123, private).

15. Cass's pamphlet is printed in William T. Young, *Sketch of the Life and Public Services of General Lewis Cass*, pp. 136–55. The Nashville *Republican Banner* of 30 Nov. 1842 praised Cass's actions in behalf of the South.

16. Cass to Guizot, 13 Feb. 1842, Disp., France (NA).

17. Cass to Webster, 13, 15, 20, 22, 24, 25 Feb., 29, 30 Apr., 17, 26 May, 3 Oct., 11 Dec. 1842, 7 Mar. 1843, ibid.; Cass to Webster, 17 Sept. 1842, U.S., Congress, *Senate Documents*, 27 Cong., 3 sess., vol. 4, no. 223, p. 34; Webster to Cass, 14 Nov., 20 Dec. 1842, ibid., pp. 6–8, 14, 18; Webster to Cass, 25 Apr. 1842, Cass Papers. Cass also received praise from Hugh Legaré, Tyler's attorney general from South Carolina (Legaré to Cass, 5 Apr. 1842, ibid.). Webster to George Ticknor, 18 Feb. 1842, WP (F16/21611); Tyler to Webster, Feb. [Mar?] 1842, WP (F16/21734); Webster to son Fletcher, 5 Oct. 1842, WP (F18/23526); Webster to Everett, 26 Apr. 1842, EP (F7/1058). Cass did not get the Democratic presidential nomination in 1844.

18. Everett to Webster, 31 Jan., 3 Mar. 1842, WP (F16/21448 and F17/21768).

19. Guizot to Cass, 26 May 1842, Disp. France (NA); Wilbur D. Jones, *The American Problem in British Diplomacy, 1841–1861*, pp. 8, 18; William L. Langer, *Political and Social Upheaval, 1832–1852*, p. 309; Norah Lofts and Margery Weiner, *Eternal France*, pp. 133–34; Cass to Webster, 30 Apr. 1842, Cass Papers; Everett to

Webster, 29 Jan. 1842, WP (F16/21434). Everett believed that France's primary motivation was its strong anti-British feeling. In 1845 the French government agreed to station a fleet along the African coast to suppress the slave trade.

20. Britain renounced peacetime visit and search in 1858.

21. See my article, "The Peculiar Institution and National Honor," pp. 28–50. Documentation on *Creole* affair in *Sen. Docs.*, 27 Cong., 2 sess., vol. 2, no. 51, pp. 1–46. Depositions by William Merritt, 9 Nov. 1841, ibid., p. 24; by Zephaniah Gifford and crew, 17 Nov. 1841, ibid., p. 16; by Blinn Curtis, 10 Nov. 1841, ibid., p. 34; and by Lucius Stevens, 10 Nov. 1841, ibid., p. 22. John Bacon [Amer. consul at Nassau] to Webster, 17 Nov. 1841, ibid., p. 16.

22. *Sen. Docs.*, 27 Cong., 2 sess., vol. 2, no. 51, pp. 37, 40, 41–42; Bacon to Webster, 30 Nov. 1841, ibid., pp. 3–4; statement of C. R. Nesbitt [col. sec.], 9 Nov. 1841, ibid., p. 6; G. C. Anderson to Gov. Francis Cockburn, 13 Nov. 1841, ibid., pp. 8–9; Bacon to Cockburn, 12 Nov. 1841, ibid., p. 6; Cockburn to Bacon, 12, 15 Nov. 1841, ibid., pp. 7, 8; depos. by Gifford, 2 Dec. 1841, ibid., pp. 42–45; by Gifford, Stevens, and Curtis, 17 Nov. 1841, ibid., p. 18; by Gifford and crew, 7 Dec. 1841, ibid., pp. 43–44; Anderson's report to Cockburn, 13 Nov. 1841, ibid., pp. 9–10; Aberdeen to Everett, 18 Apr. 1842, Disp., GB (NA); *Niles' Reg.* 61 (8 Jan. 1842): 304; Nassau *Observer* (n.d.), cited in New Orleans *Pic.*, 30 Dec. 1841.

23. New Orleans *Comm. Bulletin* (n.d.) cited in Richmond *Enq.*, 16 Dec. 1841; New Orleans *Adv.*, 4 Dec. 1841, cited in Boston *Lib.*, 24 Dec. 1841; Boston *Lib.*, 31 Dec. 1841; *Nat. Intell.*, 15 Dec. 1841; Charleston *Merc.*, 14 Dec. 1841; Mobile *Reg. & J.*, 6 Dec. 1841; Nashville *Union*, 15 Dec. 1841; *Southron* (Jackson), 9 Dec. 1841; La. Res., 14 Jan. 1842, in U.S., Congress, *House Documents*, 27 Cong., 2 sess., vol. 2, no. 116, p. 1; Miss. Res., 15 Mar. 1842, in ML (NA); Va. Res., Feb. 1842, in Richmond *Enq.*, 22 Feb. 1842; Balt. *Sun*, 20 Dec. 1841; Charleston *Cour.* (n.d.) cited in New Orleans *Pic.*, 5 Jan. 1842; Thomas Hart Benton, *Thirty Years' View*, 2:411; *CG*, 27 Cong., 2 sess., pp. 47, 116, 203–4; ibid., 26 Cong., 1 sess., p. 233; *CG, Append.*, 26 Cong., 1 sess., pp. 266–70; Richard K. Crallé, ed., *The Works of John C. Calhoun*, 3:560–83. Charles M. Wiltse, Calhoun's biographer, believes the South was afraid that British interference with the interstate slave trade was evidence of a "plot" to destroy slavery itself (see his *John C. Calhoun*, 3:63–64).

24. *U.S. v. Amistad* in Richard Peters, ed., *Reports of Cases Argued and Adjudged in the Supreme Court of the United States*, 15 (1841): 519–98; William W. Story, ed., *Life and Letters of Joseph Story*, 2:348; Edwin P. Hoyt, *The Amistad Affair*; R. Earl McClendon, "The *Amistad* Claims," pp. 386–412; Charles G. Haines and Foster H. Sherwood, *The Role of the Supreme Court in American Government and Politics, 1835–1864*, pp. 96–110. In *U.S. v. Schooner La Jeune Eugenie* (1822), Story denounced slavery as unchristian and inhumane (ibid., p. 104, n. 29). Justice Henry Baldwin argued that *New York* v. *Miln* (1837) established that blacks in a free state were free because of the state's police power (Peters, ed., *Reports*, 11 (1837): 139; ibid., 15 (1841): 549–66). Carl B. Swisher, *Roger B. Taney*, pp. 417–18; Richmond *Enq.*, 21 Dec. 1841; Mobile *Reg. & J.*, 6 Dec. 1841; Nashville *Union*, 15 Dec. 1841.

25. *Nat. Intell.*, 23 Dec. 1841; Portsmouth *J.* (n.d.) cited in Boston *Lib.*, 7 Jan. 1842; *CG*, 27 Cong., 2 sess., pp. 47–48.

26. Stevenson to Aberdeen, 21 Oct. 1841, Disp., GB (NA); Richmond *Enq.*, 2 Jan. 1841; Balt. *Sun*, 14 Dec. 1841; *Nat. Intell.*, 17 Dec. 1841. The Charleston *Mercury* of 18 March 1842 warmly praised Cass's pamphlet.

27. New Orleans *Pic.*, 24 Mar. 1842; Mobile *Reg. & J.*, 4 Dec. 1841; Balt. *Sun*, 23 Mar. 1842; N.Y. *Amer.* (n.d.) cited in Boston *Lib.*, 11 Mar., 8 Apr. 1842; Boston *Lib.*, 18 Mar. 1842; Mobile *Reg. & J.*, 1 Mar., 11 Apr. 1842; Nashville *Repub. Banner*, 30 Mar. 1842; Worcester *Spy*, 26 Feb. 1842, quoted in ibid., 11 Mar. 1842.

28. Wiltse, *Calhoun*, 3:69–70. Birney's article cited in Betty Fladeland, *James*

Gillespie Birney, p. 222. Whittier to Joseph Sturge [chmn. of Brit. and For. Anti-Slavery Soc.], 31 Jan. 1842, in Annie Heloise Abel and Frank J. Klingberg, eds., *A Side-Light on Anglo-American Relations, 1839–1858*, p. 92; Simeon Jocelyn [corresp. sec. of Amer. and For. Anti-Slavery Soc.], 1 Apr. 1842, cited in *Nonconformist*, 27 Apr. 1842, pp. 275–76 as cited in Abel and Klingberg, eds., *Side-Light*, p. 93, n. 61. Tappan to John Scoble of Brit. Soc., 1 Apr. 1842, cited in ibid., p. 94; Jocelyn to Sec. of Brit. Soc., 1 Apr. 1842, ibid., pp. 94–95; ibid., p. 83.

29. *CG*, 27 Cong., 2 sess., pp. 342, 346, 373; ibid., 28 Cong., 1 sess., pp. 534, 537–38; Samuel F. Bemis, *John Quincy Adams and the Union*, pp. 439–40. The "gag rule" in the House was in effect from 1836 to 1844. Balt. *Sun*, 23 Mar. 1842; Gilbert H. Barnes, *The Antislavery Impulse 1830–1844*, p. 286, n. 33; *Nat. Intell.*, 31 Mar., 2 Apr. 1842.

30. Peters, ed., *Reports*, 14 (1841): 540–98; Fox to Aberdeen, 28 Dec. 1841, *BFSP* 31 (1842–43): 673; Richmond *Enq.*, 21 Dec. 1841. Fox had unsuccessfully proposed a new extradition agreement (Fox to Forsyth, 12 Aug. 1840, NFBL [NA]).

31. Webster to Everett, 29 Jan. 1842, Dipl. Instr., GB (NA); Palm. to Stevenson, 7 Jan. 1837, ibid. Palmerston's argument related to the *Comet*, the *Encomium*, and the *Enterprise*.

32. Everett to Webster, 31 Jan. 1842, WP (F16/21448).

33. *Hansard's Parliamentary Debates*, 3d ser., 60 (14 Feb. 1842): 318–26; Betty Fladeland, *Men and Brothers*, pp. 330–31. If Campbell had read farther in the work, he would have realized that Wheaton could not have believed the *Creole* ever came under British jurisdiction. Extradition had no bearing on the case because the master had the right to help from the American consul (Henry Wheaton, *Elements of International Law*, p. 166, n. 62). See also Arthur Nussbaum, *A Concise History of the Law of Nations*, pp. 234–35.

34. London *Times*, 14, 19 Jan., 1, 16 Feb., 18 May, 3 June 1842; Boston *Lib.*, 1 Apr. 1842; Abel and Klingberg, eds., *Side-Light*, pp. 89–91; Aberdeen to Everett, 18 Apr. 1842, Disp., GB (NA); Timothy Darling [Amer. consul at Nassau] to Webster, 16 Apr. 1842, encl. in Webster to Lord Ashburton, 4 May 1842, Lord Ashburton Papers, FO 5/379 (PRO), pt. II (private); Richmond *Compiler* (n.d.) cited in Charleston *Merc.*, 23 Dec. 1842; New Orleans *Cour.*, 4 Dec. 1841, cited in Boston *Lib.*, 24 Dec. 1841; Fox to Aberdeen, 25 Feb. 1842, *BFSP* 31 (1842–43): 692–93.

35. Webster to Story, 17 Mar. 1842, WP (F17/21889); Everett to Aberdeen, 1 Mar. 1842, Disp., GB (NA).

Chapter 6

1. Author not identified, "France, America, and Britain," pp. 1–48.

2. Forsyth to Fox, 16, 28 Jan. 1840, NTFL, GB (NA); Sir John Harvey to Lord Sydenham, 3, 13 Nov. 1840, *HCSP* 61 (1843): 43–45; Francis Rice [j. p.] to Warden James MacLauchlan, 3 Nov. 1840, ibid., p. 47; MacLauchlan to Harvey, 9 Nov. 1840, ibid., p. 46; Sydenham to Fox, 23 Nov. 1840, ibid., p. 49; Fox to Palm., 13 Nov. 1839, 11 Jan. 1840, FO 115/69 (PRO); Palm. to Fox, 19 Feb. 1840, Lord Palmerston's Letter-Books, vol. 79. Fox repeatedly warned Washington about Maine's encroachments in the disputed area and recommended arbitration (Fox to Forsyth, 12, 26 Jan., 7, 13, 26 Mar., 22 June, 28 July, 3 Sept. 1840, NFBL [NA]). Numerous letters among New Brunswick officials indicate that they wanted only peace with Maine. See Harvey to Fox, 11, 31 Jan., 10 Feb. 1840, N.B., Disp. (PAC); Harvey to Gov. Gen. A. Thomson, 17 Jan. 1840, ibid.; Harvey to Lt. Gen. Richard Jackson, 25 Jan., 3 Feb. 1840, ibid.; Sydenham to Sir William Colebrooke, 21 May 1841, FO 5/362 (PRO).

3. Kent to Maine legis., 15 Jan. 1841, *HCSP* 61 (1843): 51–53; Maine Resolve, 15 Feb. 1841, Ala. Res., 15 Jan. 1841, Indiana Res., 24 Feb. 1841, Md. Res., 23 Mar. 1841, all in ibid., pp. 129–33; Fox to Palm., 30 Mar., 30 July 1840, ibid.; Palm. to Russell, 19

Jan. 1841, quoted in Herbert C. F. Bell, *Lord Palmerston*, 1:253; Russell to Palm., 19 Dec. 1840, Lord Palmerston Papers, GC/RU/54/1–2, by permission of the Trustees of the Broadlands Archives. *Hansard's Parliamentary Debates*, 3d ser., 61 (5 Mar. 1841): 1355–56.

4. Maine Report, 30 Mar. 1841, in *HCSP* 61 (1843): 96–128; Sydenham to Colebrooke, 21 May, 8 June 1841, ibid., pp. 150–51; M. Langevin [Catholic priest] to Harvey, 15 June 1841, ibid., p. 156.

5. Webster to Fox, 9 June, 4 Sept. 1841, ibid., pp. 141–42, 164–65; Fox to Sydenham, 27 July 1841, ibid., pp. 139–40; Fox to Webster, 11 June, 6 Sept. 1841, ibid., pp. 143–44, 166; Sydenham to Fox, 3 Aug. 1841, ibid., pp. 162–63; Sydenham to Russell, 9 Aug. 1841, ibid., 52 (1845): 1; Palm. to Fox, 31 Aug. 1841, ibid., 61 (1843): 163.

6. Frederick Merk, *Fruits of Propaganda in the Tyler Administration*, pp. 9, 59–62.

7. Smith to Van Buren, 7 Dec. 1837, with enclosure: "Instructions proposed to be given to an agent on the ne boundary & c.," Martin Van Buren Papers; Smith to Webster, 7 June 1841, WP (F40/55251).

8. Merk, *Fruits of Propaganda*, p. 63; Smith to Webster, 7 June 1841, WP (F40/55251). In the act of 1 May 1810, Congress authorized an annual appropriation "for the contingent expenses of intercourse between the United States and foreign nations." Section 3 distinguished between expenditures the president could make public and those he could keep secret "by certificates" (or vouchers) for the amount spent (*U.S. Statutes at Large*, 2:609). Everett to Webster, 15 Dec. 1841, WP (F16/20851); Webster to Kent, 21 Dec. 1841, WP (F16/20914); Webster to Everett, 28 Dec. 1841, WP (F16/20945). A note dated 19 July 1842 concerning the secret-service fund account shows that Francis Smith received $2,000 for "services connected with the N.E. boundary." On 1 February 1845, he received an additional $500 "over the amount of $2000 charged in former settlements." Two other men, "J Smith" and "A [Albert?] Smith," received $60 and $200 in matters relating to the "business of the boundary," while Albert Smith received $600 for his services (WP [F18/22959]; author of notes not identified).

9. Smith to Webster, 20 Nov. 1841, WP (F16/20694). Smith's articles reprinted in U.S., Congress, *House Reports*, 29 Cong., 1 sess., no. 684, pp. 26–35. Merk, *Fruits of Propaganda*, p. 158, n. 25; Joseph Griffin, ed., *History of the Press of Maine*, p. 65.

10. Richard N. Current, "Webster's Propaganda and the Ashburton Treaty," pp. 187–200; Portland *East. Argus*, 29 July, 4 Aug. 1842, cited in ibid., p. 190, nn. 12, 14; Chicago *Amer.*, 5 Aug. 1842; Detroit *Demo. Free Press*, 5 Aug. 1842; Detroit *Const. Democrat*, 6 Aug. 1842; Little Rock *Ark. Times and Advocate*, 22 Aug. 1842, all cited in ibid., p. 190, n. 13; Richmond *Enq.*, 16 Aug. 1842.

11. Hunter Miller, ed., *Treaties and Other International Acts of the United States of America, 1776–1863*, 4:383; Webster to Williams, 2, 18 Feb. 1842, WP (F16/21475 and 21615); Williams to Webster, 12 Feb. 1842, WP (F16/21548).

12. Sprague to Webster, 17 Feb., 26 Mar., 17 July 1842, WP (F16/21606; F17/21980 and 22914). For Sprague's payment, see "Copy of a Memorandum" of 24 Aug. 1842, by disbursing agent of State Department, but in Webster's handwriting, in WP (F40/55375). For Smith's, see secret-service fund account of 1 Feb. 1845, in WP (F18/22959).

13. Merk questions Webster's use of the executive fund (*Fruits of Propaganda*, pp. 87–92). Critics who referred to Webster's campaign in Maine as propaganda include ibid.; Current, "Webster's Propaganda and the Ashburton Treaty," pp. 187–200. See *U.S. Statutes at Large*, 2:609.

14. Author not identified, "United States' Boundary Question," *Quarterly Rev.* 67 (Dec. 1840 and Mar. 1841): 501–41; author not identified, "Relations of Foreign Powers with the Present Conservative Cabinet," *For. Quarterly Rev.* 56 (Jan. 1842): 259–73; Palm. to Fox, 19 July 1841, Palmerston's Letter-Books, vol. 79; Sir Charles Graham to Peel, 1 Aug. 1841, Charles S. Parker, ed., *Sir Robert Peel, From His Private Papers*,

2:492–93. Graham was a close friend of Peel's. For the importance of France in the Peel ministry's policymaking, see Wilbur D. Jones, *The American Problem in British Diplomacy, 1841–1861*, pp. 8, 18.

15. Peel to Aberdeen, 30 Dec. 1841, Sir Robert Peel Papers (BM, 40453); Peel to Aberdeen, 17 Nov. 1841, Lord Aberdeen Papers (BM, 43061, private); Aberdeen to Fox, 3 Jan. 1842, ibid. (43123); Fox to Palm., 16 Aug. 1840, FO 115/69 (PRO); Fox to Aberdeen, 5 Dec. 1841, 28 Jan. 1842, ibid., vols. 76 and 79. As early as February 1841, rumor in the United States was that the incoming president, William Henry Harrison, planned to send a special mission to Britain to settle Anglo-American difficulties. Fox believed the best and most probable choice for the position was Henry Clay. This rumor may have affected the Peel ministry's decision to send Ashburton to the United States. Fox to Palm, 24 Feb. 1841, ibid., vol. 69; Aberdeen to Peel, 23 Dec. 1841, Peel Papers (BM, 40453); Miller, ed., *Treaties*, 4:374; Ashb. to Aberdeen, 22 Dec. 1841, 9 Jan. 1842, Aberdeen Papers (BM, 43123, private; 43062); Peel to Aberdeen, 24 Dec. 1841, ibid. (43061); Ashb. to Croker, 22 Dec. 1841, John Croker Papers (Duke U.); Aberdeen to Queen Victoria, 24 Dec. 1841, Arthur C. Benson and Viscount Esher, eds., *The Letters of Queen Victoria*, 1:368; Queen Victoria to Aberdeen, 26 Dec. 1841, Aberdeen Papers (BM, 43041); Fox to Palm., 30 July 1840, FO 115/69 (PRO).

16. Everett to Webster, 31 Dec. 1841, Disp., GB (NA); Everett to Webster, 3 Jan. 1842, WP (F16/20984); Peel to Aberdeen, 30, 31 Dec. 1841, Aberdeen Papers (BM, 43061); Ashb. to Aberdeen, 28 Dec. 1841, ibid. (43123); London *Times*, 31 Dec. 1841.

17. Robert C. Alberts, *The Golden Voyage*, pp. 226, 423; Bradford Perkins, *The First Rapprochement*, pp. 12, 169; James E. Winston and R. W. Colomb, "How the Louisiana Purchase Was Financed," pp. 189–237; Alexander DeConde, *This Affair of Louisiana*, pp. 172–73, 188. The following letters indicate that the Baring lands in present-day Maine lay between the Schoodic and Penobscot rivers and not in the disputed territory: Alexander Baring to William Bingham, 1, 15 Feb. 1796, Baring Brothers Papers, Private Docs., no. 2491 (PRO); Bingham to Baring, 1 Feb. 1796, ibid.

18. Quoted in Alberts, *Golden Voyage*, p. 433. See Bradford Perkins, *Prologue to War*, pp. 19–20, 31. During the War of 1812, Ashburton acted as informal intermediary in London between Gallatin and the British government when the American commissioner tried to negotiate peace (Bradford Perkins, *Castlereagh and Adams*, p. 22). Dudley A. Mills, "British Diplomacy and Canada," pp. 683–712; Lady Ashb. to Webster, 12 Jan. 1842, WP (F16/21287).

19. Webster's close ties with the House of Baring become clear in Webster to Thomas Ward of Baring Bankers of London, 29 Feb. 1840, Baring Papers (PAC); Webster to Joshua Bates [Baring board chmn.], 26 Mar. 1840, ibid.; Ward to Bates, 31 Feb. 1842, 28 June, 1 Dec. 1843, Thomas Wren Ward Papers; Ralph W. Hidy, *The House of Baring in American Trade and Finance*, pp. 100, 283–84, 293, 316, 320–21, 327; Ashb. to Webster, 2 Jan. 1842, WP (F16/21210).

20. London *Morn. Chron.* (n.d.) and London *Times* (n.d.), both quoted in Richmond *Enq.*, 27 Jan. 1842; London *Examiner*, 14 May 1842, p. 311; Halifax *Novascotian*, 2 June 1842; author not identified, "Relations of Foreign Powers," p. 265; Charles C. F. Greville, *The Greville Memoirs*, 1:403; *Nat. Intell.*, 26 Jan., 1 Mar. 1842; Mobile *Reg. & J.*, 3, 8 Feb. 1842; *Madisonian* (n.d.) cited in Charleston *Merc.*, 8 Feb. 1842; Nashville *Repub. Banner*, 4 May 1842; Winthrop to Everett, 23 Apr. 1842, EP (F7/1034); Richmond *Enq.*, 27 Jan. 1842; Davis to Webster, 27 Apr. 1842, WP (F17/22284); Mangum to Col. (C. S.) [?] Green, 21 Apr. 1842, Adeline Ellery (Burr) Davis Green Papers; Wash. *Globe* (n.d.) quoted in ibid.; Boston *Cour.*, 3 Mar. 1842; Nashville *Union*, 18 Apr. 1842.

21. Bayard Tuckerman, ed., *The Diary of Philip Hone*, 2:110 (24 Jan. 1842); Webster to Everett, 29 Jan. 1842, EP (F7/0771); Everett to Aberdeen, 21 Feb. 1842, Disp., GB (NA); Gallatin to Ashb., 21 Apr. 1842, Aberdeen Papers (BM, 43123); Ashb. to

Gallatin, 12 Apr. 1842, and Gallatin to Ashb., 20 Apr. 1842, both in Albert Gallatin Papers. Numerous letters between the men before the War of 1812 show their friendship.

22. Thomas LeDuc, "The Maine Frontier and the Northeastern Boundary Controversy," pp. 31–41; W. D. Jones, *American Problem*, p. 18. Instructions in Aberdeen to Ashb., 8 Feb. 1842, Lord Ashburton Papers, FO 5/378 (PRO), pt. I. Ephraim D. Adams, "Lord Ashburton and the Treaty of Washington," pp. 764–82; Wilbur D. Jones, "Lord Ashburton and the Maine Boundary Negotiations," pp. 477–90; Hugh T. Gordon, *The Treaty of Washington, Concluded August 9, 1842, by Daniel Webster and Lord Ashburton*, pp. 173–257.

23. Aberdeen to Ashb., 8 Feb. 1842, Ashb. Papers, FO 5/378 (PRO), pt. I.

24. Aberdeen to Ashb., 9 Feb. 1842, Aberdeen Papers (BM, 43123, private); memo by Wellington, 8 Feb. 1842, in ibid.; Ashb. to Aberdeen, 10 Feb. 1842, ibid.

25. Ashb. to Aberdeen, 22, 28 Dec. 1841, ibid. (both private).

26. Ashb. to William Rives [chmn. of Sen. For. Relats. Committee], 26 Aug. 1844, William Cabell Rives Papers. The original of this letter is not in the Rives Papers, but a transcript copy is in box 104 of the collection. A search for the original in every likely box in the Rives Papers did not lead to its discovery.

27. Sparks to Webster, 15 Feb. 1842, WP (F16/21582); Franklin to Vergennes, 6 Dec. 1782, Francis Wharton, ed., *The Revolutionary Diplomatic Correspondence of the United States*, 6:120. The letter read: "I have the honor of returning herewith the map your Excellency sent me yesterday. I have marked with a strong red line, according to your desire, the limits of the United States as settled in the preliminaries between the British and American Plenipotentiaries." Franklin's letter encl. in Sparks's letter to Webster.

28. Lawrence Martin and Samuel F. Bemis, "Franklin's Red-Line Map Was a Mitchell," pp. 105–11. The d'Anville map Sparks found probably was the one entitled *Amérique Septentrionale Publiée sous les Auspices de Monseigneur le Duc d'Orleans Prémier Prince du Sang Par le Sr d'Anville MDCCXLVI Avec Privilege*. The Mitchell map most likely used by Franklin was a French edition of Mitchell's map of North America of 1755, entitled *L'Amerique Septentrionale avec les Routes, Distance en miles, Limites et Etablissements François et Angloise* (ibid., p. 105, n. 2; p. 107). Samuel F. Bemis, *John Quincy Adams and the Foundations of American Foreign Policy*, p. 479; Sparks to Webster, 15 Feb. 1842, WP (F16/21582). Sparks later found another map in the Paris archives which had the same boundary marked with a dotted red ink line, and he concluded that it was a copy of the original (Miller, ed., *Treaties*, 4:403–13).

29. Webster to Sparks, 4 Mar. 1842, WP (F17/21777); John Mulligan [Steuben's legatee] to Webster, 13 July 1838, WP (F40/55415); Webster's explanation of Steuben map, 27 Nov. 1844, in "Unpublished Testimony of the Select Committee of the House of Representatives," ibid.; Martin and Bemis, "Franklin's Map a Mitchell," p. 108; Merk, *Fruits of Propaganda*, p. 66; Miller, ed., *Treaties*, 4:403–4.

30. Everett to Aberdeen, 17 May 1842, FO 5/385 (PRO); Everett to Webster, 19 May 1842, WP (F17/22494).

31. Everett to Webster, 31 May 1843, WP (F18/24794); Miller, ed., *Treaties*, 4:407; Greville, *Memoirs*, 1:430.

32. Bemis, *Adams and Foundations*, p. 479; Sparks to Everett, 30 Jan. 1843, Herbert B. Adams, *The Life and Writings of Jared Sparks*, 2: 405–6; Webster to Everett, 14 June, 23 Dec. 1842, EP (F8a/0060 and 0756, second, "private and confidential"); Everett to Webster, 16 June 1842, WP (F17/22700). The italicized words in the text of this chapter were underlined in the original letter.

33. Martin and Bemis, "Franklin's Map a Mitchell," pp. 107, 109; Sparks to Webster, 15 Feb. 1842, WP (F16/21582); *Parl. Debates* 57 (21, 22 Mar. 1843): 1248, 1305. Sparks's red-line map disappeared after he saw it in Paris. Peel later claimed he had seen the d'Anville map around 1827 and doubted that it had been used in Paris in

1782–83, while Benjamin Disraeli told members of the House of Commons that he also had seen it and agreed it was dubious. Apparently no one has seen it since 1842. Sparks's copy, included in this chapter and entitled "Map of Maine," is with his letter to Webster of 15 February 1842, in the National Archives. The Steuben map is there also. Miller, ed., *Treaties*, 4:405; Henry S. Burrage, *Maine in the Northeastern Boundary Controversy*, p. 346, n. 2; Sparks to Everett, 30 Jan. 1843, Adams, *Life and Writings of Sparks*, 2:406; Sparks to George Gibbs, 8 Apr. 1843, ibid., p. 409; Sparks to Rives, 23 Feb. 1843, Jared Sparks Letters.

34. Martin and Bemis, "Franklin's Map a Mitchell," pp. 107–8; Everett to Webster, 28, 31 Mar. 1843, WP (F18/24750 and 24794); *Parl. Debates*, 67 (21 Mar. 1843): 1248–49; Jared Sparks, "The Treaty of Washington," pp. 452–96. A transcription of the Oswald map is in the Map Collection of the Library of Congress. Merk says the King George III map (or Oswald) was placed in the British Museum in 1828 (*Fruits of Propaganda*, p. 80). See also Ashb. to Rives, 26 Aug. 1844, Rives Papers. Ashburton's lack of knowledge of Webster's red-line maps during the negotiations will become evident in the following chapter.

35. *Parl. Debates* 46 (27 Mar. 1839): 1226–28; Anthony Panizzi [keeper in BM] to Palm., 29 Mar. 1839, FO 5/340 (PRO); Brit. warrant of 1 Apr. 1839, in ibid.

36. Everett to Webster, 31 Mar. 1843, Disp., GB (NA); Merk, *Fruits of Propaganda*, p. 63, n. 44; Featherstonhaugh to John Backhouse, 13 Feb. 1843, John Backhouse Papers.

37. George W. Featherstonhaugh, *Observations upon the Treaty of Washington, signed August 9, 1842*; London *Times*, 6 Feb. 1843.

38. Ashb. to Rives, 26 Aug. 1844, Rives Papers. I would like to thank Ann Liston for calling this letter to my attention.

39. Everett to Webster, 28 Mar. 1843, Disp., GB (NA). It perhaps is more than coincidental that during the boundary discussions between the countries in 1840, Palmerston had rejected an American proposal because, he said, the suggested examination of each country's archives would impede progress. He also objected to using a Mitchell map in any boundary negotiations because it was inaccurate. The Oswald map Palmerston impounded from the British Museum was a Mitchell. Palm. to Fox, 24 Aug. 1840, HCSP 61 (1843): 136–37.

40. Everett to Webster, 28, 31 Mar. 1843, Disp., GB (NA); Featherstonhaugh to Palm., 14 Dec. 1840, Palmerston Papers, GC/FE/10/1–2; Martin and Bemis, "Franklin's Map a Mitchell," p. 108; Albert Gallatin, *A Memoir on the North-Eastern Boundary, In Connexion with Mr. Jay's Map*, pp. 7, 52–53; Everett to Webster, 17 Apr. 1843, WP (F18/24881); Ashb. to Rives, 26 Aug. 1844, Rives Papers. The Jay map is in the New York Historical Society. Mills, "British Diplomacy," pp. 699–700; Raymond Walters, Jr., *Albert Gallatin*, pp. 374–75; Augusta J., 21 Apr. 1843; Albert Gallatin, *The Right of the United States of America to the North-Eastern Boundary Claimed by Them*; William F. Ganong, "A Monograph of the Evolution of the Boundaries of the Province of New Brunswick," pp. 139–449; Justin Winsor, "The Settlement of the Northeastern Boundary," pp. 349–69. The strongest argument for the credibility of the Oswald map is by Hunter Miller, though he bases much of his case on Everett's reasoning (Miller, ed., *Treaties*, 3:342–49).

41. *Parl. Debates* 67 (21 Mar. 1843): 1247–52; Ashb. to Aberdeen, 9 Aug. 1842, Aberdeen Papers (BM, 43123, private); Ashb. to Croker, 7, 13 Feb. 1843, John Croker Papers (U. of Mich.); Ashb. to Webster, 28 Apr. 1843, James M. McIntyre, ed., *The Writings and Speeches of Daniel Webster*, 18:191; Ashb. to Greville, 9 Feb. 1843, Greville, *Memoirs*, 1:469; Merk, *Fruits of Propaganda*, pp. 79–80, 82.

42. Merk, *Fruits of Propaganda*, pp. 86–87; Miller, ed., *Treaties*, 4:412–13. A photograph of the Aranda map is in the Library of Congress, and a photostat is in the archives of the State Department. Martin and Bemis argue that the Aranda map substantiated the American claim to the disputed territory ("Franklin's Map a Mitchell," pp. 110–11).

43. Martin and Bemis, "Franklin's Map a Mitchell," p. 108; Ashb. to Aberdeen, 21 Jan. 1843, Aberdeen Papers (BM, 43123, private); Ashb. to Croker, 7 Feb. 1843, Croker Papers (U. of Mich.); Webster to Everett, 25 Apr. 1843, EP (F9a/o117).

44. Samuel F. Bemis, *The Diplomacy of the American Revolution*, p. 228; Richard B. Morris, *The Peacemakers*, p. 346. Though Martin and Bemis maintain that by 8 October 1782, Oswald had persuaded Jay to accept the idea of a postwar settlement of the boundary by joint commission, Morris shows that Franklin first had suggested deferment of the Nova Scotia boundary. A copy of the preliminary peace articles, entitled "Articles agreed on between the American and British Commissioners," 8 Oct. 1782, is in Wharton, *Rev. Dipl. Corresp.*, 5:805–8. The last paragraph of the Articles read: "Alteration to be made in the treaty respecting the boundaries of Nova Scotia, viz: East, the true line between which, and the United States shall be settled by commissioners as soon as conveniently may be after the war" (Miller, ed., *Treaties*, 3:345).

45. Admiralty to Foreign Office, 21 Jan. 1842, FO 5/386 (PRO); Greville to Henry Reeve, 1 Apr. 1842, Arthur H. Johnson, ed., *The Letters of Charles Greville and Henry Reeve, 1836–1865*, p. 62; Richmond *Enq.*, 8 Apr. 1842; Ashb. to Aberdeen, 8 Apr. 1842, Ashb. Papers, FO 5/379 (PRO), pt. I (disp. 1).

46. N.Y. *Herald*, 7, 10 Apr. 1842; Abel Upshur to Judge N. Beverley Tucker, 20 Apr. 1842, Lyon Gardiner Tyler, *The Letters and Times of the Tylers*, 2:198; Thomas Hart Benton, *Thirty Years' View*, 2:421; *Niles' Reg.* 62 (6 Aug. 1842): 353; *CG, Append.*, 27 Cong., 2 sess., p. 444.

47. Webster to Fairfield and Davis, 11 Apr. 1842, WP (F17/22110); Webster to Fairfield, 11 Apr. 1842, McIntyre, ed., *Writings and Speeches of Webster*, 11:274. For American survey commission, see cursory report of James Renwick, James Graham, and Andrew Talcott, 6 Jan. 1841, in *HCSP* 61 (1843): 54–63.

48. Smith to Webster, 13, 16 Apr. 1842, WP (F17/22153 and 22184); Webster to Bates and Rufus Choate, 15 Feb. 1842, WP (F16/21573); Mass. Resolves, 3 Mar. 1842, U. S., Congress, *Senate Documents*, 27 Cong., 3 sess., vol. 1, pp. 63–64; Webster to Davis, 16 Apr. 1842, WP (F17/22169); Davis to Webster, 27 Apr. 1842, WP (F17/22282).

49. Webster to Sparks, 14, 16 May 1842, WP (F17/22449 and 22464); Adams, *Life and Writings of Sparks*, 2:400; Sparks to Everett, 30 Jan. 1843, in ibid., pp. 406–7; "Copy of a Memorandum," 24 Aug. 1842, in WP (F40/55375); Webster to Davis, 16 Apr. 1842, WP (F17/22169); Martin and Bemis, "Franklin's Map a Mitchell," p. 106. Though Sparks reported expenses of only $20 for his trip to Augusta, Webster allotted him $250—again from the secret-service fund. The president refused the secretary's request to pay Sparks more (Sparks to Webster, 16 May 1842, WP [F17/22471]; Webster to Tyler, 24 Aug. 1842, WP [F40/55375]; Tyler to Webster, 25 Aug. 1842, WP [F40/55376]).

50. Webster to Williams, 7, 14 May 1842, WP (F17/22410 and 22451); Webster to Kavanagh, 17 May 1842, WP (F17/22474).

51. Sprague to Webster, 18 May 1842, WP (F17/22484); Sparks to Webster, 19 May 1842, WP (F17/22498); Maine Resolutions, 26 May 1842, encl. in Fairfield to Tyler, 27 May 1842, William R. Manning, ed., *Diplomatic Correspondence of the United States*, 3:271, n. 2; William S. Jenkins, ed., *Records of the States of the United States, 1836–41. Maine: Legislative Records [Journal of the Senate, Special Session*, 22 Legis. (26 May 1842), pp. 33–34]. The day before, the state senate, by vote of 29 to 0, approved claims by the state for reimbursement of past defense expenditures for the disputed territory (ibid., p. 22).

52. Webster to Kent, 28 May 1842, WP (F17/22556); Maine commissioners to Webster, 12 June 1842, U.S., Congress, *House Documents*, 27 Cong., 3 sess., vol. 1, no. 2, p. 69; Mass. commissioners to Webster, 13 June 1842, ibid.; Webster to Everett, 14 June 1842, EP (F8a/0060).

Chapter 7

1. Ashb. to Aberdeen, 25 Apr. 1842, Lord Ashburton Papers, FO 5/379 (PRO), pt. I (disp. 2 and 3); Ashb. to Aberdeen, 26 Apr., 12, 29 May 1842, Lord Aberdeen Papers (BM, 43123, first, private; third, disp. 8).

2. Aberdeen to Sir James Kempt, Sir Howard Douglas, Lord Seaton, and Sir George Murray, 24 Feb. 1842, Aberdeen Papers (BM, 43123, confidential); Aberdeen to Ashb., 3 Mar. 1842, ibid. (private); Kempt to Aberdeen, 1 Mar. 1842, ibid. (confidential); Murray to Aberdeen, 6 Mar. 1842, ibid.; Douglas to Aberdeen, 7 Mar. 1842, ibid.; Seaton to Aberdeen, 9 Mar. 1842, ibid.; Mildmay to Aberdeen, 28 Apr. 1842, ibid.; revised instructions in Aberdeen to Ashb., 31 Mar. 1842, Ashb. Papers, FO 5/378 (PRO), pt. I.

3. Aberdeen to Ashb., 1 Apr. 1842, Aberdeen Papers (BM, 43123, private); Peel to Aberdeen, Mar. 1842, ibid. (disp. 3).

4. Colebrooke to Ashb., 12 May 1842, FO 5/388 (PRO); Ashb. to Aberdeen, 12, 29 May 1842, Aberdeen Papers (BM, 43123, second, private); Hamilton to Tyler, 29 Apr. 1842, ibid.; Aberdeen to Ashb., 3, 18 June 1842, ibid. (both private).

5. Ashb. to Webster, 21 June 1842, *HCSP* 61 (1843): 6–10; Ashb. to Aberdeen, 13 July 1842, Ashb. Papers, FO 5/380 (PRO), pt. I (disp. 13); Julia G. Tyler [president's wife] to George T. Curtis, ca. late 1842, "The Ashburton Treaty, 1812," pp. 255–56; Tyler to son Robert, 29 Aug. 1858, Lyon Gardiner Tyler, *The Letters and Times of the Tylers*, 2:242; Webster to John Denison, 26 Apr. 1842, WP (F17/22264); Ashb. to Webster, 13 June 1842, NFBL (NA). On the dinners, see "information sheet" on St. John's Parish House, 1525 H Street, N.W., Washington, D.C.

6. Ashb. to Colebrooke, 28 Apr., 17, 24 May, 29 July 1842, N.B., Disp. (PAC); Colebrooke to Ashb., 10, 27 May, 1 June 1842, FO 5/388 (PRO); Ashb. to Aberdeen, 29 June 1842, FO 881/259 (PRO); Thomas C. Grattan, British consul in Boston, implies that Webster was aware of the New Brunswick delegation's presence in Washington. See his *Civilized America*, 1:369.

7. Webster to Everett, 25 Apr. 1842, EP (F7/1045); Ashb. to Aberdeen, 25 Apr. 1842, Ashb. Papers, FO 5/379 (PRO), pt. I (disp. 3); Ashb. to Aberdeen, 14 June 1842, Aberdeen Papers (BM, 43123, private); Ashb. to Webster, 21 June 1842, *HCSP* 61 (1843): 6–8.

8. Aberdeen to Ashb., 16, 20 May, 18 June 1842, Aberdeen Papers (BM, 43123, all three private); Peel to Aberdeen, 16 May 1842, ibid. (disp. 3).

9. Webster to Everett, 28 June 1842, EP (F8a/0122); Tyler, *Letters*, 2: 172, 218.

10. Maine commissioners to Webster, 29 June 1842, *HCSP* 61 (1843): 15–22; Webster to Ashb., 8 July 1842, ibid., pp. 10–15; Ashb. to Webster, 11 July 1842, ibid., pp. 22–23; Aberdeen to Ashb., 2 July 1842, Aberdeen Papers (BM, 43123, private).

11. Ashb. to Aberdeen, 29 June 1842, Aberdeen Papers (BM, 43123, private); Ashb. to Webster, 1 July 1842, WP (F17/22802).

12. Ashb. to Aberdeen, 29 May 1842, Ashb. Papers, FO 5/379 (PRO), pt. II (disp. 8); Ashb. to Aberdeen, 14 June, 13 July 1842, Aberdeen Papers (BM, 43123, both private).

13. Grattan to Aberdeen, 14 June, 30 July 1842, Aberdeen Papers (BM, 43123, both private); Aberdeen to Ashb., 2 July 1842, ibid. (private); Ashb. to Aberdeen, 28 July 1842, ibid. (private); Grattan, *Civilized America*, 1: 365.

14. Grattan, *Civilized America*, 1:367, 368, 371–72; Ashb. to Webster, 11 July 1842, *HCSP* 61 (1843): 23–26; Ashb. to Aberdeen, 13 July 1842, Ashb. Papers, FO 5/380 (PRO), pt. I (disp. 13).

15. J. R. Baldwin, "The Ashburton-Webster Boundary Settlement," pp. 121–33; Samuel F. Bemis, *John Quincy Adams and the Foundations of American Foreign Policy*, pp. 479–80.

16. Webster to Everett, 25 Aug. 1842, 29, 30 Jan., 10, 29 Mar. 1843, EP (F8a/0380,

F8b/0949, 0955, 1139, 1190); Everett to Webster, 16 Sept. 1842, 18 Apr. 1843, WP (F18/23423 and 24900); Webster to Robert Letcher, 21 Feb. 1843, WP (F18/24407); Webster to Thomas Curtis, 12 Mar. 1843, WP (F18/24631); Everett to Tyler, 18 Apr. 1843, EP (F9a/0078).

17. Ashb. to Aberdeen, 9 Aug. 1842, Aberdeen Papers (BM, 43123, private). The "former private letter" Ashburton referred to is not in the Aberdeen Papers (Bemis, *Adams and Foundations*, pp. 479–80).

18. Ashb. to Aberdeen, 14 June 1842, Aberdeen Papers (BM, 43123, private); Aberdeen to Peel, 25 Aug. 1842, Sir Robert Peel Papers (BM, 40453). Grattan claimed that one of the Maine commissioners informed him that Webster laid the Sparks map before the Maine commission on 13 June (Grattan to Aberdeen, 31 Dec. 1842, Aberdeen Papers [BM, 43123, private]; Aberdeen to Ashb., 2 July 1842, ibid. [private]).

19. Bemis, *Adams and Foundations*, p. 480; Ashb. to Aberdeen, 14 June, 9 Aug. 1842, Aberdeen Papers (BM, 43123, both private).

20. Webster to Nathaniel Williams [Baltimore banker], 3, 4 Feb., 13 Mar., 29 Oct., 8, 12 Dec. 1842, WP (F16/21499 and 21504; F17/21855; F18/23654, 23866, 23874). Bemis, *Adams and Foundations*, p. 588.

21. Ashb. to Aberdeen, 9 Aug. 1842, Aberdeen Papers (BM, 43123, private). One might add that, technically, Ashburton did not say he paid money to anyone.

22. Ashb. to Aberdeen, 25 Apr., 13 Aug. 1842, ibid. (43062, disp. 3; 43122, private).

23. Webster to Sparks, 11 Mar. 1843, WP (F18/24619).

24. Bemis, *Adams and Foundations*, p. 481.

25. Webster to Ashb., 8 July 1842, *HCSP* 61 (1843): 10–15; Ashb. to Aberdeen, 13 July 1842, Ashb. Papers, FO 5/380 (PRO), pt. I (disp. 13).

26. Webster to Maine commissioners, 15 July 1842, James M. McIntyre, ed., *The Writings and Speeches of Daniel Webster*, 11: 276–78; Ashb. to Webster, 18 July 1842, NFBL (NA); Webster to Ashb., 18 July 1842, NTFL, GB (NA); Hunter Miller, ed., *Treaties and Other International Acts of the United States of America, 1776–1863*, 4:434.

27. Mass. commissioners to Webster, 20 July 1842, William R. Manning, ed., *Diplomatic Correspondence of the United States*, 3:758; Maine commissioners to Webster, 22 July 1842, ibid., p. 760; "Memorandum," marked "A," encl. in ibid., p. 765, n. 1. An agreement on payment of the disputed territory fund was reached in September 1846. New Brunswick paid $14,893.45 to Maine and Massachusetts (Miller, ed., *Treaties*, 4:433). Ashb. to Aberdeen, 28 July 1842, Aberdeen Papers (BM, 43123, private).

28. Joseph Delafield [surveyor] to Major D. Fraser, 20 July 1842, U.S., Congress, *House Documents*, 27 Cong., 3 sess., vol. 1, no. 2, p. 101; Robert Stuart to Webster, 7 July 1842, ibid., p. 100; James Ferguson [surveyor] to Webster, 25 July 1842, ibid., p. 104.

29. Ashb. to Webster, 16 July 1842, McIntyre, ed., *Writings and Speeches of Webster*, 11:280–82; Ashb. to Aberdeen, 9 Aug. 1842, Ashb. Papers, FO 5/380 (PRO), pt. II (disp. 17).

30. Frederick Merk, *Fruits of Propaganda in the Tyler Administration*, p. 75; Glyndon G. Van Deusen, *The Jacksonian Era*, p. 175, n. 4; Albert B. Corey, *The Crisis of 1830–1842 in Canadian-American Relations*, p. 168; Fremont P. Wirth, *The Discovery and Exploitation of the Minnesota Iron Lands*, pp. 9–11. Merk argues that both Americans and Britons knew the area held minerals, but that no one thought it rich in these goods. He cites no evidence for these statements, however. Van Deusen believes that Webster and Tyler knew of the mineral deposits, but that Ashburton did not. He also presents no evidence for these conclusions. James D. Richardson, ed., *A Compilation of the Messages and Papers of the Presidents*, 4:165.

31. For a convincing argument that Webster, Tyler, and Ashburton did not know of

the mineral deposits along the northwestern section of the boundary, see Thomas LeDuc, "The Webster-Ashburton Treaty and the Minnesota Iron Ranges," pp. 476–81. General Land Office, Records: Letters to Surveyors General, 1796–1901 (NA).

32. See Roger H. Brown, *The Struggle for the Indian Stream Territory.*

33. Webster to Ashb., 27 July 1842, McIntyre, ed., *Writings and Speeches of Webster*, 11: 284–87; Ashb. to Webster, 9 Aug. 1842, ibid., p. 289; Spencer to Webster, 11 Aug. 1842, in Dept. of State, envelope marked "Miscellaneous on Northeastern Boundary," E98 (NA); Ashb. to Webster, 26 July 1842, WP (F17/23005); Webster to Ashb., 9 Aug. 1842, *HCSP* 61 (1843): 32; *CG*, 29 Cong., 1 sess., p. 617; Fox to Webster, 25 Apr. 1843, NFBL (NA).

34. Capt. Andrew Talcott [Corps of Engineers] to Webster, 14 July 1842, *House Docs.*, 27 Cong., 3 sess., vol. 1, no. 2, p. 82; Aberdeen to Peel, 15 Aug. 1842, Aberdeen Papers (BM, 43062).

35. Allan Nevins, ed., *Diary of Philip Hone, 1828–1851*, p. 614.

Chapter 8

1. Aberdeen to Ashb., 1 Apr. 1842, Lord Aberdeen Papers (BM, 43123); Tyler to Webster, 8 May 1842, WP (F17/22413).

2. See Cass's pamphlet, *An Examination of the Question Now in Discussion Between the American & British Governments, Concerning the Right of Search*, pp. 136–65.

3. Ashb. to Aberdeen, 10 Feb. 1842, Aberdeen Papers (BM, 43123); Peel to Aberdeen, 21 Feb. 1842, ibid. (43062).

4. Webster to Ashb., 30 July 1842, WP (F17/23031); Tyler to Webster, [July, Aug.], 1 Aug. 1842, WP (F17/23070 and 23089); Webster to Ashb., 8 Aug. 1842, James M. McIntyre, ed., *The Writings and Speeches of Daniel Webster*, 11: 318–25.

5. Everett to Webster, 31 Jan. 1842, WP (F16/21448); Ashb. to Webster, 9 Aug. 1842, McIntyre, ed., *Writings and Speeches of Webster*, 11:326–27; Ashb. to Aberdeen, 12 May 1842, Lord Ashburton Papers, FO 5/379 (PRO), pt. II (disp. 7); Aberdeen to Ashb., 3 June 1842, ibid., vol. 378, pt. II (disp. 9); Everett to Webster, 15 Apr. 1842, Disp., GB (NA); Aberdeen to Ashb., 3 June, 18 July 1842, Aberdeen Papers (BM, 43123, first, private).

6. Everett to Webster, 15 Apr. 1842, Disp., GB (NA); Ashb. to Aberdeen, 12 May 1842, Ashb. Papers, FO 5/379 (PRO), pt. II (disp. 7); Ashb. to Webster, 9 Aug. 1842, McIntyre, ed., *Writings and Speeches of Webster*, 11:326–27; Aberdeen to Peel, 25 Aug. 1842, Aberdeen Papers (BM, 43062).

7. The reader will recall that the Van Buren administration renounced the unauthorized Paine-Tucker agreement on mutual search. Navy commanders Charles Bell and James Paine filed their report on 10 May 1842 (copy encl. in Ashb. to Aberdeen, 12 May 1842, *HCSP* 61 [1843]: 5–9). Tyler to son Robert, 29 Aug. 1858, Lyon Gardiner Tyler, *The Letters and Times of the Tylers*, 2:240; Ashb. to Aberdeen, 25 Apr. 1842, ibid., p. 4; Wilbur D. Jones, "The Influence of Slavery on the Webster-Ashburton Negotiations," pp. 48–58.

8. Webster to Everett, 26 Apr. 1842, EP (F7/1058).

9. Tyler's revisions explained in Ashb. to Aberdeen, 13 July 1842, Aberdeen Papers (BM, 43123, private). By 1842, Britain had signed treaties with several governments guaranteeing mutual search to suppress the African slave trade.

10. Everett to Webster, 17 May 1842, WP (F17/22479); Ashb. to Webster, [July ?] 1842, WP (F17/23066); Aberdeen to Ashb., 26 May 1842, *HCSP* 61 (1843): 4; Everett to Webster, 1 June 1842, Disp., GB (NA); Ashb. to Aberdeen, 14 June 1842, Aberdeen Papers (BM, 43123, private); Aberdeen to Ashb., 2 July 1842, ibid.; Ashb. to Aberdeen, 29 June 1842, Ashb. Papers, FO 5/379 (PRO), pt. III (disp. 12). Art. VIII of treaty in Appendix.

11. Alan R. Booth, "The United States African Squadron, 1843–1861," pp. 77–117. As mentioned earlier, France in 1845 agreed to station a fleet along the West African coast to suppress the slave trade. The Letter Books of Commodore Matthew C. Perry, commander of the American vessels comprising the African squadron, indicate the problems American naval officers had in trying to halt the traffic. See Perry to Sec. of Navy Abel Upshur, 7 Apr., 11 May, 4 Sept. 1843, Perry, Letter Books (NA); Perry to Capt. B. Kennon, 4 Aug. 1843, ibid.; Perry to Sec. of Navy David Henshaw, 26 Dec. 1843, 12 Feb., 2 Mar. 1844, ibid.

12. Perry to Upshur, 5 Sept. 1843, Perry, Letter Books (NA); Perry to Henshaw, 29 Jan. 1844, ibid. Booth blames Southerners in the Navy Department for the African squadron's failure ("U.S. African Squadron," pp. 112–13). W. E. B. Dubois, *The Suppresssion of the African Slave-Trade to the United States of America, 1638–1870*, p. 183; Warren S. Howard, *American Slavers and the Federal Law, 1837–1862*, pp. 42, 124–41; Peter Duignan and Clarence Clendenen, *The United States and the African Slave Trade, 1619–1862*, pp. 40–42; Richard W. Van Alstyne, "The British Right of Search and the African Slave Trade," pp. 37–47; Bradford Perkins, *Castlereagh and Adams*, p. 277; John B. Moore, *A Digest of International Law*, 2:946–47. The Anglo-American convention of 7 April 1862 allowed mutual search in suppressing the African slave trade.

13. Everett to Webster, 2 Feb. 1842, WP (F16/21486); Webster to [Edward ?] Curtis, [Feb./Mar. ?] 1842, WP (F16/21724); Aberdeen to Ashb., 9 Feb., 3 Mar. 1842, Aberdeen Papers (BM, 43123, both private).

14. William W. Story, ed., *Life and Letters of Joseph Story*, 2:408.

15. Story to Webster, 26 Mar., 19 Apr. 1842, WP (F17/21984 and 22221); Webster to Story, 9 Apr. 1842, WP (F17/22101); *Amistad* case in Richard Peters, ed., *Reports of Cases Argued and Adjudged in the Supreme Court of the United States*, 15 (1841): 593–94.

16. Aberdeen to Ashb., 3 June 1842, Aberdeen Papers (BM, 43123, private); Aberdeen to Ashb., 3 June 1842, Ashb. Papers, FO 5/378 (PRO), pt. II (disp. 10); Story to Webster, 26 Mar., 19 Apr. 1842, WP (F17/21984 and 22221); Webster to Story, 9 Apr. 1842, WP (F17/22101); Peters, ed., *Reports*, 15 (1841): 518.

17. Aberdeen to Ashb., 26 May, 3 June 1842, Aberdeen Papers (BM, 43123, both private); Aberdeen to Ashb., 3 June 1842, Ashb. Papers, FO 5/378 (PRO), pt. II (disp. 10); Ashb. to Aberdeen, 15 Apr., 12 May 1842, ibid., vol. 379, pt. I (disp. 2) and pt. II (disp. 6); Everett to Webster, 2 June 1842, WP (F17/22620); Webster to Everett, 28 June 1842, WP (F17/22763).

18. Ashb. to Aberdeen, 13 July 1842, McIntyre, ed., *Writings and Speeches of Webster*, 11:311.

19. Webster to Everett, 29 Jan. 1842, EP (F7/0771); Boston *Lib.*, 25 Mar., 1, 16 Apr., 30 Sept. 1842; excerpts of Channing's pamphlet in ibid., 15, 22 Apr. 1842. Webster believed that the American stand on the *Creole* case was misunderstood throughout Europe (Webster to Cass, 25 Apr. 1842, Lewis Cass Papers). Samuel May and Edward Moreton to Webster, 29 Mar. 1842, WP (F17/02201); Legaré to Webster, 29 July 1842, WP (F17/23027); Webster to [Edward ?] Curtis, [Feb./Mar. ?] 1842, WP (F16/21726); Mobile *Reg. & J.*, 5, 24 Mar., 5 May 1842. Southern newspapers praising Webster's stand included the Balt. *Sun*, 24 Feb., 15 Mar. 1842; Charleston *Merc.*, 7 Mar. 1842; New Orleans *Commerc. Bulletin* (n.d.), cited in Boston *Lib.*, 15 Apr. 1842; Wash. *Globe*, 23 Feb. 1842; Nashville *Union*, 24 Mar. 1842. The Nashville *Republican Banner* of 25 March 1842 urged the United States to prepare for war with Britain.

20. Ashb. to Webster, 31 July 1842, WP (F17/23061); Ashb. to Webster, 6 Aug. 1842, McIntyre, ed., *Writings and Speeches of Webster*, 11:313–14, 316; Webster to Ashb., 1 Aug. 1842, HCSP 61 (1843): 35–40; Aberdeen to Ashb., 26 May 1842, Aberdeen Papers (BM, 43123, private).

21. Tyler to Cass, 29 June 1842, Cass Papers; Tyler to Webster, 7 Aug. 1842, WP (F17/23112); Webster to Ashb., 8 Aug. 1842, HCSP 61 (1843): 42–43.

22. Ashb. to Aberdeen, 9 Aug. 1842, Aberdeen Papers (BM, 43123, private); Ashb. to Aberdeen, 28 Apr., 9 Aug. 1842, Ashb. Papers, FO 5/379 (PRO), pt. II (disp. 5), and vol. 380, pt. III (disp. 20). Copy of Webster-Ashburton Treaty in Appendix. Jay's Treaty stipulated that upon mutual requisition, Britain and the United States would surrender fugitives charged with murder or forgery, if there were enough evidence to justify a trial (Hunter Miller, ed., *Treaties and Other International Acts of the United States of America, 1776–1863*, 2:245–64).

23. *CG, Append.*, 27 Cong., 3 sess., pp. 1–27, 49–53; Thomas Hart Benton, *Thirty Years' View*, 2:424, 449; Charles F. Adams, ed., *Memoirs of John Quincy Adams, Comprising Portions of His Diary from 1795 to 1848*, 11:284, 285.

24. Albert B. Corey, *The Crisis of 1830–1842 in Canadian-American Relations*, pp. 169–79; Ashb. to Aberdeen, 25 Apr. 1842, Ashb. Papers, FO 5/379 (PRO), pt. I (disp. 2); Charles Bagot to Lord Stanley, 28 May 1842, FO 5/388 (PRO); James Stephen to Henry Addington, 30 June 1842, ibid.; Tyler to Webster, 7 Aug. 1842, WP (F17/23112); Everett to Webster, 1 Mar. 1843, WP (F18/24471); Ashb. to Webster, 9 Aug. 1842, *HCSP* 61(1843): 33; Concord (N.H.) *Herald of Freedom*, 23 Sept. 1842; Roman J. Zorn, "Criminal Extradition Menaces the Canadian Haven for Fugitive Slaves, 1841–1861," pp. 284–94. Approximately twelve thousand former slaves lived in Canada by 1842. Hinton to Rev. Henry Capern of Nassau, 14 Dec. 1843, Annie Heloise Abel and Frank J. Klingberg, eds., *A Side-Light on Anglo-American Relations, 1839–1858*, p. 156; Howard Temperley, *British Antislavery, 1833–1870*, p. 204; Betty Fladeland, *Men and Brothers*, pp. 317–18. The apprehension felt by the abolitionists who met with Ashburton perhaps was due partially to a recent case involving an escaped slave from Arkansas, Nelson Hackett, who had been returned by the Canadian governor to stand trial for larceny (Bagot to Stanley, 20 Jan. 1842, FO 5/386 (PRO); Balt. *Sun*, 12 Oct. 1842).

25. Ralph W. Hidy, *The House of Baring in American Trade and Finance*, pp. 79–85; U.S., Congress, *Senate Documents*, 34 Cong., 1 sess., vol. 15, no. 103, pp. 52, 241–45; Moore, *Digest of Intern. Law*, 2:358–61; James B. Scott, ed., *Cases on International Law, Selected from Decisions of English and American Courts*, pp. 252–55.

26. Tyler to Alexander Gardiner, 6 May 1845, John Tyler Papers; Oliver P. Chitwood, *John Tyler*, pp. 272–73, 278; Robert F. Dalzell, Jr., *Daniel Webster and the Trial of American Nationalism, 1843–1852*, pp. 37–39, 85; Claude M. Fuess, *Daniel Webster*, 2:96–100. The New York *Herald* was an exception. It considered the *Creole* incident the worst violation of American sovereignty ever committed by the British (N.Y. *Herald*, 25 Feb., 13, 15, 16, 17 Mar. 1842). Harvey Wish, "American Slave Insurrections Before 1861," pp. 299–320; Helen T. Catterall, ed., *Judicial Cases Concerning American Slavery and the Negro*, 1:19; Joshua Coffin, *An Account of Some of the Principal Slave Insurrections*; Clement Eaton, *The Freedom-of-Thought Struggle in the Old South*, pp. 89–117; Clement Eaton, "The Freedom of the Press in the Upper South," pp. 479–99.

27. On Hogan, see Graham Chapin to Tyler, 1 Apr. 1842, ML (NA); Utica *Daily Gazette* of 2 Apr. 1842, reprint of stories in Rochester *Daily Democrat*, 1 Apr. 1842, warning against another McLeod controversy. John Spencer to Webster, 2, 8 Apr. 1842, ML (NA); N.Y. *Herald*, 8, 9 Mar. 1842; Fox to Aberdeen, 11 Mar., 5 Apr. 1842, FO 5/377 (PRO).

28. Aberdeen to Ashb., 8 Feb. 1842, Ashb. Papers, FO 5/378 (PRO), pt. I. The duke of Wellington agreed with Aberdeen (memo, 8 Feb. 1842, Aberdeen Papers [BM, 43123]; Aberdeen to Ashb., 18 July 1842, ibid.).

29. Webster to Ashb., 27 July 1842, NTFL, GB (NA); Ashb. to Aberdeen, 28 July 1842, Ashb. Papers, FO 5/380 (PRO), pt. I (disp. 14); Tyler to Webster, 26 July 1842, WP (F17/23009).

30. Ashb. to Webster, 28 July 1842, McIntyre, ed., *Writings and Speeches of Webster*, 11: 295–301; Webster to Ashb., 27 July, 6 Aug. 1842, ibid., pp. 292–93, 302–3; Ashb. to Aberdeen, 28 July 1842, Ashb. Papers, FO 5/380 (PRO), pt. I (disp. 14);

Tyler to Webster, 26 July 1842, WP (F17/23009); George T. Curtis, *Life of Daniel Webster*, 2:121, n. 1; *U.S. Statutes at Large*, 5:539.

31. On Oregon, see Frederick Merk, *The Oregon Question*; Norman A. Graebner, *Empire on the Pacific*; Frederick Merk, "The Oregon Question in the Webster-Ashburton Negotiations," pp. 379–404 (reprinted in Merk, *Oregon*, pp. 189–215).

32. Memo of Jan. 1842, Ashb. Papers, FO 5/378 (PRO), pt. I; Aberdeen to Ashb., 8 Feb. 1842, ibid.

33. Memo by Wellington, 8 Feb. 1842, Aberdeen Papers (BM, 43123); Merk, "Oregon Question," pp. 379–404.

34. Ashb. to Aberdeen, 25 Apr. 1842, Ashb. Papers, FO 5/379 (PRO), pt. I (disp. 2). Webster, normally opposed to expansion into the Southwest, recognized San Francisco harbor's potential (Webster to Waddy Thompson [Amer. minister to Mexico], 27 June 1842, WP [F17/22754]; David M. Pletcher, *The Diplomacy of Annexation*, p. 100).

35. Aberdeen to Ashb., 18 July 1842, Aberdeen Papers (BM, 43123, private); Everett to Webster, 1 Aug. 1842, Disp., GB (NA); Everett to Webster, 17 Oct. 1842, 2 Jan. 1843, WP (F18/23568 and 24071).

36. Ashb. to Aberdeen, 29 June 1842, Ashb. Papers, FO 5/379 (PRO), pt. III (disp. 10); Aberdeen to Fox, 18 Oct. 1842, FO 115/79 (PRO); Ashb. to Aberdeen, 1 Jan. 1843, Aberdeen Papers (BM, 43123, private); Ashb. to Webster, 2 Jan. 1843, WP (F18/24063); Ashb. to Croker, 20 Feb. 1843, John Croker Papers (U. of Mich.); Kenneth Bourne, *Britain and the Balance of Power in North America, 1815–1908*, p. 123.

37. The United States had no strong claim to Puget Sound; the British had done virtually all the exploring in the area.

38. Ashb. to William Sturgis, 2 Apr. 1845, U.S., Congress, *House Documents*, 42 Cong., 3 sess., no. 1, pt. 6, p. 37; Webster's speech at Boston's Faneuil Hall, 7 Nov. 1845, McIntyre, ed., *Writings and Speeches of Webster*, 13:314.

Chapter 9

1. Webster to Rives, 10 Aug. 1842, WP (F17/23143); Tyler to Webster, 8, ca. 9 Aug. 1842, WP (F17/23130 and 23135); Webster to Everett, 29 Dec. 1842, WP (F18/23968); Webster to John Healy, 17 Aug. 1842, WP (F17/23188); Ashb. to Aberdeen, 13 Aug. 1842, Lord Ashburton Papers, FO 5/380 (PRO), pt. IV (disp. 23); *CG, Append.*, 27 Cong., 3 sess., pp. 16, 61; Fox to Aberdeen, 24 Jan. 1843, FO 115/84 (PRO); Dudley A. Mills, "British Diplomacy and Canada," pp. 683–712. For years the pact of 1842 was called the Treaty of Washington, but in 1871 the Atlantic nations signed another treaty by the same name, and the earlier agreement became known as the Webster-Ashburton Treaty.

2. *CG, Append.*, 27 Cong., 3 sess., pp. 1–27, 101–10; Thomas Hart Benton, *Thirty Years' View*, 2:424, 449.

3. *CG, Append.*, 27 Cong., 3 sess., pp. 3, 14–16, 21.

4. Ibid., pp. 16, 61; Calhoun's explanation of Jefferson map in ibid., p. 51; Benton, *Thirty Years' View*, 2: 424, 449; Thomas C. Grattan, *Civilized America*, 1: 389–91; *CG*, 27 Cong., 3 sess., p. 111.

5. *CG, Append.*, 27 Cong., 3 sess., pp. 51, 53; N.Y. *Herald*, 21 Aug. 1842. Observer not identified.

6. Richard N. Current, "Webster's Propaganda and the Ashburton Treaty," pp. 187–200; *Nat. Intell.*, 9 June, 30 July, 2 Aug. 1842; Wash. *Globe*, 9 June, 20, 22 Aug. 1842. The publisher was William Seaton.

7. Webster to Jeremiah Mason, 21 Aug. 1842, James M. McIntyre, ed., *The Writings and Speeches of Daniel Webster*, 18:146. Webster's 1846 defense of treaty in Senate in ibid., 9:79. The eight Democrats who voted against ratification were: Allen of Ohio, Arthur Bagby of Alabama, Benton of Missouri, Buchanan of Pennsylvania, Lewis Linn of

Missouri, Perry Smith of Connecticut, Daniel Sturgeon of Pennsylvania, and Reuel Williams of Maine. The lone Whig was Charles Conrad of Louisiana, former Jacksonian Democrat who had broken with the party on the bank issue (*Biographical Dictionary of the American Congress, 1774–1961*, p. 731). *Nat. Intell.*, 22 Aug. 1842; Richard N. Current, *Daniel Webster and the Rise of National Conservatism*, p. 124. The tariff of 1842 increased duties on British manufactured goods.

8. Augusta *Age*, 19 Aug. 1842, Calais *Front. J.* (n.d.), Leeds citizens, Fairfield's message to Maine legis., 7 Jan. 1843, all cited in Henry S. Burrage, *Maine in the Northeastern Boundary Controversy*, pp. 356, 360–61; Augusta *J.*, 24 Aug. 1842, 6, 13 Jan., 3 Feb. 1843; Portland *East. Argus*, 4 Aug. 1842, cited in Balt. *Sun*, 10 Aug. 1842; Bangor *Demo.* (n.d.) cited in New Brunswick *Cour.*, 13 Aug., 3 Sept. 1842; *CG*, *Append.*, 27 Cong., 3 sess., pp. 53, 56; Maine committee report summarized in Augusta *J.*, 24 Mar. 1843; Kent to Webster, 4 Jan. 1843, WP (F16/21230) [letter erroneously dated 4 Jan. 1842]. Webster's 1846 defense of treaty in Senate in McIntyre, ed., *Writings and Speeches of Webster*, 9:101. William L. Lucey, ed., "Some Correspondence of the Maine Commissioners Regarding the Webster-Ashburton Treaty," pp. 332–48.

9. Boston *Trans.*, 25, 30 Aug. 1842; Boston *Post*, 1, 13 Sept. 1842; *Niles' Reg.* 62 (27 Aug. 1842): 401; N.Y. *J. of Comm.*, 27 Aug. 1842, cited in New Brunswick *Cour.*, 3 Sept. 1842; N.Y. *Comm. Adv.*, 21 Aug. 1842, cited in Kingston *Chron. and Gaz.*, 27 Aug. 1842; N.Y. *Albion* (n.d.) cited in Kingston *Chron. and Gaz.*, 3 Sept. 1842; Chicago *Amer.*, 9 Sept. 1842; St. Louis *Repub.*, 9 Aug. through 31 Dec. 1842; Wash. *Globe*, 26 Aug., 2 Sept. 1842; Cincinnati *Enq.*, 16, 18, 27 Aug. 1842; Charles March to Webster, 23 Aug. 1842, WP (F17/23274); Quincy to Webster, 27 Sept. 1842, WP (F18/23474); Webster to Everett, 29 Dec. 1842, WP (F18/23968).

10. Richmond *Enq.*, 23 Aug. 1842; Balt. *Sun*, 16 Aug., 14, 20 Sept., 26 Oct. 1842; Charleston *Merc.*, 17, 30, 31 Aug., 7, 9, 10 Sept. 1842; Legaré's statements in Balt. *Sun*, 14 Sept. 1842; New Orleans *Pic.*, 7 Sept., 17, 19 Nov. 1842; *Southron*, 22 Sept. 1842; Nashville *Union*, 6, 20, 23 Sept. 1842; Nashville *Repub. Banner*, 10 Aug. through 31 Dec. 1842; Mobile *Reg. & J.*, 10 Aug., 7, 12 Sept., 3 Oct., 10 Nov. 1842.

11. Current, "Webster's Propaganda," p. 197. Observer was British consul in Boston, Thomas Grattan. See his *Civilized America*, 1:399. Charles F. Adams, ed., *Memoirs of John Quincy Adams, Comprising Portions of His Diary from 1795 to 1848*, 11:243.

12. Coburg *Star* (n.d.) cited in Charleston *Merc.*, 20 Sept. 1842; New Brunswick *Cour.*, 3 Sept. 1842; St. John *Morning News*, 22, 24 Aug., 21, 30 Sept. 1842; Colebrooke to Stanley, 30 Aug. 1842, N.B., Disp. (PAC); Ottawa *Adv.*, 18 Aug., 1 Sept. 1842; Halifax *Novascotian*, 1, 8 Sept., 6 Oct. 1842; Bagot's message to Canadian Parliament cited in ibid., 22 Sept. 1842; Montreal *Trans.*, 27, 30 Aug. 1842; Montreal *Cour.* (n.d.) cited in *Nat. Intell.*, 23 Jan. 1843; Toronto *Examiner*, 17, 31 Aug., 7 Sept., 14 Dec. 1842, 26 Apr. 1843; Halifax *Morning Post*, 3 Sept. 1842, cited in *Nat. Intell.*, 13 Sept. 1842; Kingston *Chron. and Gaz.*, 17 Aug. 1842; Fredericton *Sent.* (n.d.) cited in London *Times*, 11 Oct. 1842.

13. Thomas Ward to Joshua Bates [both Baring Bros. board members], 31 Aug. 1842, Thomas Wren Ward Papers; Liverpool *European*, 20 Sept. 1842, cited in St. John *Morning News*, 5 Oct. 1842; Charles Buller to Russell, 23 Oct. 1842, Lord Russell Papers; Liverpool *Shipping Gazette* (n.d.) cited in New Brunswick *Cour.*, 8 Oct. 1842; author not identified, "Treaty of Washington," *Quarterly Rev.* 71 (Dec. 1842 & Mar. 1843): 560–95; author not identified, "The Late Session," *Edinburgh Rev.* 153 (Oct. 1842): 241–74; Norman Gash, *Sir Robert Peel*, p. 500; London *Times*, 24, 26 Aug., 16, 17, 21, 27 Sept., 4 Oct. 1842.

14. Merle E. Curti, *The American Peace Crusade, 1815–1860*, pp. 58–60, 111; Warren F. Kuehl, *Seeking World Order*, pp. 15–19; N.Y. *Herald*, 17 Aug. 1842; Boston *Atlas* (n.d.) cited in *Nat. Intell.*, 2 Sept. 1842; Ashb. to Webster, 3 Sept. 1842, WP (F18/23376); Allan Nevins, ed., *The Diary of Philip Hone, 1828–1851*, p. 618; Oliver P.

Chitwood, *John Tyler*, pp. 315–16; Richmond *Enq.*, 6 Sept. 1842; N.Y. *Herald*, 3 Sept. 1842.

15. N.Y. *Herald*, 3 Sept. 1842.

16. Ibid., 3, 4 Sept. 1842.

17. London *Times*, 24 Sept. 1842.

18. Webster to William Derrick [special agent], 22 Aug. 1842, Dipl. Instr., GB (NA); Hunter Miller, "An Annotated Dashiell's Map," pp. 70–73; Webster to Everett, 22 Aug. 1842, WP (F17/23244); Everett to Webster, 19 Sept., 17, 20 Oct. 1842, WP (F18/23446, 23568, and 23609); Aberdeen to Peel, 13 Oct. 1842, Lord Aberdeen Papers (BM, 43062); Aberdeen to Fox, 18 Oct. 1842, FO 115/79 (PRO); Everett to Webster, 19 Oct. 1842, Disp., GB (NA); Tyler to L. W. Tazewell, 24 Oct. 1842, Lyon Gardiner Tyler, *The Letters and Times of the Tylers*, 2:248; Boston *Trans.*, 18 Nov. 1842; *Nat. Intell.*, 7 Nov. 1842.

19. London *Times*, 13, 23–26, 29 Aug. 1842; London *Morning Chron.*, 19–22, 24, 26, 27 Sept. 1842, all cited in *Nat. Intell.*, 26, 27, 31 Jan., 2, 4, 9, 16 Feb. 1843. There is no doubt of Palmerston's authorship; undated drafts of these articles are in his handwriting and located in Lord Palmerston Papers, PRE/B/17–22, by permission of the Trustees of the Broadlands Archives. London *Morning Herald* (n.d.), London *Punch* (n.d.), London *Evening Star* (n.d.), all cited in Richmond *Enq.*, 11 Oct., 22 Nov., 6 Dec. 1842; Everett to Webster, 19 Aug. 1842, Disp., GB (NA).

20. Charles C. F. Greville, *The Greville Memoirs*, 1:432; London *Morning Chron.*, 19, 20, 22, 24, 26, 27 Sept. 1842, all cited in *Nat. Intell.*, 26, 27 Jan., 2, 4, 9, 16 Feb. 1843; Palm. to Russell, Sept. [?] 1842, G. P. Gooch, ed., *The Later Correspondence of Lord John Russell, 1840–1878*, 1:58–59.

21. Palm. to Russell, 9, 24 Sept. 1842, Russell Papers; Palm. to Melbourne, 10 Oct. 1842, Palm. Papers, GC/ME/494/2–3; Palm. to Lord Minto, 10 Oct. 1842, ibid., GC/MI/581/2; Palm. to Lord Monteagle, 28 Oct. 1842, ibid., GC/MO/131/2–3.

22. London *Times*, 23 Sept. 1842, 3 Jan., 6 Feb., 25 Mar. 1843.

23. Ashb. to Croker, 15 Nov. 1842, 6 Jan., 27 Feb. 1844, John Croker Papers (Duke U.).

24. Aberdeen to Ashb., 26 Sept. 1842, Aberdeen Papers (BM, 43123); Greville to Reeve, 4 Oct. 1842, Arthur H. Johnson, ed., *The Letters of Charles Greville and Henry Reeve, 1836–1865*, p. 68; Greville, *Memoirs*, 1: 435, 450–51; Philip W. Wilson, ed., *The Greville Diary, Including Passages Hitherto Withheld from Publication*, 2:549, 550; London *Times*, 10 Oct. 1842; Russell to Palm., 19, 28 Sept., 16 Oct., 11 Nov. 1842, Palm. Papers, GC/RU/64–65; 66/1; 69/1–3; Russell to Melbourne, 4 Oct. 1842, ibid., GC/ME/494/2; Everett to Webster, 1, 19 Sept. 1842, WP (F18/23349 and 23446). Featherstonhaugh was a geologist who helped lead Palmerston's survey team in exploring the disputed territory in 1839.

25. Everett to Webster, 10 Feb. 1843, WP (F18/24332); Sparks to Webster, 21 Feb. 1843, WP (F18/24392); George W. Featherstonhaugh, *Observations upon the Treaty of Washington, Signed August 9, 1842*. See Featherstonhaugh's article in London *Times*, 6 Feb. 1843. Featherstonhaugh to John Backhouse, 13 Feb., 22 Nov. 1843, John Backhouse Papers; Aberdeen to Croker, 25 Feb. 1843, Louis J. Jennings, ed., *The Croker Papers*, 2:191. The Sparks map became known in England after the Senate published its secret debates of August 1842 in the following January.

26. Ashb. to Aberdeen, 21 Jan. 1843, Aberdeen Papers (BM, 43123, private); Montreal *Trans.*, 4 Feb. 1843; Ashb. to Croker, 7, 13 Feb. 1843; John Croker Papers (U. of Mich.); Ashb. to Webster, 2 Jan. 1843, WP (F18/24063); author not identified, "Treaty of Washington," p. 582.

27. Tyler's message to House, 27 Feb. 1843, in James D. Richardson, ed., *A Compilation of the Messages and Papers of the Presidents*, 4:229–32; Tyler's message to Congress, 6 Dec. 1842, ibid., pp. 194–96; Peel to Aberdeen, 6 Jan. 1843, Peel Papers (BM, 40453); Aberdeen to Fox, 18 Jan. 1843, HCSP 61 (1843): 10; London *Times*, 31

Dec. 1842; Montreal *Trans.*, 14 Mar. 1843; Toronto *Examiner*, 15 Mar. 1843; Fox to Aberdeen, 24 Feb. 1843, FO 115/84 (PRO); Ashb. to Aberdeen, 1, 6 Jan. 1843, Aberdeen Papers (BM, 43123, both private); Ashb. to Webster, 2 Jan. 1843, WP (F18/24063); Aberdeen to Croker, 25 Feb. 1843, Jennings, ed., *Croker Papers*, 2:190. Lewis Cass resigned his post in Paris because he believed the Washington government had sanctioned British search by not outlawing it in the treaty (Cass to Webster, 3 Oct., 11 Dec. 1842, Disp., France [NA]). Tyler, Webster, and Everett believed that Cass's behavior was due to his desire to become president in 1844 (Tyler, *Letters*, 2:235; Webster to son Fletcher, 5 Oct. 1842, WP [F18/23526]; Everett to Webster, 17 Oct. 1842, WP [F18/23568]; Webster to Cass, 14 Nov., 20 Dec. 1842, U. S., Congress, *Senate Documents*, 27 Cong., 3 sess., vol. 4, no. 223, pp. 6, 18; Tyler to son Robert, 14 Apr. 1846, Tyler, *Letters*, 2:454–55).

28. Augusta *J.*, 10 Mar. 1843; CG, 27 Cong., 3 sess., pp. 332–34.

29. *Hansard's Parliamentary Debates*, 3d ser., 67 (21 Mar. 1843): 1162–65; Palm's. speech in ibid., pp. 1162–1218. For critical opinion of his speech, see Everett to Webster, 28 Mar. 1843, Disp., GB (NA).

30. *Parl. Debates* 67 (21 Mar. 1843): 1184–85, 1216–17, 1218.

31. Ibid., pp. 1247–52.

32. Ibid. 68 (7 Apr. 1843): 641; (2 May 1843): 1168, 1241; Everett to Webster, 3 May 1843, Disp., GB (NA); William M. Torrens, ed., *Memoirs of the Right Honourable William, Second Viscount Melbourne*, 2: 380–81; London *Times*, 4 May 1843; Hunter Miller, ed., *Treaties and Other International Acts of the United States of America, 1776–1863*, 4: 408–10.

33. CG, 29 Cong., 1 sess., pp. 636ff., 699, 729–30; Adams, ed., *Memoirs of JQA*, 12: 266.

34. CG, 29 Cong., 1 sess., pp. 636, 643, 735. See my article, "The Attempt to Impeach Daniel Webster," pp. 31–44.

35. Depos. of Stubbs, 9–18 May 1846, in "Unpublished Testimony of the Select Committee," in WP (F40/55279); "Statement of Moneys advanced to the Secretary of State and how accounted for by him," 1 Feb. 1845, WP (F40/55312).

36. U.S., Congress, *House Reports*, 29 Cong., 1 sess. (Ser. 490), no. 684, pp. 11–17.

37. Tyler's testimony, including expurgated sections, in WP (F40/55212). Published portions in *House Reports*, 29 Cong., 1 sess. (Ser. 490), no. 684, pp. 9–11. Milo M. Quaife, ed., *The Diary of James K. Polk*, 1:430–31; Tyler to Webster, 21 Apr. 1846, WP (F20/26855).

38. *House Reports*, 29 Cong., 1 sess. (Ser. 490), no. 684, pp. 1–4.

39. CG, 29 Cong., 1 sess., pp. 999–1000; *House Reports*, 29 Cong., 1 sess. (Ser. 490), no. 684, p. 4. Polk's cabinet unanimously agreed with his refusal to turn over documents to the House (Quaife, ed., *Diary of Polk*, 1: 332).

40. Ashb. to Aberdeen, 29 Sept., 24, 27 Oct. 1842, Aberdeen Papers (BM, 43123; second, confidential); Aberdeen to Peel, 28 Sept. 1842, ibid. (43062); Peel to Aberdeen, 2, 20 Oct. 1842, ibid. (first, private); Peel to Wellington, 16 Oct. 1842, Peel Papers (BM, 40459, "Most Private"); C. [Charles?] Arbuthnot to Peel, 18 Oct. 1842, ibid. (40484); Wellington to Peel, 18 Oct. 1842, ibid. (40459); Aberdeen to Ashb., 21 Oct. 1842, ibid. (40453); Peel to Croker, 23 Feb. 1843, Jennings, ed., *Croker Papers*, 2:193.

Bibliography

MANUSCRIPT SOURCES, AMERICAN AND BRITISH

Ann Arbor, Michigan.

Clements Library, University of
  Michigan
    Lewis Cass Papers
    John Croker Papers
    Jared Sparks Letters

Boston.

Massachusetts Historical Society
    Edward Everett Papers
    Thomas Wren Ward Papers

Durham, North Carolina.

Perkins Library, Duke University
    John Backhouse Papers
    John Croker Papers
    Adeline Ellery (Burr) Davis Green
        Papers
    John Rutherfoord Papers

Hanover, New Hampshire.

Dartmouth College
    Daniel Webster Papers, Charles M.
        Wiltse, ed.

London.

British Museum, Additional Manu-
    scripts
    Lord Aberdeen Papers
    Lord Palmerston's Letter-Books,
        48495
    Sir Robert Peel Papers
Hampshire Record Office
    Lord Palmerston Papers, Broad-

lands Manuscripts, 12889 (temporarily housed in London)

Public Record Office
  Lord Ashburton Papers, Foreign
      Office
  Great Britain, Foreign Office
  Lord John Russell Papers

New York.

New York University
  Albert Gallatin Papers

Ottawa.

Public Archives of Canada
  Baring Papers
  Great Britain, Colonial Office
  Sir Allan MacNab Papers, Albemarle Manuscripts
  New Brunswick, Dispatches

Washington, D.C.

Library of Congress
  Baring Brothers Papers (photocopies taken from London, Public Record Office, Private Documents)
  John J. Crittenden Papers
  Thomas Ewing Papers
  William Cabell Rives Papers
  John Tyler Papers
  Martin Van Buren Papers

National Archives
  Department of the Navy
  The Letter Books of Commodore
      Matthew C. Perry
  Department of State
  Diplomatic Instructions, Great
      Britain
  Dispatches, France
  Dispatches, Great Britain
  Domestic Letters
  Envelope marked "Miscellaneous
      on Northeastern Boundary," E98
  Folder marked "Ne. Bdry. Negot.,"
      E89

Miscellaneous Letters

Notes from the British Legation in the United States to the Department of State, 1791–1906

Notes to Foreign Legations in the United States from the Department of State, 1834–1906, Great Britain

Department of the Treasury

Letters Sent to the President by the Secretary of the Treasury, 1833 to 1878

Department of War

Eastern Division, Letters Sent by [Winfield] Scott, Book 36

Eastern Division, Letters to [Winfield] Scott, Book 37

Letters Sent to the President, 1800–1863

Military Book No. 23, War Office, no. 210

General Land Office

Records: Letters to Surveyors General, 1796–1901

COLLECTED WORKS, AMERICAN AND BRITISH

Abel, Annie Heloise, and Klingberg, Frank J., eds. *A Side-Light on Anglo-American Relations, 1839–1858; Furnished by the Correspondence of Lewis Tappan and Others with The British and Foreign Anti-Slavery Society.* New York: Augustus M. Kelley, Publishers, 1970. Originally published in Lancaster, Pa., 1927.

Adams, Charles F., ed. *Memoirs of John Quincy Adams, Comprising Portions of His Diary from 1795 to 1848.* 12 vols. Philadelphia: Lippincott, 1874–77.

Baker, George E., ed. *The Works of William H. Seward.* 5 vols. New York: Houghton, Mifflin, 1884.

Bassett, John Spencer, ed. *The Correspondence of Andrew Jackson.* 7 vols. Washington, D.C.: Carnegie Institute, 1926–35.

Benson, Arthur C., and Esher, Viscount, eds. *The Letters of Queen Victoria: A Selection from Her Majesty's Correspondence Between the Years 1837 and 1861.* 3 vols. London: John Murray, 1908.

Benton, Thomas Hart. *Thirty Years' View; or, A History of the American Government for Thirty Years from 1820 to 1850.* 2 vols. New York: D. Appleton and Co., 1856.

Chapman, Leonard B., ed. "Rev. Caleb Bradley on the Madawaska War."

Collections and Proceedings of the Maine Historical Society, 2d ser., 9 (Portland, Maine, 1898): 418–25.

Crallé, Richard K., ed. *The Works of John C. Calhoun*. 6 vols. New York: D. Appleton and Co., 1854–60.

Fitzpatrick, John C., ed. *The Autobiography of Martin Van Buren*. In *Annual Report of the American Historical Association*, 1918, vol. 2. Washington, D.C.: U.S. Government Printing Office, 1920.

Ford, Worthington C., ed. *Writings of John Quincy Adams*. 7 vols. New York: Macmillan, 1913–17.

Gallatin, Albert. *A Memoir on the North-Eastern Boundary, In Connexion with Mr. Jay's Map*. New York: Printed for the New York Historical Society, 1843. In *Proceedings of the New York Historical Society for the Year 1843*. New York, 1844.

————. *The Right of the United States of America to the North-Eastern Boundary Claimed By Them: Principally Laid Before the King of the Netherlands*. New York: Samuel Adams, Printer, 1840.

Gooch, G. P., ed. *The Later Correspondence of Lord John Russell, 1840–1878*. 2 vols. London: Longmans, Green and Co., 1925.

Grattan, Thomas C. *Civilized America*. 2 vols. London: Bradbury and Evans, 1859.

Greville, Charles C. F. *The Greville Memoirs* (second part): *A Journal of the Reign of Queen Victoria from 1837 to 1852*. Edited by Henry Reeve. 2 vols. New York: D. Appleton and Co., 1885.

Jennings, Louis J., ed. *The Croker Papers: The Correspondence and Diaries of the Late Right Honourable John Wilson Croker, LL. D., F.R.S.* 2 vols. New York: Charles Scribner's Sons, 1884.

Johnson, Arthur H., ed. *The Letters of Charles Greville and Henry Reeve, 1836–1865*. London: T. F. Unwin, 1924.

Lucey, William L., ed. "Some Correspondence of the Maine Commissioners Regarding the Webster-Ashburton Treaty." *New England Quarterly* 15 (June 1942): 332–48.

McElroy, Robert, and Riggs, Thomas, eds. *The Unfortified Boundary: A Diary of the First Survey of the Canadian Boundary Line from St. Regis to the Lake of the Woods by Major Joseph Delafield, American Agent under Articles VI and VII of the Treaty of Ghent*. New York: private printing, 1943.

McIntyre, James M., ed. *The Writings and Speeches of Daniel Webster*. 18 vols. Boston: Little, Brown, 1903.

Moore, John B. *The Collected Papers of John Bassett Moore*. 7 vols. New Haven: Yale University Press, 1944.

Morrell, Philip, ed. *Leaves from the Greville Diary*. New York: Dutton, 1929.

Nevins, Allan, ed. *The Diary of Philip Hone, 1828–1851*. New York: Dodd, Mead and Co., 1927.

Ormsby, William G., ed. *The Grey Journals and Letters; Crisis in the Canadas: 1838–1839*. London: Macmillan, 1965.

Parker, Charles S., ed. *Sir Robert Peel, From His Private Papers.* 3 vols. London: John Murray, 1891–99.

Quaife, Milo M., ed. *The Diary of James K. Polk: During His Presidency, 1845 to 1849.* 4 vols. Chicago: A. C. McClurg and Co., 1910.

Rives, George L., ed. *Selections from the Correspondence of Thomas Barclay.* New York: Harper and Brothers Publishers, 1894.

Rush, Richard. *Memoranda of a Residence at the Court of London, Comprising Incidents Official and Personal from 1819 to 1825. Including Questions Between the United States and Great Britain.* Philadelphia: Lea and Blanchard, 1845.

Scott, Winfield. *Memoirs of Lieut.-General Scott, LL.D. Written by Himself.* 2 vols. New York: Sheldon and Co., 1864.

Seward, Frederick W., ed. *William H. Seward: An Autobiography from 1801–1834. With a Memoir of His Life, and Selections from His Letters, 1831–1846.* 3 vols. New York: Derby and Miller, 1891.

Stacey, C. P., ed. "A Private Report of General Winfield Scott on the Border Situation in 1839." *Canadian Historical Review* 21 (Dec. 1940): 407–14.

Staples, Arthur G., ed. *The Letters of John Fairfield.* Lewiston, Maine: Lewiston Journal Co., 1922.

Story, William W., ed. *Life and Letters of Joseph Story.* 2 vols. Boston: Little, Brown, 1851.

Strachey, Lytton, and Fulford, Roger, eds. *The Greville Memoirs, 1814–1860.* London: Macmillan, 1938.

Torrens, William M., ed. *Memoirs of the Right Honourable William, Second Viscount Melbourne.* 2 vols. London: Macmillan, 1878.

Tuckerman, Bayard, ed. *The Diary of Philip Hone.* 2 vols. New York: Dodd, Mead and Co., 1910.

Tyler, Lyon Gardiner. *The Letters and Times of the Tylers.* 3 vols. Richmond: Whittet and Shepperson, 1884–96. Reprint. New York: DaCapo, 1970.

————. "The Ashburton Treaty, 1842." *Tyler's Quarterly Historical and Genealogical Magazine* 3, no. 4 (April 1922): 255–56.

Wheaton, Henry. *Enquiry into the Validity of the British Claim to a Right of Visitation and Search of American Vessels Suspected to be Engaged in the African Slave-Trade.* Philadelphia: Lea and Blanchard, 1842. Located in Indiana University Library.

Wilson, Philip W., ed. *The Greville Diary, Including Passages Hitherto Withheld from Publication.* 2 vols. Garden City, N.Y.: Doubleday, Page, 1927.

DOCUMENTARY COLLECTIONS, AMERICAN

American State Papers, Foreign Relations. 6 vols. Washington, D.C.: Gales and Seaton, 1832–59.

Aroostook War. Historical Sketch and Roster of Commissioned Officers and Enlisted Men Called into Service for the Protection of the Northeastern Frontier of Maine. From February to May, 1839. Augusta, Maine: n.p., 1904.

Biographical Dictionary of the American Congress, 1774–1961. In *House Documents*, 85 Cong., 2 sess., no. 442.

Catterall, Helen T., ed. *Judicial Cases Concerning American Slavery and the Negro.* 5 vols. Washington, D.C.: Carnegie Institution, 1926–32.

"Documentary History of the North Eastern Boundary Controversy." *Historical Collections of Piscataquis County, Maine.* Dover, Maine: Observer Press, 1910. Pp. 282–327.

Gould, Marcus T. C. *Gould's Stenographic Reporter.* 2 vols. Washington, D.C.: Gould's Stenographic Reporter, 1841. In Law Division, Library of Congress. Outside of volume entitled, *Trial of Alex. McLeod for Murder of Amos Durfee–New York, 1841:* Wash. City, 1841.

Hill, Nicholas, Jr. *New York Common Law Reports, Vol. 15* (4 vols. in one). Newark, N.Y.: Lawyers' Co-operative Publishing Co., 1885.

Jenkins, William S., ed. *Records of the States of the United States, 1836–41. Maine: Executive Records.* Washington, D.C.: Library of Congress in association with the University of North Carolina, 1949.

————. *Records of the States of the United States, 1836–41. Maine: Legislative Records* [*Journal of the Lower House of the State of Maine; Journal of the Senate of the State of Maine; Journal of the Senate, Special Session; Journal of the State of Maine, Appendix* (joint meeting of House and Senate)]. Washington, D.C.: Library of Congress in association with the University of North Carolina, 1949.

Lincoln, Charles Z., ed. *Messages from the Governors, Comprising Executive Communications to the Legislature and Other Papers Relating to Legislation from the Organization of the First Colonial Assembly in 1683 to and Including the Year 1906, with Notes.* 11 vols. Albany, n.p., 1909.

Malloy, William M., et al., eds. *Treaties, Conventions, International Acts, Protocols, and Agreements Between the United States and Other Powers, 1776–1937.* 4 vols. Washington, D.C.: U.S. Government Printing Office, 1910–38.

Manning, William R., ed. *Diplomatic Correspondence of the United States. Canadian Relations, 1784–1860.* 4 vols. Washington, D.C.: Carnegie Endowment for International Peace, 1940–45.

Miller, Hunter, ed. *Treaties and Other International Acts of the United States of America, 1776–1863.* 8 vols. Washington, D.C.: U.S. Government Printing Office, 1931–48.

Moore, John B. *A Digest of International Law.* 8 vols. Washington, D.C.: U.S. Government Printing Office, 1906.

————. *History and Digest of the International Arbitrations to Which the United States Has Been a Party.* 6 vols. Washington, D.C.: U.S. Government Printing Office, 1898.

————, ed. *International Adjudications, Ancient and Modern,* Modern Series. 6 vols. New York: Oxford University Press, 1929–33.

Nevins, Allan, ed. *America Through British Eyes*. New York: Oxford University Press, 1948.

New York *Sun*. *Trial of Alexander M'Leod for the Murder of Amos Durfee and as an Accomplice in the Burning of the Steamer Caroline in the Niagara River, during the Canadian Rebellion[s] in 1837–8*. New York: New York *Sun*, 1841. Outside of volume entitled *McLeod's Trial*, L. of C., No. 2. Located in Library of Congress, Law Division.

Peters, Richard, ed. *Reports of Cases Argued and Adjudged in the Supreme Court of the United States*. 90 vols. Philadelphia, 1828–74.

Poore, Benjamin Perley. *A Descriptive Catalogue of the Government Publications of the United States, September 5, 1774–March 4, 1881*. 2 vols. Washington, D.C.: U.S. Government Printing Office, 1885.

Richardson, James D., ed. *A Compilation of the Messages and Papers of the Presidents*. 11 vols. New York: Bureau of National Literature, 1896–1910.

Scott, James B., ed. *Cases on International Law Selected from Decisions of English and American Courts*. Boston: Boston Book Co., 1902.

U.S., Congress, *Congressional Globe*, 1837–43.

————. *Congressional Globe, Appendix*, 1837–43.

————. *House Documents*, 1837–43.

————. *House Executive Documents*, 1837–43.

————. *House Reports*, 1837–43.

————. *Senate Documents*, 1837–43.

U.S. *Statutes at Large*. Multivols. Boston: Little, Brown, 1853–.

Wendell, John L. *Reports of Cases Argued and Determined in the Supreme Court of Judicature and in the Court for the Trial of Impeachments and the Correction of Errors of the State of New York, Vol. 25*. Newark, N.Y.: Lawyers' Co-operative Publishing Co., 1885. Outside of volume entitled *New York Common Law Reports. Vol. 14*.

Wharton, Francis, ed. *The Revolutionary Diplomatic Correspondence of the United States*. 6 vols. Washington, D.C.: U.S. Government Printing Office, 1889.

DOCUMENTARY COLLECTIONS, BRITISH

Great Britain. *British and Foreign State Papers*. 116 vols. London: James Ridgway and Sons, 1812–1925.

Great Britain. Parliament. *House of Commons. Sessional Papers*, 1801–1900.

Hansard, Thomas C., ed. *Hansard's Parliamentary Debates*. 3d ser. 356 vols. London: Wyman, 1830–91.

Knaplund, Paul, ed. *Letters from Lord Sydenham, Governor-General of Canada, 1839–1841, to Lord John Russell*. London: G. Allen and Unwin, 1931.

New Brunswick. Dispatches. Public Archives of Canada, Ottawa.

NEWSPAPERS, MAGAZINES, CONTEMPORARY JOURNALS, AND PAMPHLETS, AMERICAN AND BRITISH

Albany *Argus*

Augusta *Age*

Augusta *Journal*

Baltimore *Sun*

Bangor *Democrat*

Bangor *Whig*

Blackwood's Edinburgh Magazine (London)

Boston *Advertiser*

Boston *Courier*

Boston *Liberator*

Boston *Post*

Boston *Times*

Boston *Transcript*

[Cass, Lewis]. *An Examination of the Question Now in Discussion Between the American & British Governments, Concerning the Right of Search. By an American.* Paris: H. Fournier, 1842.

Charleston *Courier*

Charleston *Mercury*

Chicago *American*

Cincinnati *Enquirer*

Concord *Herald of Freedom* (New Hampshire)

Edinburgh Review (London)

Featherstonhaugh, George W. *Observations upon the Treaty of Washington, Signed August 9, 1842; with the Treaty Annexed.* London, 1843. Located in Eli Lilly Library (Indiana University).

Foreign Quarterly Review (London)

Fredericton *Sentinel* (New Brunswick)

Gleaner (Miramichi, New Brunswick)

Halifax *Morning Post*

Halifax *Novascotian*

Kingston *Chronicle and Gazette* (New Brunswick)

London *Examiner*
London *Punch*
London *Times*
Mobile *Register & Journal*
Montreal *Courier*
Montreal *Transcript*
Nashville *Republican Banner*
Nashville *Union*
National Intelligencer (Washington,
  D.C.)
New Brunswick *Courier*
New Brunswick *Royal Gazette*
New Orleans *Picayune*
New York *Herald*
Niles' Register (Baltimore)
North American Review (Boston)
Northampton *Courier* (Massa-
  chusetts)
Ottawa *Advertiser*
Palfrey, John G. "British American
  Politics." *North American Review*
  49 (Oct. 1839): 373–431.
Philadelphia *Public Ledger and Daily
  Transcript*
Pittsfield *Sun* (Massachusetts)
Portland *Advertiser*
Portland *Eastern Argus*
Quarterly Review (London)
Richmond *Enquirer*
Rochester *Daily Democrat*
Rochester *Republican*
St. John *Herald*
St. John *Morning News*
St. John *Observer*
St. Louis *Republican*
Southron (Jackson, Miss.)
Sparks, Jared. "The Treaty of Wash-
  ington." *North American Review*
  56 (Apr. 1843): 452–96.
Toronto *Examiner*
Utica *Daily Gazette*
Washington *Globe*

SECONDARY MATERIALS

Adams, Ephraim D. "Lord Ashburton and the Treaty of Washington." *American Historical Review* 17 (July 1912): 764–82.

Adams, Herbert B. *The Life and Writings of Jared Sparks: Comprising Selections from His Journals and Correspondence.* 2 vols. Boston: Houghton, Mifflin, 1893.

Alberts, Robert C. *The Golden Voyage: The Life and Times of William Bingham, 1752–1804.* Boston: Houghton-Mifflin, 1969.

Allen, Harry C. *Conflict and Concord: The Anglo-American Relationship since 1783.* New York: St. Martin's, 1959.

————. *Great Britain and the United States: A History of Anglo-American Relations (1783–1952).* New York: St. Martin's, 1955.

Amory, Thomas C. *The Life of James Sullivan: With Selections from his Writings.* 2 vols. Boston: Phillips, Sampson and Co., 1858–59.

Baldwin, J. R. "The Ashburton-Webster Boundary Settlement." *Canadian Historical Association,* 1938, pp. 121–33. Toronto, 1938.

Barnes, Gilbert H. *The Antislavery Impulse, 1830–1844.* New York: American Historical Association, 1933.

Barnes, James J. *Authors, Publishers and Politicians: The Quest for an Anglo-American Copyright Agreement, 1815–1854.* Columbus: Ohio State University Press, 1974.

Bell, Herbert C. F. *Lord Palmerston.* 2 vols. London: Longmans, Green and Co., 1936.

Bemis, Samuel F. *The Diplomacy of the American Revolution.* New York: D. Appleton-Century, 1935.

————. "Jay's Treaty and the Northwest Boundary Gap." *American Historical Review* 27 (Apr. 1922): 465–84.

————. *Jay's Treaty: A Study in Commerce and Diplomacy.* New York: Macmillan, 1923.

————. *John Quincy Adams and the Foundations of American Foreign Policy.* New York: Alfred A. Knopf, 1949.

————. *John Quincy Adams and the Union.* New York: Alfred A. Knopf, 1956.

————. *Pinckney's Treaty: America's Advantage from Europe's Distress, 1783–1800.* Baltimore: Johns Hopkins Press, 1926.

————. *American Secretaries of State and Their Diplomacy.* Vol. 5. New York: Alfred A. Knopf, 1928.

Bonham, Milledge L., Jr. "Alexander McLeod: Bone of Contention." *New York History* 18 (Apr. 1937): 189–217.

Booth, Alan R. "The United States African Squadron, 1843–1861." In Jeffrey Butler, ed., *Boston University Papers in African History,* pp. 77–117. Boston: African Studies Center of Boston University, 1964.

Bourne, Kenneth. *Britain and the Balance of Power in North America, 1815–1908.* Berkeley: University of California Press, 1967.

Brebner, John B. *North Atlantic Triangle*. New Haven: Yale University Press, 1945.

Brightfield, Myron F. *John Wilson Croker*. Berkeley: University of California Press, 1940.

Brown, Roger H. *The Struggle for the Indian Stream Territory*. Cleveland: Western Reserve University Press, 1955.

Burrage, Henry S. "The Attitude of Maine in the Northeastern Boundary Controversy." In *Collections of the Maine Historical Society*, 3d ser., 1, pp. 353–68. Portland, Maine, 1904.

————. *Maine in the Northeastern Boundary Controversy*. Portland, Maine: Marks Printing House, 1919.

————. "St. Croix Commission." Paper read before Maine Historical Society, 6 Feb. 1895.

Burt, Alfred L. *The United States, Great Britain and British North America from the Revolution to the Establishment of Peace after the War of 1812*. New Haven: Carnegie Endowment for International Peace, 1940.

Callahan, James M. *American Foreign Policy in Canadian Relations*. New York: Macmillan, 1937.

Campbell, Charles S. *From Revolution to Rapprochement: The United States and Great Britain, 1783–1900*. New York: John Wiley and Sons, 1974.

Chitwood, Oliver P. *John Tyler: Champion of the Old South*. New York: D. Appleton-Century, 1939.

Coffin, Joshua. *An Account of Some of the Principal Slave Insurrections*. New York: n.p., 1860. In *Slave Insurrections: Selected Documents*. Westport, Conn.: Negro Universities Press, 1970. No editor given. Volume originally published in 1822 by A. E. Miller, Charleston, S.C.

Corey, Albert B. *The Crisis of 1830–1842 in Canadian-American Relations*. New Haven: Carnegie Endowment for International Peace, 1941.

————. "Public Opinion and the McLeod Case." *Canadian Historical Association, 1936*, pp. 53–64. Toronto, 1936.

Creighton, D. G. "The Economic Background of the Rebellions of Eighteen Thirty-Seven." *Canadian Journal of Economics and Political Science* 3 (Aug. 1937): 322–34.

Current, Richard N. *Daniel Webster and the Rise of National Conservatism*. Boston: Little, Brown, 1955.

————. "Webster's Propaganda and the Ashburton Treaty." *Mississippi Valley Historical Review* 31 (Oct. 1947): 187–200.

Curti, Merle E. *The American Peace Crusade, 1815–1860*. Durham: Duke University Press, 1929.

Curtin, Philip D. *The Atlantic Slave Trade: A Census*. Madison: University of Wisconsin Press, 1969.

Curtis, George T. *Life of Daniel Webster*. 2 vols. New York: Appleton, 1870.

Curtis, James C. *The Fox at Bay: Martin Van Buren and the Presidency, 1837–1841*. Lexington: University Press of Kentucky, 1970.

Dalzell, Robert F., Jr. *Daniel Webster and the Trial of American Nationalism, 1843–1852*. Boston: Houghton Mifflin, 1973.

Dangerfield, George. *The Era of Good Feelings*. New York: Harcourt, Brace and World, 1952.

Davis, Calvin D. *The United States and the Second Hague Peace Conference: American Diplomacy and International Organization, 1899–1914*. Durham: Duke University Press, 1976.

Davis, Varina (Howell). *Jefferson Davis, Ex-President of the Confederate States of America: A Memoir by His Wife*. 2 vols. New York: Belford Co., 1890.

DeConde, Alexander. *This Affair of Louisiana*. New York: Charles Scribner's Sons, 1976.

Dent, John C. *The Story of the Upper Canadian Rebellion; Largely Derived from Original Sources and Documents*. 2 vols. Toronto: C. B. Robinson, 1885.

DuBois, W. E. B. *The Suppression of the African Slave-Trade to the United States of America, 1638–1870*. New York: Longmans, Green, and Co., 1896.

Duckett, Alvin L. *John Forsyth, Political Tactician*. Athens: University of Georgia Press, 1962.

Duignan, Peter, and Clendenen, Clarence. *The United States and the African Slave Trade, 1619–1862*. Stanford: Stanford University Press, 1962.

Eaton, Clement. "The Freedom of the Press in the Upper South." *Mississippi Valley Historical Review* 18 (Mar. 1932): 479–99.

————. *The Freedom-of-Thought Struggle in the Old South*. New York: Harper and Row, 1964.

Elliott, Charles W. *Winfield Scott, the Soldier and the Man*. New York: Macmillan, 1937.

Engelman, Fred L. *The Peace of Christmas Eve*. New York: Harcourt, Brace and World, 1960.

Ernst, Robert. *Rufus King: American Federalist*. Chapel Hill: University of North Carolina Press, 1968.

Faris, John T. *The Romance of the Boundaries*. New York: Harper and Bros., 1926.

Ferrell, Robert H. *American Diplomacy: A History*. New York: W. W. Norton and Co., 1959; 3d ed., 1975.

Filler, Louis. *The Crusade Against Slavery, 1830–1860*. New York: Harper and Row, 1960.

Fladeland, Betty. *James Gillespie Birney: Slaveholder to Abolitionist*. Ithaca, N.Y.: Cornell University Press, 1955.

————. *Men and Brothers: Anglo-American Antislavery Cooperation*. Urbana: University of Illinois Press, 1972.

Frothingham, Paul R. *Edward Everett, Orator and Statesman*. Boston: Houghton, Mifflin, 1925.

Fuess, Claude M. *Daniel Webster*. 2 vols. Boston: Little, Brown, 1930.

Ganong, William F. "A Monograph of the Evolution of the Boundaries of the

Province of New Brunswick." In *Proceedings and Transactions of the Royal Society of Canada*, 2d ser., 7, pp. 139–449. Ottawa, 1901.

Gash, Norman. *Sir Robert Peel: The Life of Sir Robert Peel after 1830*. London: Longman, 1972.

Gordon, Hugh T. *The Treaty of Washington, Concluded August 9, 1842, by Daniel Webster and Lord Ashburton. University of California, James Bryce Historical Prize Essays, 1905–07*, pp. 173–257. Berkeley: University of California Press, 1908.

Graebner, Norman A. *Empire on the Pacific: A Study in American Continental Expansion*. New York: Ronald Press, 1955.

Griffin, Joseph, ed. *History of the Press of Maine*. Brunswick, Maine: The Press, 1872.

Guillet, Edwin C. *The Lives and Times of the Patriots: An Account of the Rebellion in Upper Canada, 1837–38, and of the Patriot Agitation in the United States, 1837–1842*. Toronto: University of Toronto Press, 1938.

Haines, Charles G., and Sherwood, Foster H. *The Role of the Supreme Court in American Government and Politics, 1835–1864*. Berkeley: University of California Press, 1957.

Hand, Augustus N. "Local Incidents of the Papineau Rebellion." *New York History* 15 (Oct. 1934): 376–87.

Hidy, Ralph W. *The House of Baring in American Trade and Finance*. Cambridge, Mass.: Harvard University Press, 1949.

Howard, Warren S. *American Slavers and the Federal Law, 1837–1862*. Berkeley: University of California Press, 1963.

Hoyt, Edwin P. *The Amistad Affair*. London: Abelard-Schuman, 1970.

Jones, Howard. "Anglophobia and the Aroostook War." *New England Quarterly* 48 (Dec. 1975): 519–39.

———. "The Attempt to Impeach Daniel Webster." *Capitol Studies* 3 (Fall 1975): 31–44.

———. "The *Caroline* Affair." *The Historian* 38 (May 1976): 485–502.

———. "The Peculiar Institution and National Honor: The Case of the *Creole* Slave Revolt." *Civil War History* 21 (Mar. 1975): 28–50.

Jones, Wilbur D. *The American Problem in British Diplomacy, 1841–1861*. Athens: University of Georgia Press, 1974.

———. "The Influence of Slavery on the Webster-Ashburton Negotiations." *Journal of Southern History* 22 (Feb. 1956): 48–58.

———. *Lord Aberdeen and the Americas*. Athens: University of Georgia Press, 1958.

———. "Lord Ashburton and the Maine Boundary Negotiations." *Mississippi Valley Historical Review* 40 (Dec. 1953): 477–90.

Kilbourn, William. *The Firebrand: William Lyon Mackenzie and the Rebellion in Upper Canada*. Toronto: Clarke, Irwin and Co., 1956.

Kirwan, Albert D. *John J. Crittenden*. Lexington: University Press of Kentucky, 1962.

Kuehl, Warren F. *Seeking World Order: The United States and International Organization to 1920.* Nashville: Vanderbilt University Press, 1969.

Langer, William L. *Political and Social Upheaval, 1832–1852.* New York: Harper and Row, 1969.

LeDuc, Thomas. "The Maine Frontier and the Northeastern Boundary Controversy." *American Historical Review* 53 (Oct. 1947): 30–41.

————. "The Webster-Ashburton Treaty and the Minnesota Iron Ranges." *Journal of American History* 51 (Dec. 1964): 476–81.

Lofts, Norah, and Weiner, Margery. *Eternal France: A History of France, 1789–1944.* Garden City, N.Y.: Doubleday, 1968.

Longley, R. S. "Emigration and the Crisis of 1837 in Upper Canada." *Canadian Historical Review* 17 (Mar. 1936): 29–40.

Lowenthal, David. "The Maine Press and the Aroostook War." *Canadian Historical Review* 32 (Dec. 1951): 315–36.

McClendon, R. Earl. "The *Amistad* Claims: Inconsistencies of Policy." *Political Science Quarterly* 48 (Sept. 1933): 386–412.

McInnis, Edgar W. *The Unguarded Frontier: A History of American-Canadian Relations.* Garden City, N.Y.: Doubleday, Doran and Co., 1942.

Mackay, R. A. "The Political Ideals of William Lyon Mackenzie." *Canadian Journal of Economics and Political Science* 3 (Feb. 1937): 1–22.

Mahon, John K. *History of the Second Seminole War, 1835–1842.* Gainesville: University of Florida Press, 1967.

Mannix, Daniel P., and Cowley, Malcolm. *Black Cargoes: A History of the Atlantic Slave Trade, 1518–1865.* New York: Viking, 1962.

Martin, Ged. *The Durham Report and British Policy: A Critical Essay.* London: Cambridge University Press, 1972.

Martin, Lawrence, and Bemis, Samuel F. "Franklin's Red-Line Map Was a Mitchell." *New England Quarterly* 10 (Mar. 1937): 105–11.

May, Ernest R. *The Making of the Monroe Doctrine.* Cambridge, Mass.: Harvard University Press, 1976.

Merk, Frederick. *Fruits of Propaganda in the Tyler Administration.* Cambridge, Mass.: Harvard University Press, 1971.

————. *The Oregon Question: Essays in Anglo-American Diplomacy and Politics.* Cambridge, Mass.: Harvard University Press, 1967.

————. "The Oregon Question in the Webster-Ashburton Negotiations." *Mississippi Valley Historical Review* 43 (Dec. 1956): 379–404.

Miller, Hunter. "An Annotated Dashiell's Map." *American Historical Review* 38 (Oct. 1932): 70–93.

Mills, Dudley A. "British Diplomacy and Canada. The Ashburton Treaty." *United Empire: The Royal Colonial Institute Journal, New Series* 2 (Oct. 1911): 683–712.

Morgan, Robert J. *A Whig Embattled: The Presidency under John Tyler.* Lincoln: University of Nebraska Press, 1954.

Morris, Richard B. *The Peacemakers: The Great Powers and American Independence*. New York: Harper and Row, 1965.

New, Chester W. *Lord Durham: A Biography of John George Lambton, First Earl of Durham*. Oxford: Clarendon, 1929.

———. "The Rebellion of 1837 in Its Larger Setting." *Canadian Historical Association, Report*, 1937, pp. 5–17. Toronto, 1937.

Nussbaum, Arthur. *A Concise History of the Law of Nations*. New York: Macmillan, 1947.

Parks, Joseph H. *John Bell of Tennessee*. Baton Rouge: Louisiana State University Press, 1950.

Perkins, Bradford. *Castlereagh and Adams: England and the United States, 1812–1823*. Berkeley: University of California Press, 1964.

———. *The First Rapprochement: England and the United States, 1795–1805*. Berkeley: University of California Press, 1955.

———. *Prologue to War: England and the United States, 1805–1812*. Berkeley: University of California Press, 1961.

Pletcher, David M. *The Diplomacy of Annexation: Texas, Oregon, and the Mexican War*. Columbia: University of Missouri Press, 1973.

Reeves, Jesse S. *American Diplomacy under Tyler and Polk*. Baltimore: Johns Hopkins University Press, 1907.

Ridley, Jasper. *Lord Palmerston*. London: Constable, 1970.

Ritcheson, Charles R. *Aftermath of Revolution: British Policy Toward the United States, 1783–1795*. Dallas: Southern Methodist University Press, 1969.

Seager, Robert, II. *And Tyler Too: A Biography of John and Julia Gardiner Tyler*. New York: McGraw-Hill, 1963.

Shortridge, Wilson P. "The Canadian-American Frontier during the Rebellion of 1837–1838." *Canadian Historical Review* 7 (Mar. 1926): 13–26.

Soulsby, Hugh G. *The Right of Search and the Slave Trade in Anglo-American Relations, 1814–1862*. Baltimore: Johns Hopkins University Press, 1933.

Sprague, John F. "The North Eastern Boundary Controversy and the Aroostook War." *Historical Collections of Piscataquis County, Maine*, pp. 216–81. Dover, Maine: Observer Press, 1910.

Stacey, C. P. "The Myth of the Unguarded Frontier, 1815–1871." *American Historical Review* 56 (Oct. 1950): 1–18.

Steel, Anthony. "Impressment in the Monroe-Pinkney Negotiations, 1806–1807." *American Historical Review* 57 (Jan. 1952): 352–69.

Swisher, Carl B. *Roger B. Taney*. New York: Macmillan, 1935.

Temperley, Harold W. V. *The Foreign Policy of Canning, 1822–1827*. London: G. Bell and Sons, 1925.

Temperley, Howard. *British Antislavery, 1833–1870*. London: Longman, 1972.

Thistlethwaite, Frank. *The Anglo-American Connection in the Early Nineteenth Century*. Philadelphia: University of Pennsylvania Press, 1959.

———. "Atlantic Partnership." *Economic History Review* 7 (Aug. 1954): 1–17. —

Tiffany, Orrin E. *The Relations of the United States to the Canadian Rebellion of 1837–38*. In *Buffalo Historical Society Publications* 8: 1–147. Buffalo, 1905.

Tyler, Alice Felt. *Freedom's Ferment: Phases of American Social History from the Colonial Period to the Outbreak of the Civil War*. Minneapolis: University of Minnesota Press, 1944.

Tyler, Lyon G. "President John Tyler and the Ashburton Treaty." *William and Mary College Quarterly Historical Magazine* 25 (July 1916): 1–8.

Van Alstyne, Richard W. "The British Right of Search and the African Slave Trade." *Journal of Modern History* 2 (Mar. 1930): 37–47.

Van Deusen, Glyndon G. *The Jacksonian Era: 1828–1848*. New York: Harper and Row, 1959.

_____. *William Henry Seward*. New York: Oxford University Press, 1967.

Walters, Raymond, Jr. *Albert Gallatin: Jeffersonian Financier and Diplomat*. New York: Macmillan, 1957.

Watt, Alastair. "The Case of Alexander McLeod." *Canadian Historical Review* 12 (June 1931): 145–67.

Wayland, Francis P. *Andrew Stevenson: Democrat and Diplomat, 1785–1857*. Philadelphia: University of Pennsylvania Press, 1949.

Webster, Charles K. *The Foreign Policy of Castlereagh, 1815–1822: Britain and the European Alliance*. London: G. Bell and Sons, 1925.

Wheaton, Henry. *Elements of International Law*. Edited by Richard Henry Dana, Jr. Boston: Little, Brown, 1836.

Whitaker, Arthur P. *The Spanish-American Frontier, 1783–1795*. Boston: Houghton Mifflin, 1927.

Willson, Beckles. *Friendly Relations, a Narrative of Britain's Ministers and Ambassadors to America (1791–1930)*. Boston: Little, Brown, 1934.

Wiltse, Charles M. "Daniel Webster and the British Experience." In *Proceedings of the Massachusetts Historical Society* 85 (Oct. 1973): 58–77.

_____. *John C. Calhoun*. 3 vols. Indianapolis: Bobbs-Merrill Co., 1944–51.

Winsor, Justin. "The Settlement of the Northeastern Boundary." In *Proceedings of the Massachusetts Historical Society* 3, 2d ser. (Oct. 1887): 349–69.

Winston, James E., and Colomb, R. W. "How the Louisiana Purchase Was Financed." *Louisiana Historical Quarterly* 12 (Apr. 1929): 189–237.

Wirth, Fremont P. *The Discovery and Exploitation of the Minnesota Iron Lands*. Cedar Rapids, Iowa: Torch Press, 1937.

Wish, Harvey. "American Slave Insurrections Before 1861." *Journal of Negro History* 22 (July 1937): 299–320.

Woodford, Frank B. *Lewis Cass: The Last Jeffersonian*. New Brunswick, N.J.: Rutgers University Press, 1950.

Wright, Marcus T. *General Scott*. New York: D. Appleton, 1894.

Young, William T. *Sketch of the Life and Public Services of General Lewis Cass. With the Pamphlet on the Right of Search, and Some of His Speeches on the Great Political Questions of the Day*. Philadelphia: E. H. Butler and Co., 1853.

Zimmerman, James. *Impressment of American Seamen*. New York: Columbia
   University Press, 1925.
Zorn, Roman J. "Criminal Extradition Menaces the Canadian Haven for
   Fugitive Slaves, 1841–1861." *Canadian Historical Review* 38 (Dec. 1957):
   284–94.

Index

163, 165, 166, 167, 170, 171, 172, 178, 179, 180; lack of trust, xi–xii, xiii, xvi, xvii–xviii, 18, 33, 67–68, 87, 88, 100, 139, 159–60; ambivalence of, xiii, xiv, xvi, xvii; rivalry over North America, 3, 33, 38, 171, 180

Anglo-French-American relations, 61, 95, 101, 124, 137, 175–76, 180

Anglo-French relations, 61, 95, 101, 124, 137, 168, 171, 175–76, 180

Anglo-French treaties (1831 and 1833), 77

Anglophobia, 3, 6, 12, 33, 34, 39, 41, 44, 48, 68, 75, 76, 88, 131, 142, 151–52, 162

Annapolis, 113

Appleby, Gilman (cmmdr. of *Caroline*), 25

Aranda, Count de (Spanish for. min.), 112

Aranda map, 112

Arbitration, 7, 11, 13, 19, 43, 114; award by king of Netherlands (1831), 13–14, 15–16, 18, 19, 101, 102, 111, 116, 120, 121, 124, 125, 131, 133, 136, 137, 164

Aroostook River, 34, 44, 45, 89

Aroostook Valley, 14, 33, 36, 37, 38, 39, 41, 43, 44, 45, 89, 103, 123, 131

Aroostook War (1839), xv, esp. ch. 3, 89, 90, 122, 129; causes of, 33; importance of, 33

Ashburton (U.S.), 166

Ashburton, Lady (Bingham, Anne Louisa), 96, 98, 102

Ashburton, Lord (Baring, Alexander, Br. special min. to U.S.), xii, 87, 93, 101, 102, 104, 106, 107, 108, 110, 111, 116, 117, 120, 121, 124, 127, 133, 134, 138, 139, 140, 141, 142, 143, 144, 145, 146, 147, 148, 149, 150, 153, 154, 156, 157, 159, 161, 162, 163, 164, 167, 168, 170, 171, 172, 173, 174, 175, 179, 180; charges against involving money, xii; personal diplomacy emphasized, xviii; uses power politics, xviii; appointed special minister to U.S., 95–96; mission to U.S., 95ff., 138, 149, 154, 159, 175; official title on mission, 96; buys land in Maine, 96; reasons for choice to head mission to U.S., 96ff.; made Lord Ashburton, 98; British and American reactions to mission, 98ff.; instructions from Aberdeen, 100–102; departure for U.S., 102; discovers Oswald map (or George III map) in British Museum, 109; arrival in U.S., 113; believes no "red-line

map" valid, 113; entourage and lodgings in U.S., 113–14; criticizes America's democratic institutions, 118; criticizes Tyler and Webster, 118; boundary instructions stiffened, 118–20; secret diplomacy of, 122–23; rift with Aberdeen, 125, 126; informant in Washington, 128ff.; reasons for accepting northeastern boundary settlement, 131, 132; criticized by Aberdeen for Oregon negotiations, 158; return to England, 169; resolutions of thanks for, 176

Asia, 156

Astor House (N.Y.), 168

Atlantic Ocean, 5, 7, 8, 11, 16, 34, 80, 101, 151

Augusta (Maine), 39, 44, 45, 93, 94, 115, 116, 122, 128, 130, 166; state legislature, 17, 18, 36, 37, 38

Augusta *Age*, 39, 91, 165

Augusta *Journal*, 39, 165

Augusta *Patriot*, 91

Australia, 49

Austria, 74

B

Backhouse, John, 109

Bagot, Sir Charles, 168

Bahamas, 70, 79, 80, 147

Balance of power: in North America, 136, 171

Baltimore, 91

Baltimore *Sun*, 79, 81, 82, 83, 166

Bancroft, George, 145

Bangor (Maine), 38, 39, 45, 137

Bangor *Whig*, 39

Bangor *Democrat*, 165

Bankhead, Charles, 18

Bank of the U.S., 57, 170

Baring, Alexander. See Ashburton, Lord

Baring, House of, 54, 96, 98, 100, 150

Barrow, Alexander, 81

Bates, Joshua, 150

"Battle of the maps." See Map controversy

Belfast *Republican*, 39

Bell, John, 54

Bemis, Samuel F. (U.S. historian): criticizes Gallatin's role in arbitral case, 14–15; criticizes Webster in northeast boundary negotiations, 113; charges against Webster during Ashburton negotiations, 127ff.

Benton, Thomas Hart (U.S. sen. from Mo.), 28, 42, 79, 88, 114, 161, 162, 163, 164, 174

Bermuda, 62
Berrien, John, 66
Bew map (1783), 111
Bingham, Anne Louisa. *See* Ashburton, Lady
Bingham, William, 96
Birney, James G., 82
"Black Dan." *See* Webster, Daniel
"Black Friday," 163
Black Rock Dam, 23
Blackwood's Edinburgh Magazine (London), xiv
"Blue Noses," 39
Board of Trade (Gr. Br.), 98
Bonaparte, Napoleon, 9, 140
Boston, 14, 40, 94, 115, 126, 150, 166, 168, 175
Boston *Courier*, 100
Boston *Liberator*, 82, 147
Boston *Patriot*, 40
Bradley, Rev. Caleb, 39
Brazil, 72, 77, 144
British and Foreign Anti-Slavery Society, 82, 84, 85
British Constitutional Act (1791), 21
British Museum, 15, 108, 109
British North America, 87, 167; vulnerable to U.S. attack, 10, 100–101, 120, 124, 137, 170, 175
"Brother Jonathan," 51, 170, 172
Brougham, Lord Henry, 84, 176
Buchanan, James (U.S. sen. from Pa.), 36, 42, 58, 162, 176
Buffalo (N.Y.), 21, 23, 24, 26, 29, 30, 31, 49, 64
Byron, Lord, 98

C
Caldwell, Sir John, 122
Calhoun, John C. (U.S. sen. from S.C.), 27, 28, 42, 59, 80, 149, 152, 162, 164, 165, 174
California, 158
Cambridge (Mass.), 103, 168
Campbell, Lord, 84
Canada Union Act (1840), 31
Canadian National Railroad, 137
Canadian rebellion (1837–38), xv, 20, 21, 22, 29, 31, 33, 49, 50, 52, 64
Canadian Refugee Relief Association, 21
Canning, George (Br. for. sec.), 71, 157
Capitol, U.S., 114
Caribbean Islands, 148

Caroline (U.S.), xv, esp. ch. 2, 41, 48, 49, 50, 51, 52, 55, 56, 58, 59, 60, 63, 64, 65, 67, 68, 86, 139, 159, 167; arrival in Niagara region, 23; destruction of (1837), 24–25; called "pirate," 28–29, 30; views of British, 29; discussed in Webster-Ashburton negotiations, 152ff.; settlement during Webster-Ashburton negotiations, 153–54
Caroline Almanac, The, 25
Cass, Lewis (U.S. min. in Paris), 54, 75, 76–77, 78, 140, 164, 167; author of anonymous pamphlet against search, 76; rift with Webster over search issue, 77
Castlereagh, Lord (Br. for. sec.), 70
Chamber of Deputies (France), 77
Channing, Rev. William Ellery, 147
Charleston *Courier*, 79
Charleston *Mercury*, 167
Chasers, 21
Chicago *American*, 93, 166
China, xi, 32, 127, 171
Chippewa, 20, 23, 24, 64, 65
Christmas Eve, Treaty of. *See* Ghent, Treaty of
Cincinnati *Enquirer*, 166
Civil War, xi, xiv, 44, 78, 88, 145
Clay, Henry (U.S. sen. from Ky.), xvi, 27, 35, 42, 57, 80, 88, 102, 125, 161, 165
Coke, Sir Edward, 84
Colebrooke, Sir William (lt. gov. of N. B.), 120, 167–68; secretly advises Ashburton, 122, 123
Colonial Office (Gr. Br.), 60
Colonial Society (Gr. Br.), 62
Columbia River, 87, 156, 157, 158
Comet (U.S.), 80, 81
Comity, 83, 84, 146
Committee on Foreign Affairs, U.S. House of Reps., 42, 52, 66, 177
Committee on Foreign Relations, U.S. Senate. *See* Foreign Relations Committee, U.S. Senate
Commons, House of (Gr. Br.), 54, 60, 98, 175, 176
Conflict of Laws (by Joseph Story), 84
Congress (U.S.), 17, 27, 28, 33, 36, 41, 42, 43, 50, 51, 55, 56, 59, 66, 71, 72, 81, 96, 102, 132, 142, 144, 154, 161, 174, 176, 177
Connecticut River, 5, 8, 12, 14, 101, 123
Conservative party (Gr. Br.), 60, 98
Constitution, U.S., 3, 6, 62, 83, 84, 166

London *Morning Chronicle*, 98, 161, 170, 172
London *Morning Herald*, 170
London *Punch*, 170
London *Times*, 85, 96, 98, 109, 168, 169, 171–72, 174, 176
Lords, House of (Gr. Br.), 51, 84, 85, 176
"Lord Surrender," 172
Louisiana, 9, 79, 80, 81
Louisiana Insurance Company, 80
Louisiana Purchase (1803), 8–9, 10, 98
Lowell, Joshua, 114
Lower Canada, 10, 11, 14, 21, 31, 38
Loyalists (in Nova Scotia), 6, 7

M
McCormack, Shepard, 25
McIntire, Rufus (land agent from Maine), 37, 38, 39
Mackenzie, William Lyon (leader of Canadian rebels), 22, 23, 25, 62
MacLauchlan, James (N.B.'s "Warden of the Disputed Territory"), 35, 37, 38, 47, 122
McLeod, Alexander (Canadian sheriff, xv, esp. ch. 4, 86, 90, 146, 153, 154, 176; personal background, 49; arrested, 49; charged with murder and arson, 51; physical characteristics of, 63; trial of, 63ff.; prosecution's argument during trial, 63–64; defense argument during trial, 64–65; acquittal, 65; attempts to secure reparation, 67; importance of case, 67–68
McLeod, Angus, 25, 26, 49, 64–65
MacNab, Allan (colonel in Canadian militia), 20, 23, 24, 25, 26, 27, 29, 65
Madawaska, 12, 44, 89, 90, 91, 101, 123, 124, 125, 126, 129, 131, 132, 136, 167
Madawaska River, 38, 45, 89, 137
Madawaska Valley, 33
Madison, James, 8, 140
Magaguadavic River, 5, 6
Maine, xv, xvi, 13, 14, 16, 17, 19, 37, 38, 39, 40, 41, 42, 43, 44, 45, 46, 47, 48, 87, 89, 91, 92, 93, 94, 95, 96, 100, 104, 106, 111, 114, 115, 118, 120, 121, 122, 123, 124, 126, 127, 128, 129, 130, 131, 132, 133, 134, 137, 139, 154, 163, 165, 166, 167, 168, 172, 177, 178; states' rights beliefs, xviii; becomes state (1820), 12, 33; rejects arbitration award of 1831, 18; policies causing border problems, 34;

opens line of communication through Northeast, 34; virtual veto over any boundary settlement, 35; census ordered in disputed territory, 35; boundary commission established, 36; boundary commission report, 36; distrust of British, 87, 90; refuses to sell land to Gr. Br., 90, 116; special session of legislature, 115, 116; legislature approves sending commission to Webster-Ashburton negotiations, 116; commission in Washington, D.C., 116, 124–25
"Maine Battle Song," 40
Manchester (N.Y.), 49
Mangum, Willie, 100
Map controversy, xii, 5, 6, 7, 14, 15, 102–13, 115ff., 127, 128, 129, 130, 131, 132, 162, 163–64, 165, 172ff.
Map of the British and French Dominions in North America (by John Mitchell, 1755): problems created by, 5
Marcy, William, 31
Maritime Provinces (Nova Scotia and N.B.), 10, 11, 14, 33, 89
Marseilles, 54
Marshall, John, 94
Mars Hill, 14, 103
Maryland, 40, 90, 113
Masons, 21
Massachusetts, 6, 12, 16, 27, 36, 39, 40, 42, 43, 44, 54, 66, 73, 80, 92, 93, 100, 114, 115, 116, 121, 124, 125, 128, 130, 131, 132, 133, 145, 146, 147; commission to Webster-Ashburton negotiations, 116
Massachusetts Antislavery Society, 147
Massachusetts General Court, 6
Melbourne, Lord (Lamb, William; Br. prime min.), 28, 34, 35, 36, 46, 59, 60, 67, 68, 78, 94, 153, 170, 173
Menefee, Richard, 28
Merk, Frederick (U.S. historian): defends Gallatin's role in arbitral case, 15
Mesabi Range, 134, 136
Metis River, 107
Mexican War, xi, 87
Mexico, 32, 125, 157, 158
Michigan, 17, 19, 21, 48, 75, 140
"Michigander." *See* Cass, Lewis
Midwest (U.S.), 167
Mildmay, Humphrey, 113, 120
Mills, John, 116
Minnesota, 134, 136

V

Van Buren, Martin (U.S. president, 1837–41), 23, 32, 35, 36, 38, 39, 45, 47, 55, 68, 80, 88, 91; views on Canadian rebellion, 22, 27, 31; sends Scott to Niagara frontier, 27; policies during Aroostook crisis, 41, 42–43, 46; policies during McLeod crisis, 50, 51, 52

Van Rensselaer, Rensselaer, 23, 30, 31

Vaughan, Sir Charles, 18

Vergennes, Count de (French for. min.), 103, 112

Vermilion Range, 134, 136

Vermont, 5, 21, 30, 61, 101, 137

Victoria (queen of England), 25, 54, 59, 61, 62, 96, 114, 123, 168

Vienna, Congress of (1815), xi

Virginia, 29, 40, 56, 58, 59, 73, 75, 79, 80, 88, 145, 162

"Viscount Chronicle," 172

Visit, 74, 76, 78

Visit and search. *See* Search, visit and

W

Walters, Raymond (U.S. historian): criticizes Gallatin's role in arbitral case, 15

War of 1812, xi, 6, 9, 12, 13, 20, 32, 33, 45, 50, 69, 70, 98, 131, 139; shows British need for military road in North America, 10

Warspite (Gr. Br.), 102, 113, 169

Washington, George (U.S. president, 1789–97), 6, 143, 163, 166, 178

Washington *Globe*, 32, 100, 161, 164

Webster-Ashburton negotiations, 110, 112, 113, 122–23, 132, 139, 171; secret diplomacy during, xviii, decision for informality, 121–22; social functions during, 122

Webster-Ashburton Treaty (1842), xi, 111, 144, 161–62, 176; importance of, xii, xiii, 5, 136ff., 139, 160, 179–80; secret diplomacy involved in, xviii; discussed in Parliament, 107; approved by U.S. Senate, 165; reactions in Maine to, 165–66; reaction in U.S. to, 166–67; reaction in British North America to, 167–68; reaction in England to, 168; exchange of ratifications, 169

Webster, Daniel (U.S. sec. of state, 1841–43), x, xii, 58, 59, 66, 75, 77, 87, 88, 91, 95, 100, 107, 108, 110, 111, 114, 116,

117, 118, 121, 122, 123, 124, 125, 133, 134, 136, 137, 138, 139, 141, 142, 143, 145, 146, 147, 148, 149, 150, 151, 152, 153, 154, 156, 157, 158, 159, 161, 162, 163, 164, 166, 167, 169, 170, 171, 172, 173, 174, 175, 179, 180; propaganda charges against, xii, 94, 176ff.; charges against involving money, xii, 126–27, 128ff., 164, 176ff.; realist in foreign policy, xvi, xvii; uses power politics, xvi, xviii; foreign policy based on international law, xvii; influence on Tyler, xvii; wary of Gr. Br. in North America, xvii; nationalist, xvii, 68; personal diplomacy emphasized, xviii; supports joint (or mixed) commission plan, 36; considered for special mission to London (1839), 42–43; policies during Aroostook crisis, 42–43; memorandum on northeast boundary, 43; physical characteristics, 54; policies during McLeod crisis, 54, 55, 56, 67; appointed secretary of state, 54, 90; controversy over Seward's pardoning power during McLeod crisis, 55–56; decides not to resign from Tyler's cabinet, 57; recommends Joshua Spencer for U.S. district attorney in N.Y., 57; accused of interference with McLeod trial, 66–67, 176; rift with Cass over search issue, 77; policies during *Creole* affair, 83–84; never demanded British surrender of *Creole*'s mutineers, 85, 147–48; newspaper campaign in New England, 91ff., 176ff.; uses secret-service fund, 92, 94, 176ff.; invites Maine and Massachusetts to send commissions to Webster-Ashburton negotiations, 93; legal adviser for House of Baring, 98; buys Steuben map, 104; conceals Sparks and Steuben maps, 106; believes no "red-line map" valid, 113; sends Sparks to Maine, 115–16; loss of interest in diplomatic post in London, 127–28; impeachment attempt of, 161, 176ff.; newspaper editorials during Webster-Ashburton negotiations, 164–65; exonerated by House committee, 178–79

Weld, Theodore, 82, 83

Wellington, duke of, 60, 62, 101–2, 120, 157, 170, 180

Wells, William (owner of *Caroline*), 23, 25, 29, 153

West Africa. *See* Africa